www.ingramcontent.com/pod-product-compliance
Lightning Source LLC
Chambersburg PA
CBHW080728230426
43665CB00020B/2660

Dear SSAT Middle test taker,

Great job completing this study guide. The hard work and effort you put into your test preparation will help you succeed on your upcoming SSAT Middle exam. Thank you for letting us be a part of your education journey!

We have other study guides and products that you may find useful. Search for us on Amazon.com or let us know what you are looking for. We offer a wide variety of study guides that cover a multitude of subjects.

If you would like to share your success stories with us, or if you have a suggestion, comment, or concern, please send us an email at support@triviumtestprep.com.

Thanks again for choosing us!
Happy Testing
Trivium Test Prep Team

Common Suffixes

Suffix	Meaning	Examples
-strat	cover	strata
-tude	state of, condition of	aptitude
-um	forms single nouns	spectrum
-ure	state of, act, process, rank	rupture, rapture
-ward	in the direction of	backward
-y	inclined to, tend to	faulty

Common Suffixes

Suffix	Meaning	Examples
-able, -ible	able, capable	visible
-age	act of, state of, result of	wreckage
-al	relating to	gradual
-algia	pain	myalgia
-an, -ian	native of, relating to	riparian
-ance, -ancy	action, process, state	defiance
-ary, -ery, -ory	relating to, quality, place	aviary
-cian	processing a specific skill or art	physician
-cule, -ling	very small	sapling, animalcule
-cy	action, function	normalcy
-dom	quality, realm	wisdom
-ee	one who receives the action	nominee
-en	made of, to make	silken
-ence, -ency	action, state of, quality	urgency
-er, -or	one who, that which	professor
-escent	in the process of	adolescent, senescence
-esis, -osis	action, process, condition	genesis, neurosis
-et, -ette	small one, group	baronet, lorgnette
-fic	making, causing	specific
-ful	full of	frightful
-hood	order, condition, quality	adulthood
-ice	condition, state, quality	malice
-id, -ide	connected with, belonging to	bromide
-ile	relating to, suited for, capable of	puerile, juvenile
-ine	nature of	feminine
-ion, -sion, -tion	act, result, state of	contagion
-ish	origin, nature, resembling	impish
-ism	system, manner, condition, characteristic	capitalism
-ist	one who, that which	artist, flautist
-ite	nature of, quality of, mineral product	graphite
-ity, -ty	state of, quality	captivity
-ive	causing, making	exhaustive
-ize, -ise	make	idolize, bowdlerize
-ment	act of, state or, result	containment
-nomy	law	autonomy, taxonomy
-oid	resembling	asteroid, anthropoid
-some	like, apt, tending to	gruesome

Common Prefixes

Prefix	Meaning	Examples
amphi-, ambi-	round, both sides	ambivalent
ante-	before	antedate, anterior
anti-	against	antipathy
archos-	leader, first, chief	oligarchy
bene-	well, favorable	benevolent, beneficent
bi-	two	binary, bivalve
caco-	bad	cacophony
circum-	around	circumnavigate
corpus-	body	corporeal
credo-	belief	credible
demos-	people	demographic
di-	two, double	dimorphism, diatomic
dia-	across, through	dialectic
dis-	not, apart	disenfranchise
dynasthai-	be able	dynamo, dynasty
ego-	i, self	egomaniac, egocentric
epi-	upon, over	epigram, epiphyte
ex-	out	extraneous, extemporaneous
geo-	earth	geocentric, geomancy
ideo-	idea	ideology, ideation
in-	in	induction, indigenous
in-, im-	not	inexhaustible, immoral
inter-	between	interstellar
lexis-	word	lexicography
liber-	free	liberal
locus-	place	locality
macro-	large	macrophage
micro-	small	micron
mono-	one, single	monocle, monovalent
mortis-	death	moribund
olig-	few	oligarchy
peri-	around	peripatetic, perineum
poly-	many	polygamy
pre-	before	prescient
solus-	alone	solitary
subter-	under, secret	subterfuge
un-	not	unsafe
utilis-	useful	utilitarian

Common Root Words

Root	Meaning	Examples
iso	identical	isolate
ject	throw	projection
logy	study of	biology
luc	light	elucidate
mal	bad	malevolent
meta, met	behind, between	metacognition, behind the thinking
meter, metr	measure	thermometer
micro	small	microbe
mis, miso	hate	misanthrope
mit	to send	transmit
mono	one	monologue
morph	form, shape	morphology
mort	death	mortal
multi	many	multiple
phil	love	philanthropist
port	carry	transportation
pseudo	false	pseudonym
psycho	soul, spirit	psychic
rupt	to break	disruption
scope	viewing instrument	microscope
scrib, scribe	to write	inscription
sect, sec	to cut	section
sequ, secu	follow	consecutive
soph	wisdom, knowledge	philosophy
spect	to look	spectator
struct	to build	restructure
tele	far off	telephone
terr	earth	terrestrial
therm	heat	thermal
vent, vene	to come	convene
vert	turn	vertigo
voc	voice, call	vocalize, evocative

Common Prefixes

Prefix	Meaning	Examples
a-, an-	without, not	anachronism, anhydrous
ab-, abs-, a-	apart, away from	abscission, abnormal
ad-	toward	adhere

Appendix - Roots and Suffixes

Common Root Words

Root	Meaning	Examples
agere	act	agent
alter	other	alternate, alter ego
ambi	both	ambidextrous
ami, amic	love	amiable
amphi	both ends, all sides	amphibian
anthrop	man, human, humanity	misanthrope, anthropologist
apert	open	aperture
aqua	water	aqueduct, aquarium
aud	to hear	audience
auto	self	autobiography
bell	war	belligerent, bellicose
bene	good	benevolent
bio	life	biology
ced	yield, go	secede, intercede
cent	one hundred	century
chron	time	chronological
circum	around	circumference
contra, counter	against	contradict
crac, crat	rule, ruler	autocrat, bureaucrat
crypt	hidden	cryptogram, cryptic
curr, curs, cours	to run	precursory
dict	to say	dictator, dictation
dyna	power	dynamic
dys	bad, hard, unlucky	dysfunctional
equ	equal, even	equanimity
fac	to make, to do	factory
form	shape	reform, conform
fort	strength	fortitude
fract	to break	fracture
grad, gress	step	progression
gram	thing written	epigram
graph	writing	graphic
hetero	different	heterogeneous
homo	same	homogenous
hypo	below, beneath	hypothermia

7. A) Being wise is a positive trait that often develops with age just as being successful is a positive quality that often results from working hard.

8. D) This option maintains the fastening action-to-fastened object relationship.

9. D) This option maintains the immature stage-to-mature stage relationship.

10. C) This option relates a taste sensation with a causative element.

11. A) This option maintains the action-to-tool relationship.

12. A) This option maintains the positive attitude-to-negative attitude relationship.

13. D) This option relates a specific technique (*pitch* as a verb) to the corresponding sport.

14. C) Chemistry is a specific field within the broader category of science, just as volleyball is a specific sport.

15. E) This option maintains the liquid-to-container relationship.

16. C) A governor is a head administrator position of a state, just as a principal leads a school.

17. A) This option provides opposite actions involving movement of an object.

18. E) Annoyance and rage are similar emotions with different intensities, just like envy and jealousy.

19. E) *Slow* and *swift* are opposite qualities describing speed, while *clumsy* and *graceful* are opposite qualities describing movement.

20. D) This option maintains the specific action-to-object relationship.

21. B) This option represents similar actions where the second term is more intense or thorough than the first.

22. B) Nonfiction is a specific category within the broader discipline of literature.

23. C) The pair in this option represents nearly synonymous personality traits.

24. D) The pair in this option indicates a physical response to an emotion or feeling.

25. B) The pair in this option shows a specific cutting action for a particular food.

26. A) *Book* and *library* represent the relationship between an item and a facility designed to house collections of such items.

27. D) The pair in this option represents a medium through which a vehicle travels.

28. C) Studying is a more thorough, purposeful form of observing, just like the relationship between *search* and *look*.

29. B) *Protect* is a supportive function, and *armor* is the object/structure designed to perform that function.

30. D) This option's pair represents opposing actions regarding inclusion/acceptance.

Answer Explanation #3

11. D) "*Resolute* means steadfast or focused to a commendable degree."

12. E) "*Opulent* means rich on a grandiose scale."

13. A) "*Scoff* means to speak in a manner that is disdainful or mocking."

14. C) "*Forbid* means to not allow something to happen or keep someone from doing something."

15. C) "*Enigma* means something that is strange or challenging to comprehend."

16. D) "*Coerce* means to pressure the actions of others by force or threat."

17. E) "*Rigid* means stiff and inflexible."

18. C) "*Perplexed* means very confused or baffled."

19. D) "*Gallant* means brave or chivalrous, especially in a showy way."

20. A) "*Dismal* means miserable and grim."

21. C) "*Condone* means to allow offensive or immoral behavior."

22. C) "*Baffle* means to completely stump or bewilder."

23. D) "*Captivate* means to charm and capture someone's attention."

24. C) "*Quandary* means a situation that is difficult to overcome, especially when the answer is unclear."

25. E) "*Gradual* means shifting slowly and continuously over time."

26. D) "*Rebuke* means to express strong disapproval of or criticize another's behavior."

27. C) "*Adept* means demonstrating high skill and capability in performing a task.

28. E) "*Arid* means exceptionally dry, especially through not having enough rainfall to support plant life."

29. C) "*Fabricate* means to create or make something up, sometimes with misleading intentions."

30. D) "*Reconcile* means to restore harmony or make things compatible with each other."

Analogies

1. E) Just as a satellite orbits around a planet, the Moon is a satellite that orbits Earth.

2. D) This option maintains the relationship of performing a stationary action on a supporting surface.

3. A) *Tick* is the distinctive sound produced by a clock, just as ringing is the sound produced by a bell.

4. B) This option maintains the basic technique-to-sport relationship.

5. B) Just as a car uses wheels, a body uses legs for locomotion.

6. C) Like shoes, glasses are tools that aid or enable a natural ability.

37. C) The tone suggests a sense of wonder and intrigue about the painting's mysteries. Option *A* is incorrect because the presentation is not scholarly; instead, it is marked by admiration. Option *B* is incorrect because the text does not challenge traditional views of the painting. Option *D* is incorrect because the passage does not present anything about the painting's history as myth or try to debunk it. Option *E* is incorrect because the text does not express concerns about commercialization.

38. E) Dickinson's seclusion is directly contrasted with her adventurous mind. Option *A* is incorrect because the passage does not compare Dickinson with other poets. Option *B* is incorrect because Amherst is only mentioned as her location. Option *C* is incorrect because Dickinson's public persona is not discussed. Option *D* is incorrect because the passage does not distinguish between early and later works.

39. A) The passage repeatedly emphasizes how Dickinson transforms familiar things into profound revelations. Option *B* is incorrect because supernatural experiences are not identified as her main subject. Option *C* is incorrect because the passage suggests that her isolation enhanced her writing. Option *D* is incorrect because there is no evidence that Dickinson deliberately obscured meaning. Option *E* is incorrect because the passage does not discuss the reception of Dickinson's work.

40. B) The passage shows that Dickinson's calm approach to mortality can be more unsettling than outright horror. Option *A* is incorrect because her approach is presented as effective. Option *C* is incorrect because her perspective on death is portrayed as unique. Option *D* is incorrect because her work is described as unsettling, not comforting. Option *E* is incorrect because no connection is made between her writing and personal fears.

Verbal

Synonyms

1. C) *Tedious* means "irritatingly dull."

2. D) "*Serene* means undisturbed and at peace."

3. D) "*Vigilant* means keeping watch and staying alert."

4. C) "*Precarious* means lacking stability in a potentially dangerous way."

5. B) "*Dubious* means arousing suspicion."

6. E) "*Eradicate* means to get rid of something entirely."

7. D) "*Obscure* means shrouded or hidden from view."

8. B) "*Futile* means unable to yield effective results."

9. D) "*Liberate* means to release someone from control."

10. C) "*Keen* means having a heightened perception or honed edge."

interprets the metaphor too literally. Option C is incorrect because urban life is portrayed as fast-paced. Option D is incorrect because the context is about job opportunities rather than how cities change. Option E is incorrect because the text does not address tourism.

31. E) The passage mentions the problem of having few job options in rural locations. Option A is incorrect because high living costs are associated with urban environments, not rural ones. Option B is incorrect because, based on the passage, rural residents have plenty of room. Option C is incorrect because the text suggests urban areas would be noisier than rural ones. Option D is incorrect because strong neighborly bonds are depicted as features of rural communities.

32. C) The text portrays urbanites as surrounded by neighbors yet disconnected from them. Option A is incorrect because the passage describes the connections as minimal to nonexistent. Option B is incorrect because political differences are not related to neighbor relationships in the passage. Option D is incorrect because the text does not discuss the role of technology in relationships. Option E is incorrect because the passage suggests that interpersonal relationships were actually stronger in the past when people knew each other better.

33. D) The passage emphasizes how the painting raises questions while answering none, evidence of its enigmatic nature that has intrigued viewers for centuries. Option A is incorrect because technical aspects are not presented as the primary appeal but as adding to the mystery. Option B is incorrect because monetary value is not mentioned as a factor in the painting's appeal. Option C is incorrect because Lisa Gherardini is only briefly mentioned as a possible subject, not as the reason for the fascination with the painting. Option E is incorrect because the painting's journey is mentioned as a secondary aspect of its appeal.

34. A) The passage suggests a special attachment, explaining that da Vinci continually modified the painting and kept it until his death. Option B is incorrect because the passage does not suggest anything about the difficulty of the painting, just that it was continually refined by the artist. Option C is incorrect because there is no mention of profit motive, and he delivered it to no patron. Option D is incorrect because the painting is not characterized as purely experimental. Option E is incorrect because the text specifically states that da Vinci never delivered the work to anybody, not that it was rejected.

35. D) The neurological research explains the scientific basis for the way viewers' perceptions change depending on how they look at the painting. Option A is incorrect because the passage does not suggest da Vinci's neurological knowledge. Option B is incorrect because the research supports the description of the effect. Option C is incorrect because da Vinci's actions are not portrayed as exploitative. Option E is incorrect because the focus is on the phenomenon itself, not how widespread it is.

36. B) The passage describes the Mona Lisa as seemingly aware of the viewer's eyes, adjusting its gaze in response. Option A is incorrect because the interaction is specifically described as not requiring specialized knowledge. Option C is incorrect because technology is not described as diminishing the Mona Lisa's impact. Option D is incorrect because the passage emphasizes directly experiencing the painting. Option E is incorrect because the relationship is described as emotional rather than intellectual.

23. A) The passage provides an example of bartering only working when both parties want what the other is offering. Option *B* is incorrect because the text does not explore government regulation as a limitation. Option *C* is incorrect because the passage does not mention bartering constraints, such as disagreements about fair value. Option *D* is incorrect because, while transportation difficulty is mentioned, it is not presented as a significant limitation. Option *E* is incorrect because the text mentions perishability as a feature of certain currencies, not as a problem in bartering.

24. C) The passage highlights community acceptance as a key trait. Option *A* is incorrect because the text mentions regulation regarding coins, not early currency. Option *B* is incorrect because the passage does not discuss resistance to counterfeiting. Option *D* is incorrect because the text does not mention religious significance. Option *E* is incorrect because the text does not show appealing aesthetics to be an important factor.

25. D) The passage presents information in a straightforward way without opinion or judgment. Option *A* is incorrect because the text lacks a sense of concern or criticality. Option *B* is incorrect because the passage remains neutral rather than enthusiastic. Option *C* is incorrect because there is no reflection on or apology for historical events. Option *E* is incorrect because the language is accessible rather than complicated.

26. B) The text follows a clear trajectory from early trading to modern credit cards and digital money. Option *A* is incorrect because the passage relies mainly on descriptions rather than analysis of advantages and disadvantages. Option *C* is incorrect because the text does not explain economic theories. Option *D* is incorrect because the text mentions geographic regions but does not present them in any organized way. Option *E* is incorrect because the passage does not make cultural comparisons.

27. E) The passage shows currency to evolve with societal and technological change. Option *A* and *B* are incorrect because the passage does not suggest whether or not digital currency will eventually replace physical money. Option *C* is incorrect because there is no indication that society will return to bartering. Option *D* is incorrect because the text does not imply the disappearance of regulations.

28. A) The passage mentions that Americans lived close enough to walk to work before the introduction of modern technology. Option *B* is incorrect because the passage specifically indicates that this was before electronics were common. Option *C* is incorrect because the text suggests that communities were more connected in the past rather than isolated. Option *D* is incorrect because health care access is not discussed as a shared characteristic. Option *E* is incorrect because there is no mention of political harmony.

29. D) The passage presents urban environments as hurried and bustling, with residents engaging in multiple activities. Option *A* is incorrect because pedestrian activity is not connected to traffic in the text. Option *B* is incorrect because the passage does not discuss health benefits. Option *C* is incorrect because public transit is not addressed in this context. Option *E* is incorrect because the focus is on the accelerated lifestyle of a typical city rather than exercise routines.

30. B) The metaphor is presented in the context of job-hopping and career advancement and immediately followed by acknowledging the pressures of urban life. Option *A* is incorrect because it

kidneys." Readers can infer that *myo-* refers to muscles, *cardio-* refers to the heart, and *nephro-* refers to the kidneys, as in *nephritis* (inflammation of the kidneys).

15. C) In the last paragraph, the author writes, "Researchers have been studying the chemical compositions of these venoms and have been making strides in using the science behind the toxins to combat major diseases such as cancer, heart disease, and Alzheimer's." Readers can therefore infer that the author is using the phrase "making strides in using the science" to refer to making discoveries that greatly improve the ability of medical science to cure diseases.

16. B) The passage is mainly about the composition of snake venom. The other sentences give details from the passage.

17. A) In the first paragraph, the author writes, "The two key ingredients in all snake venoms are enzymes and polypeptides. Some enzymes help the snake disable its prey, and others help the snake digest its prey." Later in the passage, the author goes into more detail about these processes.

18. B) The story highlights Mary's inner conflict as she uses a magic shortcut to get good grades. Option *A* is incorrect because academic pressure is not the main topic but a secondary one. Option *C* is incorrect because the emphasis is on the moral lesson, despite the entertainment factor of the pencil's supernatural power. Option *D* is incorrect because the ethical issue of taking someone's property is not explored. Option *E* is incorrect because the passage does not focus on increasing intelligence; it only focuses on artificially inflating grades.

19. D) Mary goes from relying on the pencil to breaking it, vowing to try harder going forward. Option *A* is incorrect because it misinterprets her initial behavior as dishonest when she was unaware of the pencil's influence on her grades. Option *B* is incorrect because it ignores Mary's concerns about her academic performance. Option *C* is incorrect because there is no evidence for Mary's tactical development. Option *E* is incorrect because the story does not mention feelings of insecurity.

20. A) The phrase uses *like* to compare using the pencil to wearing someone else's clothes. Option *B* is incorrect because a euphemism is used to lessen the impact of strong language, which is not happening here. Option *C* is incorrect because the comparison does not refer to anything outside of the text. Option *D* is incorrect because the comparison has no meaning beyond the literal words. Option *E* is incorrect because the phrase does not use any words to mimic sounds.

21. C) Mary's experiment conclusively shows the pencil changing her writing. Option *A* is incorrect because the pencil works for multiple subjects. Option *B* is incorrect because the pencil is not shown to cause harm. Option *D* is incorrect because the pencil's ownership is not explored in the story. Option *E* is incorrect because the experiment does not reveal anything about the duration of the pencil's magic.

22. E) Mary feels empty when she realizes that her teachers are not truly proud of her work. Option *A* is incorrect because missing the challenge of homework is not mentioned. Option *B* is incorrect because Mary does not show signs of feeling sick anywhere in the story. Option *C* is incorrect because Mary does not display fear toward the pencil's magic but instead is stunned and disappointed that her good grades were unearned. Option *D* is incorrect because *hollow* is not being used literally, as in an empty stomach.

Reading

1. A) It is not stated in the passage that taking temperature in the ear or at the temporal artery is more accurate than taking it orally. Instead, it says the best way depends on the situation.

2. B) The author's primary purpose is to explain the methods available to measure a person's temperature and the situations in which each method is appropriate. The end of the first paragraph shows this when the author writes that the best way to get an accurate reading depends on the situation, and then goes on to describe various options and their applications.

3. B) The passage is about how the most common way people measure body temperature is orally, but there are many situations when measuring temperature orally isn't an option. The passage then describes these situations in the second and third paragraphs.

4. A) The final paragraph states that agitated patients won't be able to sit still long enough for an accurate reading. The reader can therefore infer that an agitated patient is one who is visibly upset, annoyed, or uncomfortable.

5. E) The second paragraph states that the rectum provides a much more accurate reading than other locations.

6. B) The passage is primarily informative; however, the author uses jokes like the one in the last sentence to entertain readers.

7. E) The passage makes no mention of the tongue. Readers are therefore left to infer that the tongue helps press the cold substance against the roof of the mouth.

8. C) To entertain readers, the author is referring to the following rhyme: "I scream, you scream, we all scream for ice cream."

9. B) The passage is mainly about the causes of brain freeze, as scientists believe they now understand the mechanism of ice cream headaches. The other sentences provide details that support the main idea.

10. D) In paragraph 2, the author writes, "When a cold substance... presses against the roof of your mouth, it causes blood vessels there to begin to constrict." Constrict is a synonym for *narrow* or *shrink*.

11. E) In the last sentence, the author writes, "The duration of the pain varies from a few seconds up to about a minute." Readers can therefore infer that "duration of the pain" means "how long the pain lasts."

12. B) In the first sentence, the author writes, "Many snakes produce a toxic fluid, called venom, in their salivary glands." Readers can therefore infer from this that some snakes do not produce venom. There is no support for any of the other claims.

13. C) The primary purpose of the essay is to inform; its general focus is on the composition of snake venoms. It is not primarily cautionary or advisory. The author does not tell a story about a specific research scientist.

14. D) In the last sentence in the second paragraph, the author writes, "Some cytotoxins target specific types of cells—myotoxins affect muscles, cardiotoxins attack the heart, and nephrotoxins damage the

20. E) First, use the exponential law of quotients to subtract exponents with the same base:

$$a^{-4-2}b^{-5-(-4)}c^{2-1} = a^{-6}b^{-1}c$$

Then, we use the law of negative exponents to place the expressions with negative exponents in the denominator:

$$\frac{c}{a^6 b}$$

21. C) The volume of a cylinder is $\pi r^2 h$. If h=10 and r=3, then:

$$V = \pi(3)^2 10$$

$$V = 90\pi \text{ square inches}$$

22. A) Simplify each term.

$$(a): \frac{35}{35} = 1$$

$$(b): 35^0 = 1$$

$$(c): 35 \times 0 = 0$$

Therefore, a equals b, and both are greater than c.

23. B) First, subtract both sides by 4 to obtain $|x| = 1$. Both $|-1|$ and $|1| = 1$. Therefore, there are two solutions: -1 and 1.

24. C) Set up the equation and solve for x:

$$\frac{1 \text{ acre}}{500 \text{ gal}} = \frac{x \text{ acres}}{2600 \text{ gal}}$$

$$x \text{ acres} = \frac{1 \text{ acre} \times 2600 \text{ gal}}{500 \text{ gal}}$$

$$x = \frac{26}{5} \text{ acres or } 5.2 \text{ acres.}$$

25. D) This problem presents two equivalent ratios that can be set up in a fraction equation:

$$\frac{35}{5} = \frac{49}{x}$$

$$35x = 49 \times 5$$

$$x = 7$$

13. C) Parallel lines have the same slope. The line is already given in slope-intercept form, so $m = 5$. Plug the slope and the point into the point-slope formula:

$$y - 1 = 5(x - (-1))$$

$$y - 1 = 5(x + 1)$$

$$y = 5x + 6$$

14. B) Turn this into a fraction and simplify it to show that $\frac{6}{40} = \frac{3}{20}$ students have a black backpack. We divide 3 by 20 to obtain 0.15, which is equivalent to 15%. Therefore, 15% of the students have a black backpack.

15. D) Simplify the expression by following the order of operations.

$$4 + 15 \div 3 \times 2$$

$$4 + 5 \times 2$$

$$4 + 10 = 14$$

16. C) To solve 12 less than 8 squared, write it as an equation.

$$8^2 - 12$$

$$64 - 12 = 52$$

17. D) The sum of the three angles in a triangle is 180°, and because this is an isosceles triangle, the two angles in the base of the triangle are equal. Therefore, the sum of the two missing angles is:

$$180 - 34 = 146°$$

We can then divide this amount by 2 to find the missing angle:

$$146 \div 2 = 73°$$

18. C) Stacy ran 6 or more miles on Monday, Tuesday, Thursday, and Saturday, which is 4 out of 7 days.

$$\frac{4}{7} \approx 51.1\%$$

19. A) Because the diameter of the circle is 14 cm, the radius is half that amount, which is 7 cm.

$$A = \pi r^2$$

$$A = \pi(7)^2 = 49\pi \text{ cm}^2$$

Answer Explanation #3

8. C) First find the slope, which is equal to the change in y over the change in x:

$$m = \frac{3 - (-1)}{-2 - 6} = \frac{4}{-8} = -\frac{1}{2}$$

Then, use the slope-intercept form of a line $y - y_1 = m(x - x_1)$ and plug in either point and the slope to find the equation of the line:

$$y - 6 = -\frac{1}{2}(x + 1)$$

Simplify:

$$y - 6 = -\frac{1}{2}x - \frac{1}{2}$$

$$y = -\frac{1}{2}x + \frac{11}{2}$$

9. C) To find $\frac{3}{5}$ of 100, multiply.

$$\frac{3}{5} \times 100 = 60$$

10. B) First, find the slope of the given line by putting it into slope-intercept form $y = mx + b$.

$$5x + 6y = 12$$

$$6y = -5x + 12$$

$$y = -\frac{5}{6}x + 2$$

The slope of this line is $-\frac{5}{6}$. Therefore, the slope of a line perpendicular is the negative reciprocal of this number, which is $\frac{6}{5}$.

11. A) The law of negative exponents states that $x^{-a} = \frac{1}{x^a}$. Therefore, $6^{-2}2^{-4}8^3 = \frac{8^3}{6^2 2^4}$. Only the expressions that have negative exponents go into the denominator.

12. C) This is a right triangle, so we can use the Pythagorean Theorem, $a^2 + b^2 = c^2$, where a and b are the lengths of the sides and c is the length of the hypotenuse.

$$6^2 + b^2 = 10^2$$

$$36 + b^2 = 100$$

$$b = 8$$

2. B) Create an equation where a is the number being solved for.

$$\frac{5}{7} \times a = 35$$

$$a = \frac{7}{5} \times 35 = 49$$

3. C) Let x be the original number of marbles. After Vic's share is given, $.75x$ remains. After giving Robbie 20% of the remaining share what remains is:

$$0.75x \times 0.80$$

After giving Jules 10%, what remains is:

$$0.75x \times 0.8 \times 0.9$$

Roland gives his brother $\frac{6}{20}$ of this amount, so what is left is:

$$0.75x \times 0.80 \times 0.90 \times \left(1 - \frac{6}{20}\right) = 0.378x$$

If there are 378 marbles left, then:

$$0.378x = 378$$

$$x = 1,000$$

4. B) Find all of the prime numbers that multiply to give the numbers. For 2, the prime factor is 2; for 3, the prime factor is 3; for 4, the prime factors are 2, 2; and for 5, the prime factor is 5. Note the maximum times of occurrence of each prime and multiply these to find the least common multiple (LCM). The LCM is:

$$2 \times 2 \times 3 \times 5 = 60$$

5. E) To find 2 multiplied by the sum of 11 and 3, write it as an equation.

$$2(11 + 3)$$

$$2(14) = 28$$

6. E) Each subsequent value is determined by adding 7 to the previous value; therefore, to determine the first value in the sequence, subtract 7 from 13 to obtain 6.

7. A) There are 11 balls in the bag; therefore, 11 is the total number of possible outcomes. Out of the values 1–11, the following are odd numbers: 1, 3, 5, 7, 9, 11. This gives 6 total odd values; therefore, the probability of selecting an odd numbered ball is $\frac{6}{11}$.

23. B) The numbers in the series are increasing. The difference between the values increases by 10 with each number.

$$720 - 710 = 10$$
$$740 - 720 = 20$$
$$770 - 740 = 30$$
$$810 - 770 = 40$$

To find the next number, add 50 to the previous number.

$$810 + 50 = 860$$

24. D) Expand $(2m^3)^5$ by distributing the exponent.

$$2^5 m^{3 \times 5} = 32m^{15}$$

If $32m^{15} = 32m^{k+1}$, solve for k.

$$k + 1 = 15$$
$$k = 14$$

25. D) If the number is divisible by 2, d should be even. If the number is divisible by 5, then d has to equal 0. Go through the options to see which one of them meets these criteria. Then check if those remaining are divisible by 7.

Quantitative Section #2

1. B) The difference between the first and third number and the third and fifth is 8.

$$15, \_\_, 23, \_\_, 31$$
$$23 - 15 = 8$$
$$31 - 23 = 8$$

Divide by 2 to find the difference between each consecutive number:

$$8 \div 2 = 4$$

To find the missing numbers, add 4 to the previous number:

$$15 + 4 = 19$$
$$23 + 4 = 27$$

21. B) To find the combined average, first find the sum for each given set. The average is found by dividing the sum by the number of items in a number set. Since the average and number of data points are given, the sums can be found using the formula for the average.

$$\frac{sum}{data\ points} = mean$$

The sum of the first six entries:

$$\frac{x_1}{6} = 12$$

$$x_1 = 72$$

The sum of the next two entries:

$$\frac{x_2}{2} = 20$$

$$x_2 = 40$$

The sum of the remaining four entries:

$$\frac{x_3}{4} = 4$$

$$x_3 = 16$$

To find the average of the entire data set, add each sum together and divide by the total number of data points:

$$\frac{72 + 40 + 16}{12} = 10.67$$

22. A) Rewrite each value as a decimal.

(a): 30% = 0.3

(b): 0.3

(c): $\frac{3}{100}$ = 0.03

Therefore, a is equal to b, and both are greater than c.

Answer Explanation #3

18. B) The entire paycheck is $500. 20% of $500 goes to bills:

$$\$500 \times 0.20 = \$100$$

Find the remaining amount:

$$\$500 - \$100 = \$400$$

30% of the remainder ($400) goes to pay entertainment.

$$\$400 \times 0.30 = \$120$$

Find the remaining amount:

$$\$400 - \$120 = \$280$$

10% of the remainder ($280) is put into a retirement account:

$$\$280 \times 0.10 = \$28$$

Find the remainder:

$$\$280 - \$28 = \$252$$

The question states "approximately." Using rounding rules, $252 would be rounded down to $250, so $250 is the correct answer.

19. D) In this series, each digit in the four-digit number increases by 1.

$$1234, 2345, 3456, \_\_\_, 5678, 6789$$

To find the missing number, add 1 to each digit in the previous number.

$$3456 \rightarrow 4567$$

20. D) To find the combined scores, first find the sum of the scores for each test. The average is found by dividing the sum by the number of items in a number set. Since the number of items and the average are given, the sum can be calculated. If the average for test A is 21 for 5 tests, then sum of test A is:

$$21 \times 5 = 105$$

If the test B average is 23 for 13 tests, then the sum of test B is:

$$23 \times 13 = 299$$

Calculate the average of all tests by adding the sums together and dividing by the total number of tests:

$$\frac{299 + 105}{5 + 13} = \frac{404}{18} = 22.44$$

13. B) The bar graph should show that 10 students prefer vanilla, 6 students prefer strawberry, and 23 students prefer chocolate ice cream; therefore, Benjamin completed the graph correctly.

14. E) In this series, the numbers 1 and −1 alternate with a zero between each one.

$$1, 0, -1, 0, 1, 0, \ldots$$

The next number in the series will follow a zero, so it will be either 1 or −1. Because the number before the last zero is 1, the next number will be −1.

15. B) Find all the factors of 42.

$$42 = 1 \times 42$$
$$42 = 2 \times 21$$
$$42 = 3 \times 14$$
$$42 = 6 \times 7$$

The factors of 42 are 1, 2, 3, 6, 7, 14, 21, and 42. The prime factors are 2, 3, and 7. (1 is neither prime nor composite.) Subtract the smallest value from the largest to find the range.

$$7 - 2 = 5$$

16. C) The series is geometric with a common ratio of $\frac{1}{2}$, meaning each number is multiplied by $\frac{1}{2}$ or divided by 2 to find the next number.

$$\frac{12}{24} = \frac{1}{2}$$
$$\frac{6}{12} = \frac{1}{2}$$
$$\frac{3}{6} = \frac{1}{2}$$

To find the next number, multiply the previous number by $\frac{1}{2}$:

$$3 \times \frac{1}{2} = \frac{3}{2} = 1.5$$

17. E) The entire class has 42 students, 18 of which are boys, meaning the number of girls is:

$$42 - 18 = 24$$

Out of these 24 girls, 2 leave; 22 girls are left. The total number of students is now $42 - 2 = 40$. To find the percentage of remaining students that are girls, divide the number of girls by the total number of students and multiply by 100.

$$22 \div 40 \times 100 = 55\%.$$

Answer Explanation #3

5. D) When adding 7 points to each test, the mean, median, and modes will all increase by 7 points.

$$\text{mean} = 85$$
$$\text{median} = 81$$
$$\text{mode} = 84$$

The range, which is the difference between the lowest and highest score, will not change as a result of adding points.

6. D) The graph of $x = 3$ is a vertical line. It crosses the x-axis at 3 but has an undefined slope.

7. C) The numbers in the series are increasing by 1.1.

$$\_\_, 5, 6.1, 7.2, 8.3$$
$$6.1 - 5 = 1.1$$
$$7.2 - 6.1 = 1.1$$
$$8.3 - 7.2 = 1.1$$

To find the first number, subtract 1.1 from the number that follows it.

$$5 - 1.1 = 3.9$$

8. A) First, identify the variables. If m is the number of lawns Justin mows, and he earns $40 per lawn, then income= 40m. If x is the number of weeks, and he pays $35 each week, then expenses=35x.

$$\text{Profit} = \text{income} - \text{expenses}$$
$$\text{Profit} = 40m - 35x$$

9. B) The given problem is solved using subtraction:

$$7 - 2 = 5 \text{ pencils}$$

Problem B is also solved using subtraction: Selena brought 10 carrot sticks for lunch. How many carrots sticks were left after she ate 6?

$$10 - 6 = 4 \text{ carrot sticks}$$

10. B) Order the fractions by comparing the denominators.

$$\frac{1}{2} > \frac{1}{3} > \frac{1}{7} > -\frac{1}{6} > -\frac{1}{5} > -\frac{1}{4}$$

11. B) Each of the decimal numbers is expressed in ten-thousandths. The number 55 is between 47 and 162, so 0.0055 is between 0.0047 and 0.0162.

12. E) The given sequence is formed by subtracting 3. The new sequence would therefore start with 41 and decrease by 3 with each term: 41, 38, 35, 32, ...

Answer Explanation #3

Quantitative Section #1

1. B) In this series, a new number is found by adding the two previous numbers.

$$1, 1, 2, 3, 5, 8, \ldots$$

$$1 + 1 = 2$$

$$1 + 2 = 3$$

$$2 + 3 = 5$$

$$3 + 5 = 8$$

The next number is $5 + 8 = 13$.

2. A) The numbers in the series are decreasing by 106.

$$8021 - 8127 = -106$$

$$7915 - 8021 = -106$$

$$7809 - 7915 = -106$$

To find the next number, subtract 106 from the previous number.

$$7809 - 106 = 7703$$

3. E) Multiply the exponents raised to a power.

$$\frac{(10^2)^3}{(10^{-2})^2} = \frac{10^6}{10^{-4}}$$

Subtract the exponent in the denominator from the exponent in the numerator.

$$10^{6-(-4)} = 10^{10}$$

4. C) The numbers in the series are decreasing by 2.

$$71, 69, \underline{}, \underline{}, 63, 61$$

To find the missing numbers, subtract 2 from the previous number.

$$69 - 2 = 67$$

$$67 - 2 = 65$$

28. Search is to look as
    A) Jog is to sprint
    B) Listen is to understand
    C) Study is to observe
    D) Show is to tell
    E) Locate is to misplace

29. Support is to scaffold as
    A) Belt is to fasten
    B) Protect is to armor
    C) Heal is to nourish
    D) Explode is to firework
    E) Guide is to navigate

30. Exile is to embrace as
    A) Turn is to twist
    B) Enter is to exit
    C) Block is to prevent
    D) Deny is to accept
    E) Punishment is to reward

21. Clean is to disinfect as
    A) Wash is to sterilize
    B) Burn is to incinerate
    C) Dust is to dirt
    D) Tidy is to organize
    E) Wet is to flooded

22. Biology is to science as
    A) Math is to geometry
    B) Nonfiction is to literature
    C) Past is to future
    D) Communication is to English
    E) Molecule is to chemistry

23. Naïve is to gullible as
    A) Powerful is to invincible
    B) Meek is to malicious
    C) Timid is to shy
    D) Novice is to master
    E) Angry is to malevolent

24. Laugh is to humor as
    A) Grin is to smile
    B) Happy is to face
    C) Joke is to punchline
    D) Grimace is to disgust
    E) Upset is to cry

25. Slice is to pie as
    A) Serve is to cake
    B) Carve is to turkey
    C) Drink is to water
    D) Eat is to meal
    E) Combine is to ingredients

26. Animal is to zoo as
    A) Book is to library
    B) Student is to school
    C) Zucchini is to garden
    D) Shark is to water
    E) Branch is to tree

27. Air is to jet plane as
    A) Fuel is to car
    B) Rail is to train
    C) Desert is to scorpion
    D) Water is to boat
    E) Sky is to rocket

Practice Test #3

14. Volleyball is to sport as
    A) Score is to game
    B) Player is to field
    C) Chemistry is to science
    D) Ball is to game
    E) Numbers is to math

15. Soup is to bowl as
    A) Plate is to table
    B) Dish is to sink
    C) Bread is to butter
    D) Spoon is to cereal
    E) Coffee is to mug

16. Principal is to school as
    A) Coach is to sport
    B) Professor is to college
    C) Governor is to state
    D) Tutor is to student
    E) Patriarch is to family

17. Insert is to remove as
    A) Push is to pull
    B) Combine is to separate
    C) Create is to destroy
    D) Sprint is to crawl
    E) Up is to down

18. Envy is to jealousy as
    A) Gluttony is to satiety
    B) Fear is to cowardice
    C) Happy is to sad
    D) Glee is to giggling
    E) Annoyance is to rage

19. Clumsy is to graceful as
    A) Clever is to smart
    B) Honest is to transparent
    C) Bold is to brave
    D) Strong is to intimidating
    E) Slow is to swift

20. Flip is to page as
    A) Play is to sport
    B) Kick is to ball
    C) Open is to door
    D) Turn is to dial
    E) Ride is to bicycle

7. Old is to wise as
    A) Hardworking is to successful
    B) Young is to experienced
    C) Muscular is to athletic
    D) Naïve is to ignorant
    E) Wealthy is to greed

8. Click is to seatbelt as
    A) Flick is to switch
    B) Pull is to tab
    C) Push is to open
    D) Clasp is to necklace
    E) Wind is to clock

9. Seedling is to tree as
    A) Root is to soil
    B) Pollen is to bee
    C) Bark is to trunk
    D) Puppy is to dog
    E) Grass is to dirt

10. Sweet is to sugar as
    A) Spicy is to heat
    B) Bitter is to chocolate
    C) Salty is to sodium
    D) Sour is to lemon
    E) Hot is to coal

11. Type is to keyboard as
    A) Write is to pen
    B) Text is to message
    C) Listen is to speak
    D) Read is to journal
    E) Treadmill is to gym

12. Compassion is to indifference as
    A) Attraction is to repulsion
    B) Worried is to uncaring
    C) Kindness is to smile
    D) Apathy is to boredom
    E) Fear is to bravery

13. Grapple is to wrestling as
    A) Goal is to field
    B) Win is to race
    C) Team is to football
    D) Pitch is to baseball
    E) Defense is to offense

Analogies

Directions: The first two words in each question have a relationship. Choose the response that recreates that same relationship in the second set of words.

1. Satellite is to planet as
    - A) Star is to galaxy
    - B) Car is to roundabout
    - C) Airplane is to sky
    - D) Ship is to ocean
    - E) Moon is to Earth

2. Stand is to ground as
    - A) Walk is to shoe
    - B) Sleep is to pillow
    - C) Sprint is to track
    - D) Sit is to chair
    - E) Fly is to air

3. Ring is to bell as
    - A) Tick is to clock
    - B) Chirp is to bird
    - C) Loud is to ear
    - D) Strum is to guitar
    - E) Music is to record player

4) Strike is to karate as
    - A) Stance is to boxing
    - B) Dribble is to basketball
    - C) Touchdown is to football
    - D) Goal is to soccer
    - E) Score is to win

5. Car is to wheel as
    - A) Bicycle is to pedal
    - B) Body is to leg
    - C) House is to foundation
    - D) Boat is to hull
    - E) Kite is to string

6. Shoe is to walk as
    - A) Mitten is to hand
    - B) Ring is to finger
    - C) Glasses is to see
    - D) Umbrella is to rain
    - E) Sock is to foot

24. QUANDARY
    A) Question
    B) Miracle
    C) Dilemma
    D) Solution
    E) Hallucination

25. GRADUAL
    A) Abrupt
    B) Mediated
    C) Partial
    D) Hesitant
    E) Slow

26. REBUKE
    A) Rebound
    B) Encourage
    C) Request
    D) Criticize
    E) Offend

27. ADEPT
    A) Novice
    B) Quick
    C) Skilled
    D) Careful
    E) Alert

28. ARID
    A) Humid
    B) Flat
    C) Mountainous
    D) Cold
    E) Dry

29. FABRICATE
    A) Distribute
    B) Orchestrate
    C) Produce
    D) Dismantle
    E) Conduct

30. RECONCILE
    A) Describe
    B) Conclude
    C) Befriend
    D) Harmonize
    E) Resist

17. RIGID
    A) Smooth
    B) Bumpy
    C) Bouncy
    D) Flexible
    E) Stiff

18. PERPLEXED
    A) Exhausted
    B) Enlightened
    C) Confused
    D) Enslaved
    E) Disordered

19. GALLANT
    A) Tall
    B) Serious
    C) Reserved
    D) Brave
    E) Fearful

20. DISMAL
    A) Gloomy
    B) Upbeat
    C) Distant
    D) Abysmal
    E) Harsh

21. CONDONE
    A) Study
    B) Participate
    C) Disregard
    D) Deny
    E) Withdraw

22. BAFFLE
    A) Amuse
    B) Illuminate
    C) Confound
    D) Intimidate
    E) Halt

23. CAPTIVATE
    A) Begin
    B) Inspire
    C) Instruct
    D) Enthrall
    E) Hone

10. KEEN
    A) Full
    B) Blurry
    C) Sharp
    D) Grateful
    E) Nervous

11. RESOLUTE
    A) Defensive
    B) Happy
    C) Aloof
    D) Determined
    E) Cowardly

12. OPULENT
    A) Enormous
    B) Fixed
    C) Shiny
    D) Dull
    E) Luxurious

13. SCOFF
    A) Deride
    B) Hum
    C) Gather
    D) Believe
    E) Whisper

14. FORBID
    A) Regret
    B) Allow
    C) Ban
    D) Encourage
    E) Ignore

15. ENIGMA
    A) Chaos
    B) Problem
    C) Mystery
    D) Message
    E) Question

16. COERCE
    A) Share
    B) Neglect
    C) Perceive
    D) Force
    E) Continue

3. VIGILANT
    A) Violent
    B) Revolutionary
    C) Confused
    D) Watchful
    E) Neglectful

4. PRECARIOUS
    A) Ordinary
    B) Studious
    C) Unstable
    D) Expensive
    E) Annoying

5. DUBIOUS
    A) Impossible
    B) Bogus
    C) Believable
    D) Joyful
    E) Comforting

6. ERADICATE
    A) Disappear
    B) Introduce
    C) Develop
    D) Dissolve
    E) Eliminate

7. OBSCURE
    A) Obsolete
    B) Famous
    C) Weathered
    D) Unclear
    E) Transparent

8. FUTILE
    A) Amusing
    B) Useless
    C) Simple
    D) Unnecessary
    E) Worthy

9. LIBERATE
    A) Revolt
    B) Catch
    C) Politicize
    D) Free
    E) Locate

Dickinson reveals the primal terror of death with a disturbing calmness. She creates a carriage ride in "Because I could not stop for Death" that is more unsettling than a horror film. It is a portrayal of a courteous drive instead of a last stop. The domestic picture of mortality as polite company who "kindly stopped" for her strips it of its terror. It urges the reader to linger on the inevitability of the end.

38. The main contrast established in the first paragraph is between
    A) Dickinson and other poets of her era.
    B) Amherst and other literary communities.
    C) Dickinson's private and public lives.
    D) Dickinson's early and later works.
    E) Dickinson's physical and mental spaces.

39. Which of the following conclusions about Dickinson's poetry is best supported by the passage?
    A) Her work transforms the ordinary by revealing hidden significance.
    B) She mainly wrote about supernatural experiences.
    C) Her loneliness kept her from writing effectively about human connections.
    D) She purposefully obscured meaning to confuse the reader.
    E) Her poetry was well-received despite her inexperience.

40. What does the passage suggest about Dickinson's approach to writing about death?
    A) That it is less effective than more graphic depictions
    B) That it is more ominous than standard horror due to its calmness
    C) That it is like how most poets of her time wrote about death
    D) That it is intended to comfort readers rather than unsettle them
    E) That it is a way to confront her own fear of mortality

Verbal

Synonyms

Directions: Find the synonym or the word closest in meaning.

1. TEDIOUS
    A) Swift
    B) Exciting
    C) Boring
    D) Complex
    E) Deflating

2. SERENE
    A) Jittery
    B) Silent
    C) Musical
    D) Peaceful
    E) Colorful

34. What is a likely assumption about da Vinci's relationship with the painting?
   A) He felt a personal connection that prevented him from parting with it.
   B) He viewed it as an impossible task, refusing to complete it.
   C) He created it mainly to profit from it through wealthy patrons.
   D) He used it for experimentation, testing out different techniques.
   E) He finished the portrait, but it was ultimately rejected by the buyer.

35. What purpose does the function of the neurological research mentioned in the passage serve?
   A) To propose that da Vinci understood complex visual principles
   B) To challenge interpretations of the artwork's effect
   C) To imply that da Vinci had exploited visual perception
   D) To provide a logical reason why the smile changes when viewed
   E) To argue that the painting's effect is universal across all viewers

36. Which option best describes the relationship between the Mona Lisa and its viewers?
   A) It is dependent on viewers knowing about Renaissance art principles.
   B) It is interactive, as if the painting knowingly responds to being observed.
   C) It is diminishing due to the technology's demystification of the portrait's secrets.
   D) It is based on cultural word of mouth rather than firsthand observation.
   E) It is primarily intellectual and based on historical understanding.

37. How can the tone of the passage when discussing the Mona Lisa best be described?
   A) Scholarly and focused on facts
   B) Skeptical about traditional interpretations
   C) Fascinated by the enduring mystery
   D) Objective in balancing myth with reality
   E) Concerned about classical art's commercialization

Passage 8

Emily Dickinson secluded herself in a small bedroom in Amherst, Massachusetts. Most others would wither in isolation. Yet she was still able to wander. In her reclusion, she helped uncover the existential meaning of ordinary events, like a fly's intrusive buzzing.

Dickinson often introduces familiar imagery before turning it into something profound. In "Hope is the thing with feathers," she doesn't just compare hope to a bird; she turns it into a creature that "perches in the soul" and sings "without words." Hope is animal-like but distinctly nonhuman. The bird of hope sings "in the Gale," keeping the melody going through storms and harsh conditions without ever asking the poet for even a "crumb." This is how Dickinson takes an abstract concept and makes it recognizable and deeply personal.

Simple observations like buzzing bees or slanting afternoon light are transformed into revelations. They may seem like mundane details, but by Dickinson's hand, they become gateways to profound understanding. In "A narrow Fellow in the Grass," she describes a creature—most likely a snake—that divides grass "as with a Comb." Her encounter happens by chance but becomes something sinister and unnerving and reveals a sense of primal fear. The composure with which she describes the menacing creature—"a Whip lash / Unbraiding in the Sun"—can be more disturbing than explicit horror.

31. Which of the following is mentioned as a challenge of rural living?
    A) High cost of living
    B) Lack of personal space
    C) Constant noise pollution
    D) Weak social bonds
    E) Limited job prospects

32. Which one of the following best characterizes the relationship between neighbors in urban environments as suggested by the passage?
    A) Deeply connected due to proximity
    B) Strained due to political disagreement
    C) Distant despite physical closeness
    D) Strengthened by technology
    E) Friendlier than in previous generations

Passage 7

The Mona Lisa's smile seems to know when you're looking. The painting is Leonardo da Vinci's masterpiece, and it has inspired intrigue over the last several centuries. It does a good job of raising countless questions while answering none.

Sometime between 1503 and 1519, da Vinci captured one of art's great enigmas. It seems to just be a smile. Many think that the gesture belongs to Lisa Gherardini, an Italian noblewoman. Yet da Vinci never delivered this work to anybody. He kept the portrait until the very end, occasionally changing it through the years—adding a shadow here, applying a thin layer of oil glaze there. Why did he do this? Was there something personal about it? Or was he just a perfectionist? X-ray scans show at least three different versions underneath the surface of the final image. The setting doesn't match any real Italian vistas. The answer died with da Vinci, leaving us with the unanswered questions.

Part of the secret was da Vinci's use of sfumato—a technique that blends colors and leaves no visible transitions. It gives art a hazy, dreamy quality. It is also what causes the Mona Lisa's smile to melt away when looking directly at her mouth. Glance away, and it feels like her gaze is following you. Her smile is just reappearing in your periphery letting you know you are being watched. Neurological research tells us that our brains process central and peripheral vision differently. This might explain the strange interaction countless people have experienced with this painting.

The Mona Lisa's journey is as wild as the portrait itself. She has been stolen and vandalized, even used as a decoration on Napoleon's bedroom wall. Now she is safe behind bulletproof glass—at the Louvre—keeping her secrets from roughly 11 million visitors annually.

33. Based on the passage, which one of the following best explains the Mona Lisa's enduring appeal?
    A) Da Vinci's technical mastery
    B) High monetary and historical value
    C) The subject, Italian noblewoman Lisa Gherardini
    D) An unsolved mystery that raises questions
    E) Centuries of ownership and a dramatic life

Passage 6

The gap between city and countryside is steadily growing. Their divergent paths have inspired cultural and political rivalries. Sometimes these differences spill into American culture.

Both ways of life used to share similarities. In a time before electronics and the internet, Americans lived within walking distance of their jobs. They also knew their neighbors well.

Fast forward to today. Urbanites speed-walk across city blocks. They engage unceasingly in multiple tasks, riding the elevator to their high-rise apartments when the working day is done. High-speed internet is essential for life and for food delivery—it is easier to navigate a touchscreen than it is to be stuck in city traffic. Urbanites are natural job-hoppers. They go from one project to another looking for their next big break. The city might be a sea of opportunity, but some have no choice but to grind through each day due to the high cost of living.

Rural life is more relaxed. The pace is much slower in the country. Internet networks are not unheard of, but connection to the natural world is more important here. Folks do use modern technology to do things like automating farm equipment. Strong communal ties keep everything together. Rural residents have space to stretch, take a deep breath, and listen to nature's sounds. This can be difficult in the perpetual thrum of the city. The remote nature of rural living does make access to hospitals a bit tricky. Job options and entertainment are also limited. Online shopping and the closure of small-town stores have quieted several rural main streets.

In the city, people have hundreds of neighbors but barely know them. In the country, communities are strong but spread over great distances. By understanding the growing divide between urban and rural life, we can build bridges toward a more unified future.

28. According to the passage, what was a shared characteristic between urban and rural Americans in the past?
    A) Living within walking distance of their jobs
    B) Relying on electronic communication
    C) Preferring to live in isolated communities
    D) Having equal access to health care
    E) Maintaining social and political harmony

29. What does the description of urbanites "speed-walking across city blocks" illustrate?
    A) Then dangerous traffic conditions in cities
    B) The health benefits of city living
    C) The inefficiency of public transportation
    D) The fast pace of urban life
    E) The exercise habits of city residents

30. The metaphor "sea of opportunity" in the second paragraph suggests what about cities?
    A) That they are usually located near bodies of water
    B) That they have countless, but possibly overwhelming, options
    C) That they create a relaxing environment for residents
    D) That they are constantly changing like the ocean's tides
    E) That they attract tourists with interest in maritime activities

Paper money and coins presented a turning point. These items were not perishable or fragile like a shell. They were durable and could be more easily regulated. Metal coins were first minted around 3,000 years ago by the Lydian civilization of modern-day Turkey. Paper money came around 1800 years later. The Tang Dynasty of China is first recorded to have used it as a convenient alternative to lugging around heavy coin purses.

As societies grew, so too did the complexity of currency use. Banks were created to hold vast sums of money, safely holding people's cash. All one had to do was make a deposit and request a banknote. Today, these are known as bills. The use of credit cards came much later, accelerating spending and bringing into question what we can call cash. Now, cryptocurrencies and digital payments serve as the newest heirs in the line of succession started by seashells and cacao beans of the past.

23. What does the passage suggest was the primary limitation to bartering?
    A) Transactions depended on the mutual needs of traders.
    B) Governments were not able to regulate or tax these exchanges.
    C) People could not agree on fair exchanges.
    D) Items were too difficult to move between communities.
    E) Traded goods often spoiled too quickly.

24. Which characteristic was most important for early forms of currency?
    A) Government regulation and approval
    B) Resistance to counterfeiting
    C) Wide community acceptance
    D) Religious or spiritual significance
    E) An item's physical attractiveness

25. Which pair of adjectives best describes the tone of the passage?
    A) Critical and concerned
    B) Enthusiastic and positive
    C) Reflective and apologetic
    D) Informative and objective
    E) Technical and academic

26. How does the passage primarily organize information?
    A) By listing the advantages and disadvantages of each currency system
    B) By presenting currency systems in chronological order
    C) By explaining increasingly complex economic theories
    D) By discussing the spread of monetary concepts by geographical region
    E) By comparing different cultural approaches

27. What does the passage suggest about the future of currency?
    A) Digital currency is unlikely to replace physical money.
    B) Money will likely be fully digital.
    C) Society will eventually return to bartering.
    D) Government regulation of money will disappear completely.
    E) Currency will continue evolving with technology.

18. What is the primary purpose of the passage?
    A) To shine a light on the pressure to do well in school
    B) To show the psychological impact of taking shortcuts
    C) To entertain readers with a story about a supernatural object
    D) To caution against taking things that do not belong to you
    E) To demonstrate how intelligence can be increased

19. Throughout the story, how does Mary's character develop?
    A) From dishonest to ethical
    B) From ambitious to indifferent
    C) From gullible to tactical
    D) From dependent to self-reliant
    E) From confident to insecure

20. The phrase "it felt like wearing someone else's clothes" is an example of what?
    A) Simile
    B) Euphemism
    C) Allusion
    D) Idiom
    E) Onomatopoeia

21. What is the most important result of Mary's experiment?
    A) It revealed that the pencil only worked with certain subjects.
    B) It demonstrated the harm caused by the pencil.
    C) It confirmed Mary's suspicions about the pencil.
    D) It proved that the pencil belonged to Mary's teacher.
    E) It showed the temporary effects of the pencil.

22. Based on the context, what does the author mean by Mary feeling "hollow inside"?
    A) She missed the challenge of homework.
    B) She felt physically ill from using the pencil.
    C) She was afraid of the pencil's magic.
    D) She forgot to eat lunch that day.
    E) She lacked the satisfaction of doing it herself.

Passage 5

Think about how you pay for the latest gaming console—you exchange a specific amount of money for it. Now, instead of money, imagine paying with chicken eggs or with vegetables from your garden. Before dollars and cents, there was bartering. People traded goods directly instead of making a purchase. Bartering had limitations, though. For example, what if the game maker wasn't hungry?

That's where the concept of money comes in. People began to use designated objects as payment—beads, tea, salt, and even livestock were used as forms of currency. These items were usually valuable in some way and widely accepted by the community. They were also easy to transport. People in ancient China used the shell of the cowry (a type of sea snail). Native Americans also used shell money, trading wampum beads for various things. In Central America, the highly prized cacao bean was used as money by the Aztecs and the Mayans.

16. Which sentence best summarizes the passage's main idea?
    A) Many snakes produce a toxic fluid, called venom, in their salivary glands.
    B) There are many different types of snake venom, composed of various combinations of toxic and nontoxic substances.
    C) Some cytotoxins target specific types of cells— myotoxins affect muscles, cardiotoxins attack the heart, and nephrotoxins damage the kidneys.
    D) Researchers have been studying the chemical compositions of these venoms and have been making strides in using the science behind the toxins to combat major diseases such as cancer, heart disease, and Alzheimer's.
    E) Scientists have also been looking at the venom itself as a possible source of medical benefits.

17. According to the passage, how does venom benefit snakes, besides the fact that this fluid allows snakes to kill their prey?
    A) It helps snakes to disable and digest their prey.
    B) It can heal snakes' diseases, such as cancer and Alzheimer's.
    C) It terrifies snakes' prey, momentarily paralyzing these creatures.
    D) It discourages other predators from pursuing and eating snakes.
    E) It acts as a natural pain reliever for snakes.

Passage 4

Mary was struggling with her classwork when she dropped her eraser. Peering under her desk, she found a pencil. It was in much better shape than her current one. It was just an ordinary yellow No. 2 pencil. It was even perfectly sharpened. She slipped it in her pencil case without a second thought.

The pencil stayed in Mary's case until the following week, when she rushed to do her science homework before class. She grabbed the pencil and began writing about photosynthesis. The words had an odd shimmer. That's probably why the pencil's previous owner abandoned it.

Mary stared at her paper in confusion after getting it back from her teacher. It had "A+" written at the top with a big happy face next to it. The same thing happened in history class. The teacher's note read: "Brilliant citation of the text!" Mary couldn't recall citing anything.

Although Mary's grades skyrocketed, she felt hollow inside. She felt guilty when she reached for her magic pencil during her math exam. She stopped before touching it. "These aren't my own answers," she thought to herself. "My teachers aren't really proud of me."

Mary had to try an experiment. She took a piece of paper and folded it in half. She wrote the same sentence on both halves, one side using a normal pencil, the other side using the new pencil. Mary was stunned by the results the following morning. One sentence remained the same, but the other transformed into a well-written paragraph.

The pencil began as a gift, but now it felt like wearing someone else's clothes. It started to feel heavy in her bag. She realized that without understanding the concepts, appearing intelligent didn't quite feel right. Breaking the pencil in half, Mary was determined to start fresh and work harder than ever before.

neurotoxins, and cytotoxins. Hemotoxins affect the blood by interfering with the process of blood coagulation. In some cases, hemotoxins inhibit the process of blood clotting, and in other cases they cause excessive clotting. Neurotoxins target the nervous system rather than body tissues; they disrupt the messages sent by neurotransmitter production and reception throughout the body. Neurotoxins can paralyze muscles, causing respiratory failure and possibly death. Cytotoxins cause liquefactive necrosis of body cells; they dissolve cells, leading to the death of tissues or organs. Some cytotoxins target specific types of cells—myotoxins affect muscles, cardiotoxins attack the heart, and nephrotoxins damage the kidneys.

In addition to research on various antivenoms to combat the potentially deadly effects of snake venom, scientists have also been looking at the venom itself as a possible source of medical benefits. Researchers have been studying the chemical compositions of these venoms and have been making strides in using the science behind the toxins to combat major diseases such as cancer, heart disease, and Alzheimer's. For instance, a drug called captopril, used to treat hypertension, is based on a toxin in the venom of a pit viper found in Brazil.

12. What can the reader infer from the passage?
    A) That all snakes produce venom
    B) That some snakes are not venomous
    C) That a venomous snake never bites other members of its own species
    D) That a Brazilian pit viper's venom is not poisonous to humans
    E) That snakes make good pets

13. What is the author's primary purpose in writing this essay?
    A) To advise readers on ways to treat patients with snakebites
    B) To warn readers that most snakes are venomous
    C) To inform readers about the contents of snake venom
    D) To tell a story about a scientist who used venom as a medicine
    E) To discuss how venom can be used medicinally

14. In the last sentence in the second paragraph, what is most likely the meaning of the word part *nephro-* in the word *nephrotoxins*?
    A) Poison
    B) Heart
    C) Muscle
    D) Kidney
    E) Brain

15. In the last paragraph, what does the word *strides* mean?
    A) Long steps
    B) Heavy stomping
    C) Improvements
    D) Experiments
    E) Goals

7. Which body part is NOT mentioned in the passage?
   A) The roof of the mouth
   B) The trigeminal nerve
   C) The face
   D) The forehead
   E) The tongue

8. Why does the author use the word *screaming* in the last sentence?
   A) To show how painful "brain freeze" can be
   B) To show that ice cream headaches are dangerous
   C) To jokingly refer to a play on words: "I scream for ice cream"
   D) To rhyme with other words in the passage
   E) To describe how people respond to having a brain freeze

9. Which sentence best summarizes the passage's main idea?
   A) Have you ever devoured a tasty snow cone only to experience the agony of 'brain freeze'?
   B) Well, scientists now believe they understand the mechanism of these so-called ice cream headaches.
   C) When a cold substance (delicious or otherwise) presses against the roof of your mouth, it causes blood vessels there to begin to constrict, and your body starts to sense that something is awry.
   D) Because the trigeminal nerve also serves the face, the brain misinterprets these signals as coming from your forehead.
   E) The duration of the pain varies from a few seconds up to about a minute.

10. According to the passage, what happens immediately after the roof of the mouth grows cold?
    A) Blood vessels on the roof of the mouth begin to expand.
    B) The body pumps blood to the roof of the mouth to warm it up.
    C) The trigeminal nerve sends rapid signals to the brain.
    D) Blood vessels on the roof of the mouth begin to narrow.
    E) The brain misinterprets these signals as coming from your forehead.

11. In the last sentence, what does the word *duration* mean?
    A) Endurance
    B) Skin surface
    C) Intensity
    D) Strength
    E) Time period

Passage 3

Many snakes produce a toxic fluid, called venom, in their salivary glands. The two key ingredients in all snake venoms are enzymes and polypeptides. Some enzymes help the snake disable its prey, and others help the snake digest its prey. The victim of the snakebite has a much less beneficial experience with these enzymes: snake venoms can speed up chemical reactions that lower blood pressure, paralyze muscles, destroy tissues, deconstruct red blood cells, or cause internal bleeding.

There are many different types of snake venom, composed of various combinations of toxic and nontoxic substances. Toxins in snake venom are often divided into three categories: hemotoxins,

3. What is the best summary of this passage?
   A) It is important for everyone to know the best way to take a person's temperature in any given situation.
   B) The most common method of taking a person's temperature—orally—is not appropriate in some situations.
   C) The most accurate way to take a temperature is by placing a digital thermometer in the rectum.
   D) There are many different ways to take a person's temperature; the appropriate method will depend on the situation.
   E) Nurses and parents must take special steps when taking the temperatures of fussy babies.

4. What is the meaning of the word *agitated* in the last paragraph?
   A) Obviously upset
   B) Quickly moving
   C) Violently ill
   D) Slightly dirty
   E) Physically comfortable

5. According to the passage, why is it sometimes preferable to take a person's temperature rectally?
   A) People who are ill may not be able to sit still long enough to have their temperatures taken through their ears or temporal arteries.
   B) Many people cannot sit still long enough to have their temperatures taken orally.
   C) Temperature readings can vary widely between regions of the body.
   D) Many people do not have access to quick-acting thermometers.
   E) Rectal readings are more accurate than oral readings.

Passage 2

Have you ever devoured a tasty snow cone only to experience the agony of "brain freeze"? Have you ever wondered why or how that happens? Well, scientists now believe they understand the mechanism of these so-called ice cream headaches. It begins with the icy temperature of the snow cone (or any cold food, or sometimes even exposure to cold air). When a cold substance (delicious or otherwise) presses against the roof of your mouth, it causes blood vessels there to begin to constrict, and your body starts to sense that something is awry. In response, blood is pumped to the affected region to try to warm it up, causing rapid dilation of the same vessels. This causes the neighboring trigeminal nerve to send rapid signals to your brain. Because the trigeminal nerve also serves the face, the brain misinterprets these signals as coming from your forehead. The duration of the pain varies from a few seconds up to about a minute. Regardless of the time spent wincing, the danger of the ice cream headache certainly will not stop people for screaming for their favorite frozen treat in the future.

6. What is the author's purpose in writing this passage?
   A) To inform and persuade
   B) To inform and entertain
   C) To warn and persuade
   D) To amuse and entertain
   E) To persuade and entertain

Reading

Directions: For each passage, read the excerpt and answer the questions that follow.

Passage 1

Taking a person's temperature is one of the most basic and common health care tasks. Everyone from nurses to emergency medical technicians to concerned parents should be able to grab a thermometer and take a patient's or loved one's temperature. But what's the best way to get an accurate reading? The answer depends on the situation.

The most common way people measure body temperature is orally. A simple digital or disposable thermometer is placed under the tongue for a few minutes, and the task is done. There are many situations, however, when measuring temperature orally isn't an option. For example, when a person can't breathe through her nose, she won't be able to keep her mouth closed long enough to get an accurate reading. In these situations, it's often preferable to place the thermometer in the rectum or armpit. Using the rectum also has the added benefit of providing a much more accurate reading than other locations can provide.

It's also often the case that certain people, like <u>agitated</u> patients or fussy babies, won't be able to sit still long enough for an accurate reading. In these situations, it's best to use a thermometer that works much more quickly, such as one that measures temperature in the ear or at the temporal artery. No matter which method is chosen, however, it's important to check the average temperature for each region, as it can vary by several degrees.

1. Which statement is NOT a detail from the passage?
   A) Taking a temperature in the ear or at the temporal artery is more accurate than taking it orally.
   B) If an individual cannot breathe through the nose, taking his or her temperature orally will likely give an inaccurate reading.
   C) The standard human body temperature varies depending on whether it is measured in the mouth, rectum, armpit, ear, or temporal artery.
   D) The most common way to measure temperature is by placing a thermometer in the mouth.
   E) Some patients are unable to sit still long enough for an accurate reading using an oral thermometer.

2. What is the author's primary purpose in writing this essay?
   A) To advocate for the use of thermometers that measure temperature in the ear or at the temporal artery
   B) To explain the methods available to measure a person's temperature and the situations in which each method is appropriate
   C) To warn readers that the average temperature of the human body varies by region
   D) To discuss how nurses use different types of thermometers depending on the type of patient they are examining
   E) To inform readers of the proper procedure for taking a baby's temperature

21. Find the volume of a cylinder with a height of 10 inches and a radius of 3 inches.
    A) 900π square inches
    B) 90π inches
    C) 90π square inches
    D) 30π square inches
    E) 60π square inches

22. Examine (a), (b), and (c) to determine the correct answer.
    (a) $\frac{35}{35}$

    (b) 35^0

    (c) 35×0

    A) $(a) = (b) > c$
    B) $(b) = (c) > (a)$
    C) $(a) = (b) = (c)$
    D) $(a) = (b) < c$
    E) There is not enough information to determine the answer.

23. Solve for x.

    $$|x| + 4 = 5$$

    A) 1
    B) -1 and 1
    C) 9
    D) -9 and 9
    E) 0

24. One acre of wheat requires 500 gallons of water. How many acres can be watered with 2600 gallons?
    A) 10 acres
    B) 5 acres
    C) 5.2 acres
    D) 50 acres
    E) 6 acres

25. If $35 : 5 :: 49 : x$, find x.
    A) $x = 5$
    B) $x = 9$
    C) $x = 4$
    D) $x = 7$
    E) $x = 11$

18. The following table shows the number of miles run by Stacy last week.

Day	Miles
Monday	6
Tuesday	8
Wednesday	2
Thursday	9
Friday	0
Saturday	13
Sunday	2

What percentage of the days did Stacy run 6 or more miles? Round your answer to the nearest tenth of a percent.
- A) 42.9%
- B) 71.4%
- C) 51.1%
- D) 32.9%
- E) 50.1%

19. Find the area of a circle with a diameter of 14 cm.
- A) 49π cm²
- B) 196π cm²
- C) 49π cm
- D) 14π cm²
- E) 28π cm

20. Rewrite the following with positive exponents in its simplest form:

$$\frac{a^{-4}b^{-5}c^2}{a^2b^{-4}c}$$

- A) $\frac{a^6 c}{b}$
- B) $\frac{1}{a^6 bc}$
- C) $\frac{c}{a^4 b}$
- D) $\frac{bc}{a^6}$
- E) $\frac{c}{a^6 b}$

Practice Test #3

15. Simplify.

$$4 + 15 \div 3 \times 2$$

- A) 3.2
- B) 19
- C) 6.5
- D) 14
- E) 10

16. What number is 12 less than 8 squared?
    - A) 4
    - B) 76
    - C) 52
    - D) 32
    - E) 50

17. Find the missing angle in the following isosceles triangle:

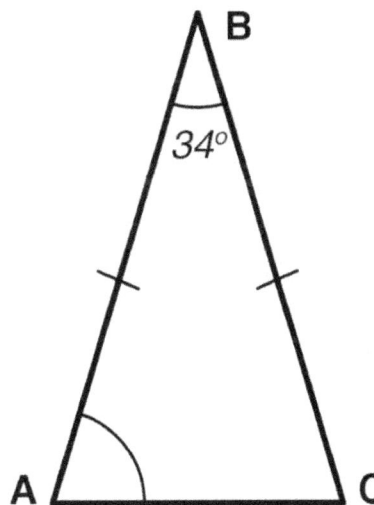

- A) 56°
- B) 34°
- C) 146°
- D) 73°
- E) 63°

11. Rewrite the following expression with positive exponents: $6^{-2}2^{-4}8^3$.
    A) $\dfrac{8^3}{6^2 2^4}$
    B) $\dfrac{1}{6^2 2^4 8^3}$
    C) $\dfrac{6^2 8^3}{2^4}$
    D) $6^2 2^4 8^3$
    E) $\dfrac{2^4 8^3}{6^2}$

12. A right triangle is shown below. Find the length of the missing side.

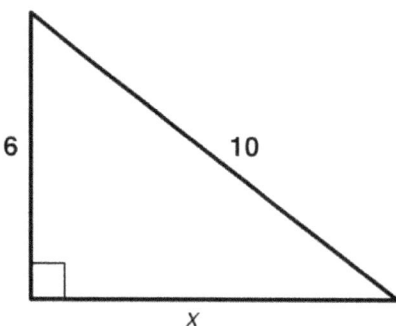

    A) 4
    B) 6
    C) 8
    D) 9
    E) 10

13. Find the equation of the line parallel to $y = 5x + 4$ that goes through the point $(-1, 1)$.
    A) $y = 5x - 6$
    B) $y = 5x$
    C) $y = 5x + 6$
    D) $y = -5x + 1$
    E) $y = -\dfrac{1}{5}x - \dfrac{6}{5}$

14. If 6 out of 40 students in a class have a black backpack, what percentage of the students have a black backpack?
    A) 6%
    B) 15%
    C) 30%
    D) 0.15%
    E) 20%

Practice Test #3

6. Which number should fill in the blank in the sequence?

$$\_\_, 13, 20, 27, 34.$$

   A) 2
   B) 3
   C) 4
   D) 5
   E) 6

7. A bag contains balls labeled with numbers 1 through 11. A person randomly selects one value. What is the probability that the ball has an odd number on it?

   A) $\frac{6}{11}$
   B) $\frac{5}{11}$
   C) $\frac{3}{5}$
   D) $\frac{1}{2}$
   E) $\frac{7}{11}$

8. Determine the equation of the line that runs through the points $(6, -1)$ and $(-2, 3)$.

   A) $y = 2x + \frac{19}{2}$
   B) $y = -\frac{1}{2}x - \frac{13}{2}$
   C) $y = -\frac{1}{2}x + \frac{11}{2}$
   D) $y = \frac{1}{2}x + \frac{11}{2}$
   E) $y = -2x + 8$

9. What number is $\frac{3}{5}$ of 100?

   A) 35
   B) 53
   C) 60
   D) 6
   E) 25

10. Find the slope of a line perpendicular to the line $5x + 6y = 12$.

   A) $-\frac{6}{5}$
   B) $\frac{6}{5}$
   C) $\frac{5}{6}$
   D) $\frac{12}{5}$
   E) $\frac{-5}{12}$

Quantitative Section #2

1. Which two numbers should fill in the blanks in the series?

    $$15, \_\_, 23, \_\_, 31$$

    A) 17, 27
    B) 19, 27
    C) 19, 28
    D) 18, 25
    E) 17, 24

2. $\frac{5}{7}$ of what number is equal to 35?
    A) 2
    B) 49
    C) 25
    D) 5
    E) 55

3. Roland has some marbles. He gives 25% to Vic, 20% of the remainder to Robbie, and 10% of that remainder he gives to Jules. Roland then gives $\frac{6}{20}$ of the remaining amount to his brother, and he keeps the rest for himself. If Roland ends up with 378 marbles, how many did he have to begin with?
    A) 800
    B) 833
    C) 1,000
    D) 378
    E) 900

4. What is the least common multiple of 2, 3, 4, and 5?
    A) 30
    B) 60
    C) 120
    D) 40
    E) 50

5. What number is 2 multiplied by the sum of 11 and 3?
    A) 32
    B) 18
    C) 196
    D) 7
    E) 28

21. A set of data has 12 entries. The average of the first 6 entries is 12, the average of the next two entries is 20, and the average of the remaining entries is 4. What is the average of the entire data set?
    A) 10
    B) 10.67
    C) 11
    D) 12.67
    E) 10.5

22. Examine (a), (b), and (c) to determine the correct answer.
    (a) 30%

    (b) 0.3

    (c) $\frac{3}{100}$

    A) (a) and (b) are equal and greater than (c)
    B) (b) and (c) are equal and less than (a)
    C) (a) and (c) are equal and less than (b)
    D) (a), (b), and (c) are all equal
    E) (c) is greater than (a) and (b)

23. Which number should come next in the series?

    $$710, 720, 740, 770, 810, ...$$

    A) 850
    B) 860
    C) 870
    D) 855
    E) 845

24. What is k if $(2m^3)^5 = 32m^{k+1}$?
    A) 11
    B) 12
    C) 13
    D) 14
    E) 15

25. If the number $56,8cd$ should be divisible by 2, 5, and 7, what could be the values of the digits c and d?
    A) 56,835
    B) 56,830
    C) 56,860
    D) 56,840
    E) 56,800

16. Which number should come next in the series?

$$24, 12, 6, 3, ...$$

- A) 2
- B) 1
- C) 1.5
- D) 0
- E) 0.75

17. In a class of 42 students, 18 are boys. Two girls get transferred to another school. What percent of students remaining are girls?
- A) 14%
- B) 16%
- C) 52.4%
- D) 60%
- E) None of the above

18. A payroll check is issued for $500.00. If 20% goes to bills, 30% of the remainder goes to pay entertainment expenses, and 10% of what is left is placed in a retirement account, then approximately how much is remaining?
- A) $150
- B) $250
- C) $170
- D) $350
- E) $180

19. Which number should fill in the blank in the series?

$$1234, 2345, 3456, \_\_\_, 5678, 6789$$

- A) 3567
- B) 4678
- C) 4680
- D) 4567
- E) 4582

20. If test A is taken 5 times with an average result of 21, and test B is taken 13 times with an average result of 23, what is the combined average?
- A) 22.24
- B) 22.22
- C) 22.00
- D) 22.44
- E) 24.22

Practice Test #3

13. Students are asked if they prefer vanilla, chocolate, or strawberry ice cream. The results are tallied on the table below. Four students then display the information from the table in a bar graph. Which student completes the bar graph correctly?

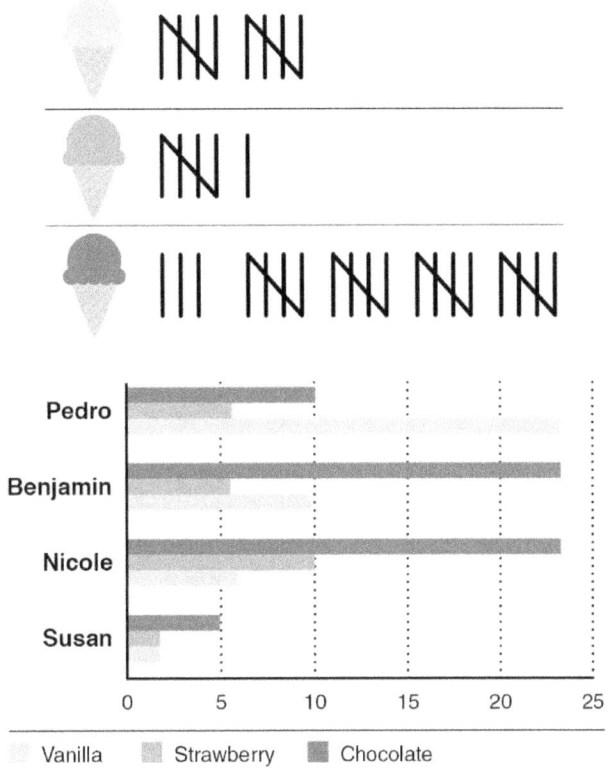

A) Pedro
B) Benjamin
C) Nicole
D) Susan
E) All of the students complete the bar graph correctly.

14. Which number should come next in the series?

$$1, 0, -1, 0, 1, 0, \ldots$$

A) 0.75
B) 0
C) 1
D) $\frac{1}{2}$
E) -1

15. A set of numbers contains all of the prime factors of 42. What is the range of the set?
A) 1
B) 5
C) 19
D) 41
E) 12

10. Which of the following is listed in order from greatest to least?
    A) $\frac{1}{2}, \frac{1}{3}, \frac{1}{7}, -\frac{1}{5}, -\frac{1}{6}, -\frac{1}{4}$
    B) $\frac{1}{2}, \frac{1}{3}, \frac{1}{7}, -\frac{1}{6}, -\frac{1}{5}, -\frac{1}{4}$
    C) $\frac{1}{2}, \frac{1}{7}, \frac{1}{3}, -\frac{1}{4}, -\frac{1}{5}, -\frac{1}{6}$
    D) $\frac{1}{2}, \frac{1}{3}, \frac{1}{7}, -\frac{1}{6}, -\frac{1}{4}, -\frac{1}{5}$
    E) $\frac{1}{7}, \frac{1}{3}, \frac{1}{2}, -\frac{1}{6}, -\frac{1}{4}, -\frac{1}{5}$

11. If the value of y is between 0.0047 and 0.0162, what could be the value of y?
    A) 0.0035
    B) 0.0055
    C) 0.0185
    D) 0.0238
    E) 0.0621

12. Which sequence follows the same rule as the following sequence?

    $$30, 27, 24, 21, \ldots$$

    A) 41, 39, 37, 35, ...
    B) 41, 44, 47, 50, ...
    C) 41, 37, 33, 29, ...
    D) 41, 36, 35, 32, ...
    E) 41, 38, 35, 32, ...

Practice Test #3

5. Mr. Smith has decided to curve his tests by adding 7 points to each of the test scores in his class. Which value will remain the same after he curves the scores?
- A) Mean
- B) Median
- C) Mode
- D) Range
- E) None of the above

6. Which of the following statements is true for the line $x = 3$?
- A) It has a slope of 3.
- B) It has a y-intercept of 3.
- C) It does not have an x-intercept.
- D) It has an undefined slope.
- E) It is a horizontal line.

7. Which number should fill in the blank in the series?

$$\_\_, 5, 6.1, 7.2, 8.3$$

- A) 4.1
- B) 3.5
- C) 3.9
- D) 4.9
- E) 2.2

8. Justin has a summer lawn care business and earns $40 for each lawn he mows. He also pays $35 per week in business expenses. Which of the following expressions represents Justin's profit after x weeks if he mows m number of lawns?
- A) $40m - 35x$
- B) $40m + 35x$
- C) $35x(40 + m)$
- D) $35(40m + x)$
- E) $40m + x(35)$

9. Which problem has the same mathematical structure as the following problem:

Selena had 7 pencils. She gave 2 pencils to her friend Amy. How many pencils does she have now?

- A) Selena brought 3 friends to the end-of-summer party. Amy brought 2 friends. Together, how many friends did they bring?
- B) Selena brought 10 carrot sticks for lunch. How many carrots sticks were left after she ate 6?
- C) Selena earned 2 stickers every school day this week, Monday through Friday. How many stickers did she earn?
- D) Selena has 7 markers. Amy has 3 more markers than Selena does. How many markers does Amy have?
- E) Selena has 5 movie tickets. Selena wants to keep 1 ticket for herself and distribute the other 4 tickets to her friends. She has 6 friends—Harrison, Paisley, Jayden, Maria, Conner, and Brenda—and is trying to determine which friends should get a ticket. How many different combinations of friends can receive the 4 extra tickets?

Practice Test #3

Quantitative Section #1

1. Which number should come next in the series?

$$1, 1, 2, 3, 5, 8, \ldots$$

- A) 11
- B) 13
- C) 16
- D) 9
- E) 12

2. Which number should come next in the series?

$$8127, 8021, 7915, 7809, \ldots$$

- A) 7703
- B) 7721
- C) 7697
- D) 7715
- E) 7701

3. If the following expression is written in the form $10n$, what is the value of n?

$$\frac{(10^2)^3}{(10^{-2})^2}$$

- A) 2
- B) 5
- C) 6
- D) 7
- E) 10

4. Which two numbers should fill in the blanks in the series?

$$71, 69, \_\_, \_\_, 63, 61$$

- A) 65, 64
- B) 68, 64
- C) 67, 65
- D) 68, 65
- E) 68, 67

9. E) The stomach is needed for digestion; the lungs are needed for breathing.

10. B) A knife is used to slice; a fork is used to pierce.

11. E) A snake slithers along the ground; a kangaroo bounds across the land.

12. A) A seagull is one member of a flock; a wolf is one member of a pack.

13. C) A sock covers a foot; a glove covers a hand.

14. A) A key opens a lock; a handle opens a door.

15. B) A sweater is worn in the winter; a swimsuit is worn in the summer

16. C) An airport houses planes; a garage houses cars.

17. A) Obscure means "hidden"; malicious means "wicked."

18. E) An elephant lumbers through the jungle; a hummingbird flits through the air.

19. D) A pebble is a small rock, while a boulder is a huge one; a hut is a small building, while a mansion is a huge one.

20. C) A sentence is part of a paragraph; a stanza is part of a poem.

21. C) Drawing is the action that creates the picture, just as signing is the action that creates a signature.

22. C) Chalk is a medium applied to a surface, just as paint is applied to a canvas.

23. A) Option *A* is correct because it maintains the access tool-to-secured object relationship.

24. E) This answer option maintains the relationship between a body part and a smaller, digit-like component.

25. D) Like a mouse, a remote is a physical input device that is used to control an object or other device.

26. B) This answer option maintains the professional-to-workplace relationship.

27. E) Water is a fluid that flows through a pipe as its channel, just as blood is a fluid that flows through an artery as its channel.

28. D) This answer option maintains the general-to-specific synonym relationship dealing with adjectives describing thickness.

29. A) *Start* and *finish* are opposite actions describing the beginning and end of a process.

30. D) *Shake* (head) is a physical gesture that communicates *no*, maintaining the physical gesture-to-meaning relationship.

11. E) *Aptitude* means "ability, capacity."

12. A) *Abolish* means "to get rid of or eliminate" something.

13. A) *Gigantic* means "huge or humongous."

14. D) *Sleek* means "smooth, glossy, and shiny."

15. C) *Substantial* means "a lot or plentiful."

16. D) *Fidelity* means "allegiance or a commitment to someone or something."

17. A) *Briskly* means "energetically, quickly."

18. A) *Cacophony* means "unpleasant noises."

19. E) *Deflated* means "collapsed, let down."

20. B) *Jar* means "to jolt or shake."

21. B) *Illegible* means "impossible to read or indecipherable."

22. C) *Scarce* means "hard to find, or rare."

23. B) *Beckon* means "to call or summon."

24. C) *Antics* are "playful tricks or exploits."

25. B) *Abate* means "to decrease or lessen."

26. C) *Meager* means "insufficient."

27. B) *Diligent* means "showing persistent effort and care while working."

28. D) *Hinder* means "to make it difficult for something to happen."

29. E) *Guarantee* means "to give assurance that certain conditions will be fulfilled."

30. A) *Wary* means "careful about potential danger."

Analogies

1. C) A classroom is where teaching takes place. A park is where playing takes place.

2. D) A joey is a baby kangaroo; a puppy is a baby dog.

3. B) Typing is done on a computer; texting is done on a phone.

4. E) Clean and dirty are opposites; small and big are opposites.

5. A) A piece is a part of the puzzle; a player is part of a team.

6. B) Feathers cover a bird; fur covers a dog.

7. D) *Facilitate* means "assist"; *obliterate* means "destroy."

8. D) A pedal is one part of a bicycle; a zipper is one part of a jacket.

37. C) Option *C* is correct because the opening intentionally contrasts Franklin's importance and his origins as the son of a struggling family. Option *A* is incorrect because the passage does not mention his expertise in finance. Option *B* is incorrect because the text does not mention any disapproval of this practice. Option *D* is incorrect because the passage does not suggest that Franklin created the $100 bill. Option *E* is incorrect because the text emphasizes Franklin's modest background, not his wealth.

38. D) Option *D* is correct because Franklin is shown to have a practical streak in his inventions while choosing to share his designs rather than profit from them. Option *A* is incorrect because his inventions were successfully applied instead of solely theorized. Option *B* is incorrect because Franklin specifically avoided commercializing his inventions by avoiding patents. Option *C* is incorrect because Franklin's inventions were noted as useful solutions to common problems. Option *E* is incorrect because Franklin freely shared his creations and did not keep them hidden.

39. B) Option *B* is correct because the phrase places contrasting elements side by side for effect. Option *A* is incorrect because the description is not an exaggeration. Option *C* is incorrect because the description is literal. Option *D* is incorrect because the description does not hint at future events. Option *E* is incorrect because no inanimate objects are given human-like qualities.

40. E) Option *E* is correct because Franklin's achievements in science, diplomacy, inventing, and more exemplify the concept of a Renaissance man as someone with expertise in multiple domains. Option *A* is incorrect because the passage does not highlight artistic abilities. Option *B* is incorrect because the passage does not discuss classical learning or its revival. Option *C* is incorrect because Franklin's appearance is only mentioned as a diplomatic choice. Option *D* is incorrect because the passage emphasizes Franklin's American authenticity.

Verbal

Synonyms

1. B) *Tremble* means "to shiver or shake."

2. E) *Hesitate* means "to pause or falter."

3. C) *Meager* means "insufficient or inadequate."

4. C) *Dormant* means "sleeping, quiet, or inactive."

5. E) *Pacify* means "to soothe," or "to make someone or something become more peaceful."

6. B) *Acclaim* means "applause, praise."

7. B) *Haphazard* means "disorganized, messy, or chaotic."

8. D) *Meander* means to wander, roam, or amble around on a winding, twisting route.

9. A) *Ascend* means "to move upward, rise."

10. C) *Quench* means "to satisfy," usually used in terms of thirst.

are not mentioned. Option *E* is incorrect because cultural pride is not suggested to be Alex's father's motivation; instead, his response suggests understanding and a desire to accommodate Mia's family so that his son can see his friend.

31. A) Option *A* is correct because Alex does not seem to fully comprehend Mia's situation, but he does have some understanding based on his grandparents' experience. Option *B* is incorrect because his understanding is shown to be lacking, indicated by his confusion toward her fears. Option *C* is incorrect because his parents appear supportive and sympathetic. Option *D* is incorrect because Alex clearly has much to learn about the situation. Option *E* is incorrect because Alex clearly has some understanding of the situation.

32. A) Option *A* is correct because the passage explains that art communicates through basic visual elements that do not require specialized knowledge. Option *B* is incorrect because the passage never mentions art's accessibility to children. Option *C* is incorrect because cave paintings are used as examples of art's universality rather than reasons for why art is universal. Option *D* is incorrect because cultural bias is not addressed when comparing language and art. Option *E* is incorrect because the passage does not suggest that the presence of art is more natural than that of language.

33. D) Option *D* is correct because the passage emphasizes that visual art appreciation requires nothing but functioning eyesight. Options *A*, *C*, and *E* are incorrect because they are all examples of specialized knowledge, and the passage argues against the need for special knowledge to appreciate art. Option *B* is incorrect because the text does not mention cultural understanding as a requirement for engaging with art.

34. B) Option *B* is correct because the passage presents these art movements as evoking opposite emotional effects through their distinctive elements. Option *A* is incorrect because no chronological or developmental relationships are established. Option *C* is incorrect because the movements are not presented as competing, just as having contrasting aesthetics. Option *D* is incorrect because generational changes are not discussed. Option *E* is incorrect because the two artistic styles are presented as fundamentally different approaches rather than related variations.

35. B) Option *B* is correct because the passage explicitly describes symbolism as essential to an artist's vocabulary, drawing a direct parallel to language. Option *A* is incorrect because colors are not presented as having the communicative function of words but only that they are capable of evoking certain emotions. Option *C* is incorrect because shapes are discussed for their sensory impacts rather than any semantic functions. Option *D* is incorrect because texture is not addressed. Option *E* is incorrect because lines are mentioned as basic visual elements with no comparison to language components.

36. D) Option *D* is correct because the text states that, unlike language, art does not require literacy or special knowledge. Option *A* is incorrect because the passage acknowledges that everyone reacts differently to artwork based on personal experience. Option *B* is incorrect because the passage emphasizes how different visual elements trigger specific emotional responses. Option *C* is incorrect because the passage describes how different artists use visual elements to create their own approaches to communication. Option *E* is incorrect because the conclusion specifically mentions that personal experience influences individuals' reactions to artwork.

23. B) Option B is correct because the boys are bored by these discussions and prefer playing games, showing a lack of interest. Option A is incorrect because they are not curious about their heritage. Option C is incorrect because the boys are not actively resentful, just disinterested. Option D is incorrect because the boys do not sympathize with their elders' experiences. Option E is incorrect because respect would require attentiveness, which the boys do not display.

24. A) Option A is correct because references to folk songs, foreign languages, taken land, and images of chaos indicate ethnic conflict. Option B is incorrect because the passage does not mention religion. Option C is incorrect because there is no indication of competition between shop owners. Option D is incorrect because there is no indication of disagreement among neighbors. Option E is incorrect because parenting strategies are not relevant to the conflict.

25. C) Option C is correct because the passage has a consistently serious, melancholy tone as it reveals details about underlying historical trauma. Option A is incorrect because the writing is literary instead of analytical. Option B is incorrect because the tone is serious overall despite initially lighter elements. Option D is incorrect because there is no indication of fondness regarding the past. Option E is incorrect because the passage is not judging the characters or their situations.

26. D) Option D is correct because the abandoned Lego project directly represents how the boys' friendship has suffered due to revelations about past conflicts. Option A is incorrect because the project symbolizes the present situation, not past events or locations. Option B is incorrect because the boys did not gradually grow out of playing with Legos—it was more abrupt. Option C is incorrect because the Lego project represents the boys' bond and is not a depiction of real events. Option E is incorrect because the passage does not indicate traditional play being replaced by technology.

27. C) Option C is correct because the text explores cultural and family circumstances that affect Alex and Mia's friendship. Option A is incorrect because romance is not the focus here, despite hints of attraction. Option B is incorrect because teamwork is not a central theme but a minor one. Option D is incorrect because Mia's adjustment to the new school is not a developed theme. Option E is incorrect because the passage does not highlight the educational value of bilingualism.

28. B) Option B is correct because Alex becomes curious after noticing Mia's intelligence and wants to know more about her. Option A is incorrect because the two are not portrayed as competitors. Option C is incorrect because Alex immediately shows interest without overt signs of skepticism. Option D is incorrect because Alex is shown following Mia's lead in lab work. Option E is incorrect because Alex engages with Mia; he does not maintain distance.

29. A) Option A is correct because the story hints at certain concerns that might be too difficult or risky to talk about publicly. Option B is incorrect because no communication issues are presented, despite the language barrier. Option C is incorrect because Alex is attentive to Mia. Option D is incorrect because there is no indication that Mia's parents have censored her. Option E is incorrect because the context does not indicate deceitful actions.

30. D) Option D is correct because Alex's father appears to understand the situation and offers an alternative. Option A is incorrect because Alex's father does not express frustration at all. Option B is incorrect because Alex's father expresses support. Option C is incorrect because distractions at school

15. B) The author explains that tens of thousands of people joined Gandhi in his march; therefore, his march was widely supported by Indian citizens.

16. C) The author explains that Indians were only allowed to buy salt from British merchants while paying a heavy salt tax, which would bring in more money for Britain.

17. E) Option E is correct because the passage highlights both the material and intellectual exchanges as the Silk Road's most significant impacts. Option A is incorrect because tax systems are not presented as either features or outcomes. Option B is incorrect because China is only mentioned briefly, and the text does not establish it as a dominant world power. Option C is incorrect because the passage does not mention documentation of trading practices. Option D is incorrect because, while cultural exchange occurred, the passage does not frame cultural tolerance as a function of the Silk Road.

18. C) Option C is correct because the "relay race" metaphor suggests that traders worked in specific segments and did not use the entire network of roads. Option A is incorrect because the metaphor implies multiple participants rather than control by a few merchants. Option B is incorrect because speed is not the aspect of a relay that is being highlighted. Option D is incorrect because the main comparison involves the segmented nature of a relay race, not coordination. Option E is incorrect because market competition is not the focus of the comparison.

19. A) Option A is correct because the passage shows several examples of technologies and practices spreading naturally alongside commercial activity. Option B is incorrect because the passage does not suggest that cultural exchanges were deliberately planned. Option C is incorrect because the passage gives equal credit to both cultural and economic considerations. Option D is incorrect because profit appears to be a primary motive rather than cultural curiosity. Option E is incorrect because there is no indication in the passage that cultural differences created challenges.

20. B) Option B is correct because the text describes the dangerous obstacles faced by traders, suggesting their willingness to risk harm for potential rewards. Option A is incorrect because the text does not characterize the traders as political representatives. Option C is incorrect because the passage does not mention the traders' cultural insensitivities. Option D is incorrect because the text does not present religious missionary work as a motive. Option E is incorrect because the passage suggests broad participation in the Silk Road beyond the immediate region.

21. C) Option C is correct because the longevity of the Silk Road in the face of several challenges shows how trade networks can endure serious obstacles over centuries. Option A is incorrect because the passage does not address the economic impact on the Ottoman Empire. Option B is incorrect because there is no value comparison between intellectual and material goods. Option D is incorrect, as the text makes no comparison to modern trade. Option E is incorrect because the passage presents both market cities and connecting routes as integral to the Silk Road's networks.

22. D) Option D is correct because the passage is about the effect of historical conflicts between the families' homelands on the boys' friendship. Option A is incorrect because the focus of the passage is not on friendship itself but how it is affected by the families' histories. Option B is incorrect because the difficulty is not necessarily the understanding of history but the revelation of troubling truths. Option C is incorrect because outgrowing games is not thematic but a consequence of growing up. Option E is incorrect because tensions between generations are not meaningfully explored.

24. B) Use dimensional analysis to determine the length of time.

$$4500 \text{ words} \times \frac{1 \text{ minute}}{45 \text{ words}} = 100 \text{ minutes}$$

25. C) Ken has 6 scores that average 92%.

$$\text{Total number of points: } 92 \times 6 = 552$$

$$\text{Total of first 5 grades: } 90 + 100 + 95 + 83 + 87 = 455$$

Subtract to find the score on the sixth test.

$$552 - 455 = 97$$

Reading

1. C) The passage explains weight loss and how each of the other answer choices impact one's ability to lose weight.

2. A) The bulk of the passage is dedicated to showing that conventional wisdom about "fewer calories in than calories out" isn't true for many people and is more complicated than previously believed.

3. B) The text says that hormone levels can affect how our bodies process calories, which impacts a person's ability to lose weight.

4. C) The author cites several scientific studies to support the argument.

5. D) People misreporting the amount of food they ate would introduce errors into studies on weight loss and might make the studies that the author cites unreliable.

6. C) The passage explains that scientists believe that if they can restore the grassland, they will be able to slow climate change by slowing the thawing of the permafrost that lies beneath the tundra.

7. A) The author explains that the development of forests was not good for the environment: scientists believe grasslands would slow climate change.

8. E) This passage is about the subarctic steppe grassland ecosystem that flourished during the last Ice Age.

9. D) The passage says that scientists believe the forested terrain was not a natural development, which means humans must have planted the trees.

10. E) Scientists hope to bring back the wildlife, especially the wooly mammoth, to this region in order to help with the clearing of trees.

11. E) While thousands in Dandi participated in Gandhi's act of nonviolent resistance by picking up a chunk of salt, millions in coastal towns across India did as well.

12. E) The author describes a situation in which civil disobedience had an enormous impact.

13. D) Because salt was a vital part of the Indian diet, the tax on salt impacted Indian families significantly.

14. A) The passage explains why the march started, who was involved, and how it ended.

Subtract to find the difference in liters.

$$10\text{ L} - 7.57\text{ L} = 2.43\text{ L}$$

19. D) Find the daily distance by adding $\frac{1}{4}$ mile to each day.

Day	Monday	Tuesday	Wednesday	Thursday	Friday
Distance	$3\frac{2}{4}$	$3\frac{1}{2}+\frac{1}{4}=3\frac{3}{4}$	$3\frac{3}{4}+\frac{1}{4}=4$	$4+\frac{1}{4}=4\frac{1}{4}$	$4\frac{1}{4}+\frac{1}{4}=4\frac{2}{4}$

Add each daily distance to find the total.

$$3\frac{2}{4}+3\frac{3}{4}+4+4\frac{1}{4}+4\frac{2}{4}=18\frac{8}{4} \to 18+2=20$$

20. A) Find the amount of sugar the patient will need to cut from his diet.

$$part = whole \times percent$$

$$40 \times 0.25 = 10$$

Subtract this amount from the initial value.

$$40 - 10 = 30 \text{ grams}$$

21. D) Add the lengths of the pipe pieces.

$$26.5 + 18.9 + 35.1 = 80.5 \text{ in}$$

22. D) Portion the shape into squares and rectangles. Find the area of each smaller shape.

Rectangle:

$$A = l \times w$$

$$A = 8 \times 2 = 16$$

The area of the center square is:

$$A = s^2$$

$$A = 8^2 = 64$$

Add the area of the four rectangles and the center square.

$$4(16) + 64 = 128$$

23. D) To solve, first isolate x by subtracting two from each side, then divide by 4.

$$-4x + 2 = -34$$

$$-4x = -36$$

$$x = 9$$

Answer Explanations #2

11. B) Change the percentage to a decimal.

$$40\% = 0.4$$

Multiply the decimal by the whole (number of voters) to find the part (number of votes for Pauline).

$$175 \times 0.4 = 70$$

12. B) Let x be the number of people to attend the party.

$$4x + 6 = 50$$

Solve for x.

$$4x + 6 - 6 = 50 - 6$$
$$4x = 44$$
$$x = 11$$

13. C) Find the percent change.

$$\frac{\text{original} - \text{new}}{\text{original}}$$

$$\frac{92 - 88}{92} = 0.0435$$

Convert to a percent. 4.35% is between 4% and 5%.

14. C) Find the number of combinations:

$$4 \text{ meats} \times 3 \text{ cheeses} \times 2 \text{ breads} \times 4 \text{ condiments} = 96 \text{ different sandwiches}$$

15. B) Multiply the car's speed by the time traveled to find the distance.

$$1.5(65) = 97.5 \text{ miles}$$
$$2.5(50) = 125 \text{ miles}$$
$$97.5 + 125 = 222.5 \text{ miles}$$

16. E) Subtract the amount used from the original yards.

$$6 - 4\frac{5}{8} \rightarrow 5\frac{8}{8} - 4\frac{5}{8} = 1\frac{3}{8} \text{ yd}$$

17. D) There are 10 sides, and each side is 2 mm in length. Add the length of each side to find the total.

$$P = 2(10) = 20 \text{ mm}$$

18. B) Convert gallons to liters.

$$2 \text{ gal} \times \frac{3.785 \text{ L}}{1 \text{ gal}} = 7.57 \text{ L}$$

5. C) Use the area formula to find the length of one side of the square.

$$A = s^2$$

$$5625 = s^2$$

$$\sqrt{5625} = s$$

$$s = 75 \text{ ft}$$

Multiply the side length by 4 to find the perimeter.

$$P = 4s$$

$$P = 4(75 \text{ ft}) = 300 \text{ ft}$$

6. A) Find the total weight of the three books.

$$0.8 + 0.49 + 0.89 = 2.18 \text{ lb}$$

Subtract the weight of the books from the maximum weight for the shipping box.

$$2.5 - 2.18 = 0.32 \text{ lb}$$

7. B) Find the circle's radius.

$$4 \text{ km} \div 2 = 2 \text{ km}$$

Use the radius to find the circumference of the circle.

$$C = 2\pi r$$

$$2\pi(2) = 4\pi$$

Arc AB is a semicircle, which means its length is half the circumference of the circle.

$$\frac{4\pi}{2} = 2\pi \text{ km}$$

8. C) Multiply the number of outcomes for each individual event.

$$(70)(2)(5) = 700 \text{ outfits}$$

9. B) Find the circumference of the bucket.

$$r = 5$$

$$C = 2\pi(5) = 10\pi \text{ or } 31.4 \text{ inches}$$

The python coils around the bucket six times. Multiply the circumference by 6.

$$31.4 \times 6 = 188.4 \approx 188 \text{ inches}$$

10. E) There are 7 seats and 9 people playing. There is a 7 out of 9 chance or 78% chance a person is not eliminated.

Quantitative Section #2

1. E) Use the volume to find the length of the cube's side.

$$V = s^3$$

$$343 = s^3$$

$$s = 7 \text{ m}$$

Find the area of each side.

$$7(7) = 49 \text{ m}$$

Multiply by the total number of sides (6) to find the total surface area.

$$49(6) = 294 \text{ m}^2$$

2. A) Use the combination formula to find the number of ways to choose 2 people out of a group of 20.

$$C(20,2) = \frac{20!}{2!\,18!}$$

$$\frac{(20)(19)}{2} = 190$$

3. D) Rearrange the formula for probability to solve for the number of possible outcomes.

$$P = \frac{\text{number of favorable outcomes}}{\text{number of possible outcomes}}$$

$$\text{number of possible outcomes} = \frac{\text{number of favorable outcomes}}{P}$$

$$\text{number of possible outcomes} = \frac{3}{0.0004} = 7{,}500$$

4. D) Find the area of the complete rectangle.

$$A = lw$$

$$(20 + 2 + 2) \times (10 + 2 + 2) = 336 \text{ cm}^2$$

Find the area of the missing corners:

$$A = 4(lw) = 4(2 \times 2) = 16 \text{ cm}^2$$

Subtract the area of the missing corners.

$$336 - 16 = 320 \text{ cm}^2$$

20. D) Set up a proportion and solve by cross-multiplying.

$$\frac{8}{650} = \frac{12}{x}$$

$$12(650) = 8x$$

$$x = 975 \text{ miles}$$

21. A) Substitute 4 for j and simplify.

$$2(j-4)^4 - j + \frac{1}{2}j$$

$$2(4-4)^4 - 4 + \frac{1}{2}(4)$$

$$2(0) - 4 + 2 = -2$$

22. B) Substitute the given values into the equation and solve for t.

$$d = r \times t$$

$$4000 = 500 \times t$$

$$t = 8 \text{ hours}$$

23. B) Multiply the number of bottles by the amount each holds.

$$24 \times 0.75 = 18$$

24. A) Because the scenario describes monthly payments, first figure out how many monthly payments make up 3 years. Then set up an equation using the known variables.

$$1 \text{ year} = 12 \text{ months}$$

$$3 \text{ years} = 3 \times 12 = 36 \text{ monthly payments}$$

$$\text{Down payment} + \text{months paid} \times \text{monthly payment} = \text{total paid}$$

$$\$3000 + 36(\$216)$$

$$\$3000 + \$7776 = \$10{,}766$$

25. A) Use the equation for the perimeter of a rectangle.

$$P = 2l + 2w$$

$$42 = 2(13) + 2w$$

$$w = 8$$

15. C) Each student receives 2 notebooks.

$$16 \times 2 = 32 \text{ notebooks}$$

Subtract to determine the notebooks that are left. $50 - 32 = 18$ notebooks are left.

16. E) Use the equation for percentages.

$$whole = \frac{part}{percent} = \frac{17}{0.4} = 42.5$$

17. C) Set up a proportion.

$$\frac{regular}{total}$$

$$\frac{3}{4} = \frac{x}{24}$$

Cross-multiply.

$$4x = 72$$

$$x = 18$$

18. C) Isolate the variable on the left side of the inequality.

$$6x + 5 \geq -15 + 8x$$

$$-2x + 5 \geq -15$$

$$-2x \geq -20$$

Reverse the direction of the inequality when dividing by a negative number.

$$x \leq 10$$

19. A) Find the slope using the values in the table.

$$m = \frac{y_2 - y_1}{x_2 - x_1}$$

$$\frac{15 - 11}{5 - 3}$$

$$\frac{4}{2} = 2$$

Alternatively, substitute an ordered pair from the table into the equations.

$$y = 2x + 5$$

$$11 = 2(3) + 5$$

$$11 = 11$$

8. A) Substitute 5 for x in the equation.

$$2(5) - 5$$
$$10 - 5 = 5$$

9. E) The decimal part ends in the hundredths place. Place the decimal over 100.

$$2\frac{61}{100}$$

10. C) The total number of children is described within the parentheses. Since each hot dog costs $2, that total is multiplied by 2.

$$2 \times (6 + 9) = \$30$$

11. A) Graphing $y = -3x - 2$ gives a line with a slope of –3 and a y-intercept of –2. Because the symbol is greater than or equal to ($\geq$), the line is solid and the graph is shaded above the line:

$$y \geq -3x - 2$$

12. A) Use order of operations to simplify the expression.

$$(5^2 + 1)^2 + 3^3 \rightarrow$$
$$(25 + 1)^2 + 3^3$$
$$676 + 27 = 703$$

13. D) To solve this, first divide the decimals.

$$\frac{7.2 \times 10^6}{1.6 \times 10^{-3}}$$
$$7.2 \div 1.6 = 4.5$$

Subtract the exponents.

$$6 - (-3) = 9$$
$$4.5 \times 10^9$$

14. B) Work backwards and write a proportion to find the number of runners in the competition (c).

$$\frac{2}{c} = \frac{10}{100}$$
$$c = 20$$

Substitute to find the number of runners on the team (r).

$$\frac{20}{r} = \frac{25}{100}$$
$$r = 80$$

Answer Explanations #2

Answer Explanations #2

Quantitative Section #1

1. B) To find the value of $8x$, multiply each side by 2.

$$4x = 3$$
$$2(4x) = 2(3)$$
$$8x = 6$$

2. C) For the sum of two numbers to be odd, one number must be odd and the other number must be even. Adding two odd numbers together results in an even sum, making Option A incorrect. While either x or y can be equal to 0, neither of them must be; therefore, Option B is incorrect. Multiplying an odd number with an even number results in an even product, so Option D is incorrect.

3. C) Order the data from smallest to largest and find the middle value.

$$17, 26, 38, 41, \mathbf{42}, 45, 46, 46, 50.$$

4. D) The remainder of a division problem must be less than the divisor, so the remainder cannot be 3.

5. B) The expression 15×99 has factors of 3, 5, and 11. The numbers 66, 42, and 28 are all even numbers so they can all be divisible by 2.

6. A) Find the amount the state will spend on infrastructure and education.

$$\text{Infrastructure} = 0.2(3{,}000{,}000{,}000) = 600{,}000{,}000$$
$$\text{Education} = 0.18(3{,}000{,}000{,}000) = 540{,}000{,}000$$

Find the difference.

$$600{,}000{,}000 - 540{,}000{,}000 = \$60{,}000{,}000$$

7. D) Write an equation to find the number of people wearing neither white nor blue. Subtract the number of people wearing both colors so that they are not counted twice.

total applicants
$$= (\text{applicants wearing blue}) + (\text{applicants wearing white})$$
$$- (\text{applicants wearing both blue and white})$$
$$+ (\text{applicants wearing neither blue nor white})$$

$$21 = 7 + 6 - 5 + \text{neither}$$

$$\text{neither} = 13$$

28. Broad is to wide as
    A) Fast is to tall
    B) Short is to narrow
    C) Minuscule is to humongous
    D) Thin is to slender
    E) Heavy is to weight

29. Enter is to exit as
    A) Start is to finish
    B) Leave is to gone
    C) Begin is to race
    D) Open is to closed
    E) Gone is to go

30. Nod is to yes as
    A) Grin is to smile
    B) Blink is to eye
    C) Spin is to twirl
    D) Shake is to no
    E) Hello is to wave

21. Draw is to picture as
    A) Art is to artist
    B) Portrait is to paint
    C) Sign is to signature
    D) Color is to markers
    E) Book is to author

22. Paint is to canvas as
    A) Lead is to pencil
    B) Ink is to pen
    C) Chalk is to chalkboard
    D) Write is to engrave
    E) Sculpt is to clay

23. Key is to lock as
    A) Password is to computer
    B) Sleeve is to jacket
    C) Switch is to lightbulb
    D) Button is to remote
    E) Doorknob is to door

24. Hand is to finger as
    A) Ear is to head
    B) Arm is to elbow
    C) Leg is to knee
    D) Torso is to chest
    E) Foot is to toe

25. Mouse is to computer as
    A) Charger is to laptop
    B) Battery is to toy
    C) Engine is to car
    D) Remote is to television
    E) Cursor is to screen

26. Teacher is to school as
    A) Parent is to child
    B) Doctor is to hospital
    C) Book is to shelf
    D) Student is to principal
    E) Patient is to hospital

27. Blood is to artery as
    A) Bike is to trail
    B) Food is to esophagus
    C) Fabric is to sew
    D) Mail is to post office
    E) Water is to pipe

14. Key is to lock as handle is to
    A) Door
    B) Safety
    C) Open
    D) Exit
    E) Turn

15. Sweater is to winter as swimsuit is to
    A) Pool
    B) Summer
    C) Heat
    D) Clothing
    E) Vacation

16. Airport is to planes as garage is to
    A) Wheels
    B) Sheds
    C) Cars
    D) Mechanic
    E) Basement

17. Obscure is to hidden as malicious is to
    A) Wicked
    B) Lonely
    C) Shy
    D) Greedy
    E) Tasty

18. Elephant is to lumbers as hummingbird is to
    A) Scurries
    B) Slinks
    C) Trots
    D) Squirms
    E) Flits

19. Pebble is to boulder as hut is to
    A) Shack
    B) Building
    C) Colossal
    D) Mansion
    E) Restaurant

20. Sentence is to paragraph as stanza is to
    A) Essay
    B) Play
    C) Poem
    D) Line
    E) Dissertation

7. Facilitate is to assist as obliterate is to
    A) Create
    B) Question
    C) Bother
    D) Destroy
    E) Surround

8. Pedal is to bicycle as zipper is to
    A) Closure
    B) Metal
    C) Button
    D) Jacket
    E) Crate

9. Stomach is to digestion as lungs are to
    A) Organ
    B) Chest
    C) Oxygen
    D) Carbon dioxide
    E) Breathing

10. Knife is to slice as fork is to
    A) Slurp
    B) Pierce
    C) Gorge
    D) Spoon
    E) Share

11. Snake is to slithers as kangaroo is to
    A) Amphibians
    B) Furry
    C) Marsupials
    D) Pouches
    E) Bounds

12. Seagull is to flock as wolf is to
    A) Pack
    B) Canine
    C) Predator
    D) Deer
    E) Dog

13. Sock is to foot as glove is to
    A) Winter
    B) Cold
    C) Hand
    D) Toes
    E) Cover

Analogies

Directions: The first two words in each question have a relationship. Choose the response that recreates that same relationship in the second set of words.

1. Classroom is to teaching as park is to
    A) Sleeping
    B) Eating
    C) Playing
    D) Dancing
    E) Sitting

2. Joey is to kangaroo as puppy is to
    A) Cat
    B) Fish
    C) Frog
    D) Dog
    E) Goat

3. Computer is to typing as phone is to
    A) Social media
    B) Texting
    C) Ringing
    D) Watching
    E) Streaming

4. Clean is to dirty as small is to
    A) Smelly
    B) Sparkly
    C) Spiffy
    D) Shady
    E) Big

5. Puzzle is to piece as team is to
    A) Player
    B) Soccer
    C) Base
    D) Goal
    E) Jersey

6. Feather is to bird as fur is to
    A) Frog
    B) Dog
    C) Scales
    D) Turkey
    E) Gills

25. ABATE
    A) Promote
    B) Reduce
    C) Intensify
    D) Enact
    E) Increase

26. MEAGER
    A) Sufficient
    B) Excessive
    C) Scant
    D) Average
    E) Greedy

27. DILIGENT
    A) Skeptical
    B) Hardworking
    C) Brilliant
    D) Reckless
    E) Creative

28. HINDER
    A) Support
    B) Observe
    C) Define
    D) Obstruct
    E) Expel

29. GUARANTEE
    A) Complete
    B) Criticize
    C) Assist
    D) Imply
    E) Promise

30. WARY
    A) Cautious
    B) Gullible
    C) Self-conscious
    D) Unaware
    E) Indifferent

18. CACOPHONY
    A) Harsh sound
    B) Melodious music
    C) Artificial flavor
    D) Sweet taste
    E) Inauthentic

19. DEFLATED
    A) Tangled
    B) Changed
    C) Lifted
    D) Intensified
    E) Collapsed

20. JAR
    A) Annoy
    B) Shake
    C) Steady
    D) Contain
    E) Open

21. ILLEGIBLE
    A) Printed
    B) Indecipherable
    C) Readable
    D) Understandable
    E) Illicit

22. SCARCE
    A) Frightened
    B) Opaque
    C) Rare
    D) Broken
    E) Fake

23. BECKON
    A) Dismiss
    B) Summon
    C) Push
    D) Detain
    E) Shout

24. ANTICS
    A) Activities
    B) Tasks
    C) Exploits
    D) Findings
    E) Medications

11. APTITUDE
    A) Talent for socializing
    B) Constant hunger
    C) Probability
    D) Lofty height
    E) Capacity to learn

12. ABOLISH
    A) Eliminate
    B) Establish
    C) Continue
    D) Inaugurate
    E) Make shiny

13. GIGANTIC
    A) Humongous
    B) Petite
    C) Dangerous
    D) Delicate
    E) Overwhelming

14. SLEEK
    A) Narrow
    B) Wet
    C) Transparent
    D) Smooth
    E) Sneaky

15. SUBSTANTIAL
    A) Partial
    B) Inferior
    C) Plentiful
    D) Upright
    E) Nourishing

16. FIDELITY
    A) Disloyalty
    B) Noncommittal
    C) Wavering
    D) Allegiance
    E) Strict

17. BRISKLY
    A) Energetically
    B) Slowly
    C) Methodically
    D) Carefully
    E) Harshly

4. DORMANT
    A) Awake
    B) Modern
    C) Inactive
    D) Loud
    E) Boring

5. PACIFY
    A) Harm
    B) Transport
    C) Motivate
    D) Nurture
    E) Soothe

6. ACCLAIM
    A) Pity
    B) Praise
    C) Interest
    D) Assistance
    E) Steal

7. HAPHAZARD
    A) Dangerous
    B) Chaotic
    C) Cautious
    D) Creative
    E) Safe

8. MEANDER
    A) Relax
    B) Whimper
    C) Sprint
    D) Wander
    E) Graze

9. ASCEND
    A) Rise
    B) Imagine
    C) Find
    D) Recline
    E) Deliver

10. QUENCH
    A) Stimulate
    B) Ignite
    C) Satisfy
    D) Encourage
    E) Capture

39. The following is an example of which literary device?

Showing off his fur cap to French courtesans prancing around in powdered wigs.

- A) Hyperbole
- B) Juxtaposition
- C) Metaphor
- D) Foreshadowing
- E) Personification

40. The description of Franklin as a "Renaissance man" most directly refers to which one of the following?
- A) Artistic abilities and affinity for the arts
- B) Efforts to revive classical Greco-Roman education
- C) Physical appearance and sense of fashion
- D) Preference for European cultural traditions
- E) Diverse talents and broad accomplishments

Verbal

Synonyms

Directions: Find the synonym or the word closest in meaning.

1. TREMBLE
    - A) Squeak
    - B) Shiver
    - C) Steadfast
    - D) Calm
    - E) Low

2. HESITATE
    - A) Persevere
    - B) Continue
    - C) Float
    - D) Resolve
    - E) Pause

3. MEAGER
    - A) Sufficient
    - B) Plentiful
    - C) Inadequate
    - D) Substantial
    - E) Excited

36. The author would most likely DISAGREE with which statement?
    A) Art allows for multiple interpretations.
    B) Visual elements can trigger emotional responses.
    C) Different artists express unique vocabularies.
    D) Formal education is necessary to appreciate art.
    E) Personal experience influences artistic interpretation.

Passage 8

Who would have thought that the man whose face appears on our $100 bills would have had such a modest upbringing? Born in Boston to a struggling candlemaker, young Ben dropped out of school at age 10. At age 12, he began the dream job of a printing shop apprentice. These were the unlikely makings of one of the greatest American icons. Franklin went on to do practically anything he wanted, experimenting with lightning, charming the French in his plain garb, and penning bits of wisdom we use today to sound smart. Through it all, he remained determined to lead a scruffy band of colonies, shaping it into a new nation.

Franklin had a practical streak, figuring out things we still use. He risked frying himself with his famous kite experiment, leading to the lightning rods we mount on buildings to keep them from burning in a thunderstorm. Sick of fumbling for two different pairs of glasses, he cut their lenses in half and stuck them together, creating bifocal lenses. The Franklin stove—his 1742 creation—kept colonists warm without burning through all their wood. The best part is that he never even patented any of this. Rather than getting rich quick, he thought he might as well share his solutions.

Even more impressive was his diplomatic career. He spent several years reasoning with the British before revolution became the only option. Later, as a 70-something-year-old, he went to France dressed a simple American, showing off his fur cap to French courtesans prancing around in powdered wigs. The French ate up his authenticity, pledging military support that helped win American independence.

We lost the American Renaissance man when he died in 1790. He was original and self-made. He was the kind of guy who could charm his way through negotiations and invent his own solutions without asking for anything in return.

37. What does the passage suggest by opening with a reference to Franklin's face on the $100 bill?
    A) Franklin was mainly known for his financial expertise.
    B) Americans disapprove of putting historical figures on currency.
    C) Franklin's later reputation contrasts with his humble beginnings.
    D) The $100 bill was one of Franklin's important creations.
    E) Franklin was wealthy compared to other founding fathers.

38. Based on the passage, which option best describes Franklin's approach as an inventor?
    A) Theoretical and abstract
    B) Commercially driven
    C) Scientifically sound but impractical
    D) Pragmatic and altruistic
    E) Competitive and secretive

literacy and formal education. Visual art has no such requirements, and it is not as precise as words. One needs only a pair of eyes to appreciate it.

Color can evoke a variety of emotions. Artists leverage this fact to trigger many sensations. Think of hot and cool colors. Colors like red can give art energy. They can signal alarm, like in the color fields of abstract expressionist Mark Rothko. Bluish hues can have more of a calming effect. The tranquilizing feeling of Monet's water lilies can attest to this. This is also why hospitals utilize cool colors. Likewise, the sharp lines and jagged shapes of German Expressionism generate anxiety and distress, while the decorative curves of Art Nouveau feel natural and organic.

An artist's silent vocabulary is incomplete without symbolism. Picasso did not need words or captions to communicate the horrors of war. In his painting "Guernica," one can see the carnage laid upon the eponymous Spanish town by German forces. The flames and shattered bodies speak volumes. Now consider Frida Kahlo's "The Broken Column." It combines traditional Mexican motifs with painful images. It shows a spine in fragments and a torn landscape. Thorns pierce the subject's body. The symbols reflect the artist's ongoing problems resulting from a traffic accident—the details are clear and startling.

Art lets people communicate in a way that is more evocative and immediate than words. It is an interpretive language, a wordless dialogue that happens between artist and viewer, and everyone has a different reaction to an artwork based on personal experience.

32. According to the passage, why is art is more universal than language?
    A) Because it uses visual cues that are more easily accessible
    B) Because it utilizes imagery that is easily understood by children
    C) Because it originated in prehistoric cave paintings
    D) Because it exhibits fewer cultural biases than words
    E) Because it appears more naturally in the human environment

33. What does the passage suggest one needs in order to engage with visual art?
    A) Knowledge of artistic time periods
    B) Understanding of different cultures
    C) Training in artistic techniques
    D) Functioning vision to see it
    E) Familiarity with famous artists' styles

34. What relationship is established between Art Nouveau and German Expressionism?
    A) Linear development from one style to another
    B) Contrasting feelings evoked by different artistic elements
    C) Competing art movements from around the same time
    D) The evolution of artistic techniques across generations
    E) Local variations on the same artistic approach

35. Based on the passage, which artistic element seems to function most like language?
    A) Colors and their emotional associations
    B) Symbols that represent specific meanings
    C) Shapes that define objects and figures
    D) Textures that suggest physical sensations
    E) Lines that create structure

"They don't like to stay out too late or go to public places," Mia explained after refusing Alex's beach barbecue invitation. He was confused by her concerns, especially the unspoken ones. Alex's grandparents had similar fears years ago, from before they got their "papers" in order. Alex didn't fully understand their fear of documents, public places, and simple questions.

Later, as they prepared to pack the car, Alex's father sensed his brooding. "Where's your friend?" Alex explained the situation, and his father understood. "Maybe we could just have our lunch at home. Something smaller and more private so your friend can join us." Alex looked up as his father concluded, "Things can get complicated, mijo, but this shouldn't have to be."

27. What is this passage mainly about?
    A) Challenges of having a middle school crush
    B) Value of teamwork in school
    C) Impact of culture on friendship
    D) Difficulty of adjusting to a new school
    E) Importance of bilingual education

28. How can Alex's attitude toward Mia best be characterized?
    A) Competitive
    B) Curious and admiring
    C) Initially skeptical but gradually accepting
    D) Patronizing
    E) Sympathetic but distant

29. What does the phrase "unspoken ones" when referring to Mia's concerns suggest?
    A) That some fears are too sensitive to openly discuss
    B) That there is a language barrier
    C) That Alex is not listening closely enough
    D) That Mia's parents strictly forbade her from speaking about certain topics
    E) That Mia is deceiving Alex

30. What does Alex's father's response to the situation regarding the barbecue invitation demonstrate?
    A) Frustration with immigration policies
    B) Disapproval of Alex's friendship
    C) Concern about distractions at school
    D) Empathy and accommodation
    E) Pride in his cultural heritage

31. Which one of the following best describes Alex's understanding of Mia's situation?
    A) Work in progress
    B) Near perfect
    C) Hindered by his parents
    D) Well-rounded
    E) Poor

Passage 7

Art is more universal than language. Instead of words and sentences, it uses much more easily accessible visual cues: lines, shapes, and colors. This is true of both modern digital art and ancient cave paintings. Understanding language means having special knowledge—it requires

23. Which of the following best characterizes the boys' attitudes toward their families' discussions about the "old country"?
    A) Curious
    B) Indifferent
    C) Resentful
    D) Sympathetic
    E) Respectful

24. Which of the following is most likely the source of conflict between the families?
    A) Historical events involving ancestral homelands
    B) Religious differences in the community
    C) Competition for customers at the local market
    D) Personal disagreements regarding the neighborhood's future
    E) Parenting styles among households

25. Which of the following best describes the tone in the passage?
    A) Scientific
    B) Lighthearted
    C) Somber
    D) Nostalgic
    E) Critical

26. What does the abandoned block kingdom most likely symbolize?
    A) Their families' lost homelands
    B) Maturing out of childhood games
    C) The destruction depicted in the old book
    D) The damaged friendship
    E) Outdated toys being replaced by technology

Passage 6

Alex was born and raised in San Diego. He lived in the same home his entire life: a Spanish-style bungalow facing the Pacific Ocean. He attended Oceanview Middle School and couldn't help glancing at the school's newest arrival—Mia Reyes. She enrolled last month, and her quiet intelligence had become immediately apparent, at least to Alex. He noticed the way she paused before sharing her thoughts. He wondered why she sketched in the margins of her notes so much.

Ms. Gomez assigned the two as lab partners. Alex's palms started to sweat. He scooted his stool closer to Mia. He helped her read the material in English and realized that Mia had a much better grasp of the topic than he thought. He was fine translating scientific terms while Mia took the lead, solving the problems with ease)

They gradually spent more time together. It started with eating at the same lunch table and continued with weekend studying.

Mia grew up in Mexico, and her parents were constantly working. Her father was a carpenter, and her mother made the best tamales. She had a younger brother who also went to Oceanview. Alex learned all of this through their conversations, which blended Spanish and English.

21. Which conclusion is best supported by the information in the passage?
    A) The Ottoman Empire's economy was devastated by its ban on trade with China.
    B) The most valuable items traded on the Silk Road were intellectual rather than material.
    C) Complex trading networks can survive for centuries despite physical obstacles.
    D) Modern trade routes face more challenges than historical ones.
    E) Market cities were more important than the routes connecting them.

Passage 5

Mehmet and Aram lived in a small town. They were quite the duo. They rode bikes and traded collectible cards. They built impressive towers out of building blocks in Aram's basement. Their favorite pastime was arguing about which superhero is more powerful. Neither boy understood their families' boring lectures about the "old country." They'd much rather play cops and robbers.

Mehmet's grandfather was a stoic man, famous for his handlebar mustache. He walked around singing Turkish folk songs with an emotion Mehmet did not understand.

Aram had a grandmother who could often be heard muttering something about "taken land." She would spend most of her time kneading dough for the day's bread. There was a sadness on her face that irritated Aram.

The town had markets every other week with picnics, food stands, and artisanal crafts. There was always a silent tension that the boys never noticed. Mehmet's grandfather stopped sharing stories when Aram's grandmother arrived. He'd go to the tea stand and order "something strong." Aram's grandmother's smile would fade into a cold wariness. The boys continued playing tag.

That evening, Aram worked on his and Mehmet's block towers when he found an old book. The discolored pages showed faded photos with captions in Armenian. It was his family's history. There were pictures of normal life and then images of people fleeing and houses burning.

When Mehmet asked about the book, his grandfather responded angrily in Turkish. Mehmet couldn't decipher the words, but his stomach twisted into a knot nonetheless. A few blocks away, Aram's grandmother wept as she recounted her family's story of hardship and something called "diaspora."

The boys hadn't felt the weight of their family's past before this night. They felt a darkness extending its slimy tentacles toward their near-indestructible bond. The block kingdom they once built sat half-finished in Aram's basement, abandoned.

22. How can the main theme of the passage best be described?
    A) The evolution of friendship during childhood
    B) The difficulty of understanding cultural heritage
    C) How children grow out of immature games
    D) The impact of historical trauma on relationships
    E) The tension between younger and older generations

People rarely traveled the entire Silk Road. Instead, goods changed hands multiple times in a 4,000 mile-long relay race. Vibrant market cities like Samarkand (Uzbekistan) and Chang'an (China) connected the roads. Ideas were shared and spread out—for example, Buddhism spread to Central Asia and China from India. Moreover, technologies, like the one used to make paper, were shared across China, the Middle East, and Europe. Knowledge was also shared, from mathematical and astronomical concepts to medical practices. Languages evolved together and new variations formed, as traders needed a common way to communicate. Even common foods of today—like noodles and oranges—were first shared along the Silk Road.

The routes that wove together the Silk Road were laced with danger. Extreme climate and terrain challenged the boldest and toughest of traders. Some people put foot to burning sand on desert paths, while others braved steep inclines on rocky mountainsides to reach the next checkpoint. Even if they found the next city or watering hole, they could still face drought and flash floods. Many did not survive, but their successors might have found fortune.

The Ottoman Empire decided to ban its trade with China in the early-to-mid-15th century. This meant the end of activity on the Silk Road. The "road" provided vital services for several nations over several generations. Its spirit lives on in today's commercial and intellectual trade across the globe.

17. Which statement best captures the primary historical significance of the Silk Road?
    A) It created a system of taxation for international markets.
    B) It established China as the dominant economic world power.
    C) It methodically documented ancient trading practices for future societies.
    D) It promoted religious and cultural tolerance between diverse communities.
    E) It facilitated the exchange of goods and ideas across continents.

18. What does the description of the Silk Road as a "relay race" most likely suggest?
    A) That goods were controlled by only a few merchants
    B) That the journey was usually completed quickly
    C) That most travelers only participated in specific segments
    D) That trading required careful coordination between everyone involved
    E) That traders competed with each other for market control

19. What can be inferred about the relationship between trade and culture from this passage?
    A) Trade routes naturally aided the spread of ideas and practices.
    B) Cultural exchange was an intended consequence of trade.
    C) Economic interests were more important than cultural ones.
    D) Trade was mainly motivated by cultural curiosity rather than profit.
    E) Trading relationships suffered from cultural differences.

20. Based on the passage, how would a historian best characterize the traders who used the Silk Road?
    A) Diplomats representing their empires for political gain
    B) Risk-taking entrepreneurs willing to face great danger
    C) Culturally insensitive merchants focused only on profit
    D) Religious missionaries using trade as a cover
    E) Local men who specialized only in commerce

11. According to the passage, how many people participated in Gandhi's act of nonviolent resistance?
    A) Under a hundred
    B) Hundreds
    C) Thousands
    D) Tens of thousands
    E) Millions

12. With which of the following claims about civil disobedience would the author most likely agree?
    A) Civil disobedience is a disorganized form of protest easily quashed by government.
    B) Civil disobedience requires extreme violations of existing law to be effective.
    C) Civil disobedience can only work on a small scale to effect local change.
    D) Civil disobedience is only effective in countries that already have democracy.
    E) Civil disobedience is an effective strategy for effecting political change.

13. Why was the heavy salt tax placed on Indians by the British so significant?
    A) Salt taxes were already very expensive.
    B) Indians were not used to paying taxes.
    C) Gandhi worked to stop the law from being passed.
    D) Salt was a vital part of the Indian diet.
    E) Indians made their own salt.

14. What is this paragraph mostly about?
    A) A march organized by Gandhi
    B) British laws regarding salt
    C) The arrest of sixty thousand Indians
    D) Getting salt from saltwater
    E) The Indian diet

15. Based on the passage, what can be concluded about the march organized by Gandhi?
    A) It was not successful in its mission to resist the British.
    B) It was widely supported by Indian citizens.
    C) It was poorly planned based on its eventual outcome.
    D) It was meant to show a sign of respect to the British.
    E) It was an attempt to eliminate salt tax altogether.

16. Why did the British prohibit Indians from collecting or selling salt?
    A) Salt was an important part of the British diet.
    B) The Indians were being punished for resisting.
    C) The British wanted to profit from the sale of salt in India.
    D) Salt was too expensive for most families to afford.
    E) It would push the Indians to leave Britain.

Passage 4

China began the Silk Road in 130 BC, and the Ottoman empire put an end to it in 1453 CE. It served both the Eastern and Western worlds for well over a millennium. Although its name is a misnomer—it was not a single road, nor was the only commodity silk—it was one of the most influential trading routes in human history. Countless goods were transported along the vast network of routes. Ideas and cultures also proliferated during this time.

6. By slowing the thawing of permafrost, what do scientists believe they will be able to do?
   A) Bring back the wooly mammoth
   B) Preserve a region of Siberia
   C) Slow global warming
   D) Clear the trees in the forest
   E) Remove predatory threats

7. In the fourth sentence, what does the word *advantageous* most nearly mean?
   A) Beneficial
   B) Damaging
   C) Useful
   D) Appropriate
   E) Irrelevant

8. This paragraph is chiefly concerned with the revitalization of what?
   A) The wooly mammoth
   B) Permafrost
   C) Rainforests
   D) Climate
   E) Grassland

9. Based on the passage, what can we infer about trees in this region?
   A) They were an important part of the subarctic steppe grassland ecosystem of the last Ice Age.
   B) They must increase in order for scientists to slow the thawing of permafrost.
   C) They ward off wildlife in order to stabilize the climate of this area.
   D) They exist today as a result of human interference with the natural ecosystem.
   E) They diminished with the rising climate.

10. Based on the passage, what does the word *revive* most likely mean?
    A) Remove
    B) Avoid
    C) Support
    D) Reverse
    E) Bring back

Passage 3

One of the most dramatic acts of nonviolent resistance in India's movement for independence from Britain came in 1930, when independence leader Mahatma Gandhi organized a 240-mile march to the Arabian Sea. The goal of the march was to make salt from seawater, in defiance of British law. The British prohibited Indians from collecting or selling salt—a vital part of the Indian diet—requiring them instead to buy it from British merchants and pay a heavy salt tax. Along the way the crowd of marchers grew to tens of thousands of people. In Dandi, Gandhi picked up a small chunk of salt and broke British law. Thousands in Dandi followed his lead as did millions of fellow protestors in coastal towns throughout India. In an attempt to quell the civil disobedience, authorities arrested more than sixty thousand people across the country, including Gandhi himself.

2. Which one of the following would provide the best conclusion to the passage?
    A) It turns out that conventional dieting wisdom doesn't capture the whole picture of how our bodies function.
    B) Still, counting calories and tracking exercise is a good idea if you want to lose weight.
    C) In conclusion, it's important to lose weight responsibly: losing too much weight at once can negatively impact the body.
    D) It's easy to see that diets don't work, so we should focus less on weight loss and more on overall health.
    E) In fact, counting calories is so stressful that it causes many dieters to give up on their weight loss efforts altogether.

3. According to the text, what is true about hormone levels?
    A) They are not related to nutrition.
    B) They can impact a person's ability to lose weight.
    C) They will change based on a person's diet.
    D) They make a person think they are losing weight even if they are not.
    E) They were the subject of a new study released this year.

4. Which of the following type of argument is used in the passage?
    A) Emotional argument
    B) Appeal to authority
    C) Specific evidence
    D) Rhetorical questioning
    E) Logical reasoning

5. Which one of the following would weaken the author's argument?
    A) A new diet pill from a pharmaceutical company that promises to help patients lose weight by changing intestinal bacteria
    B) The personal experience of a man who was able to lose a significant amount of weight by taking in fewer calories than he used
    C) A study showing that people in different geographic locations lose different amounts of weight when on the same diet
    D) A study showing that people often misreport their food intake when they are part of a scientific study on weight loss
    E) A calorie-counting program that offers a money-back guarantee to participants who do not reach their weight goals

Passage 2

In a remote nature preserve in northeastern Siberia, scientists are attempting to recreate the subarctic steppe grassland ecosystem that flourished there during the last Ice Age. The area today is dominated by forests, but the lead scientists of the project believe the forested terrain is neither a natural development nor environmentally <u>advantageous</u>. They believe that if they can restore the grassland, they will be able to slow climate change by slowing the thawing of the permafrost that lies beneath the tundra. Key to this undertaking is restoring the wildlife to the region, including wild horses, musk oxen, bison, and yak. Most ambitiously, the scientists hope to <u>revive</u> the wooly mammoth species, which was key in trampling the ground and knocking down the trees, helping to keep the land free for grasses to grow.

24. Harvey types at an average speed of 45 words per minute. Approximately how long will it take for him to type a newsletter that is 4,500 words in length?
- A) 89 minutes
- B) 100 minutes
- C) 180 minutes
- D) 3,955 minutes
- E) 75 minutes

25. Ken has taken six tests in his English class. Each test is worth 100 points. Ken has a 92% average in English. If Ken's first five grades are 90, 100, 95, 83, and 87, what was Ken's score on the sixth test?
- A) 80
- B) 92
- C) 97
- D) 100
- E) 89

Reading

Directions: For each passage, read the excerpt and answer the questions that follow.

Passage 1

We've been told for years that the recipe for weight loss is fewer calories in than out. In other words, eat less and exercise more, and your body will take care of the rest. As many who've tried to diet can attest, this edict doesn't always produce results. If you're one of those folks, you might have felt that you just weren't doing it right—that the failure was all your fault.

However, several new studies released this year have suggested that it might not be your fault at all. For example, a study of people who'd lost a high percentage of their body weight (more than 17 percent) in a short period of time found that they could not physically maintain their new weight. Scientists measured their resting metabolic rate and found that they'd need to consume only a few hundred calories a day to meet their metabolic needs. Basically, their bodies were in starvation mode and seemed to desperately hang on to each and every calorie. Eating even a single healthy, well-balanced meal a day would cause these subjects to start packing the pounds back on.

Other studies have shown that factors like intestinal bacteria, distribution of body fat, and hormone levels can affect the manner in which our bodies process calories. There's also the fact that it's actually quite difficult to measure the number of calories consumed during a particular meal and the number used while exercising.

1. This passage is chiefly concerned with what?
    - A) Calories
    - B) Exercise
    - C) Weight loss
    - D) Metabolic needs
    - E) Nutrition

20. A doctor advises her patient to decrease his sugar consumption by 25%. If the patient currently consumes 40 grams of sugar per day on average, how many daily grams of sugar should his new target be?
   A) 30 g
   B) 24 g
   C) 16 g
   D) 10 g
   E) 15 g

21. Andre welded together 3 pieces of metal pipe measuring 26.5 inches, 18.9 inches, and 35.1 inches. How long was the welded pipe?
   A) 10.3 in
   B) 27.5 in
   C) 42.7 in
   D) 80.5 in
   E) 15.4 in

22. What is the area of the following shape?

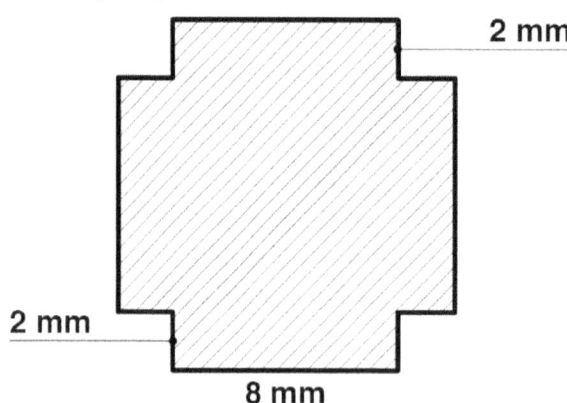

   A) 6 mm²
   B) 16 mm²
   C) 64 mm²
   D) 128 mm²
   E) 32 mm²

23. Solve:

$$-4x + 2 = -34$$

   A) −9
   B) −8
   C) 8
   D) 9
   E) 14

16. Justine bought 6 yards of fabric to make some curtains, but she only used $4\frac{5}{8}$ yards. How many yards of fabric does she have left?

   A) $\frac{3}{8}$

   B) $\frac{5}{8}$

   C) $1\frac{3}{4}$

   D) $2\frac{5}{8}$

   E) $1\frac{3}{8}$

17. What is the perimeter of the following shape?

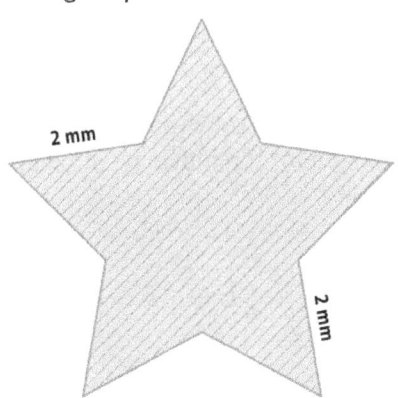

   A) 2 mm
   B) 4 mm
   C) 10 mm
   D) 20 mm
   E) 40 mm

18. A 10 liter container will hold how much more liquid than a 2-gallon container? (1 gal = 3.785 L)
   A) 2.00 L
   B) 2.43 L
   C) 6.22 L
   D) 8.00 L
   E) 1.25 L

19. Alice ran $3\frac{1}{2}$ miles on Monday, and she increased her distance by $\frac{1}{4}$ mile each day. What was the total distance Alice ran from Monday to Friday?

   A) $17\frac{1}{2}$ mi
   B) $18\frac{1}{2}$ mi
   C) 19 mi
   D) 20 mi
   E) $15\frac{1}{4}$ mi

11. Pauline is running for class president. All 175 students voted in the election, and she received 40% of the vote. How many students voted for Pauline?
    A) 40
    B) 70
    C) 135
    D) 438
    E) 60

12. Tamara is hosting a birthday party at the movie theater. Her mother gives her $50 to spend on movie tickets for her friends. The theater charges $4 per person and a $6 service charge for the order. How many friends can she invite to the party?
    A) 5
    B) 11
    C) 12
    D) 40
    E) 22

13. A movie runs for 92 minutes. For it to air on television, it must be edited down to 88 minutes to make room for commercials. What percent of the movie must be edited?
    A) Between 2 and 3%
    B) Between 3 and 4%
    C) Between 4 and 5%
    D) Between 5 and 6%
    E) Between 2 and 5%

14. A sandwich shop offers 4 different types of meat, 3 types of cheese, 2 types of bread, and 4 condiments. If each sandwich must have 1 meat, 1 cheese, 1 type of bread, and 1 condiment, how many different sandwiches can be made?
    A) 13
    B) 32
    C) 96
    D) 300
    E) 120

15. A car traveled at 65 miles per hour for $1\frac{1}{2}$ hours and then traveled at 50 miles per hour for $2\frac{1}{2}$ hours. How many miles did the car travel?
    A) 200 miles
    B) 222.5 miles
    C) 237.5 miles
    D) 260 miles
    E) 198 miles

7. The following circle shows a walking path through a park. If the distance from A to B is 4 km, how far will someone walking along arc AB travel?

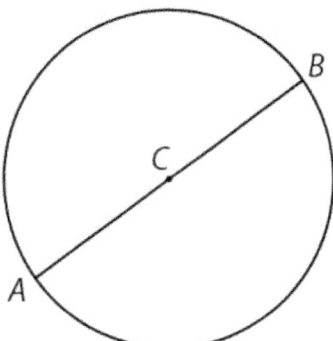

A) 4 km
B) 2π km
C) 8 km
D) 4π km
E) 5.5 km

8. How many combinations can be made from a wardrobe that consists of 70 shirts, 2 ties, and 5 sets of cufflinks?
A) 77
B) 350
C) 700
D) 3,500
E) 850

9. A python coils 6 times around a round plastic bucket whose radius is 5 inches. How long is the python? (Round to the nearest whole number.)
A) 471 inches
B) 188 inches
C) 94 inches
D) 60 inches
E) 240 inches

10. In a game of musical chairs, there are 9 people playing and 7 available seats. Those who do not get a seat by the time the music ends are eliminated. What is the probability that a person is NOT eliminated?
A) 11%
B) 22%
C) 17%
D) 89%
E) 78%

4. The figure below shows a rectangle with 4 square cutouts made to each corner. What is the area of the resulting shape?

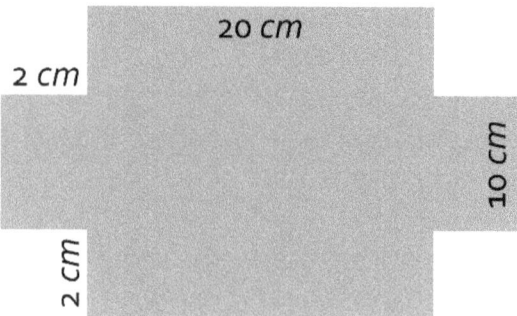

- A) 142 cm²
- B) 200 cm²
- C) 296 cm²
- D) 320 cm²
- E) 275 cm²

5. Melissa is ordering fencing to enclose a square garden with 5625 square feet. What is the number of feet of fencing that she needs?
- A) 75
- B) 150
- C) 300
- D) 1405
- E) 1275

6. Juan is packing a shipment of three books weighing 0.8 pounds, 0.49 pounds, and 0.89 pounds. The maximum weight for the shipping box is 2.5 pounds. How much more weight will the box hold?
- A) 0.32 lb
- B) 0.48 lb
- C) 1.21 lb
- D) 2.18 lb
- E) 0.57 lb

25. The perimeter of a rectangle is 42 mm. If the length of the rectangle is 13 mm, what is its width?
   A) 8 mm
   B) 13 mm
   C) 20 mm
   D) 29 mm
   E) 16 mm

Quantitative Section #2

1. If the volume of a cube is 343 cubic meters, what is the cube's surface area?
   A) 49 m^2
   B) 84 m^2
   C) 196 m^2
   D) 78 m^2
   E) 294 m^2

2. In a class of 20 students, how many conversations must take place so that every student talks to every other student in the class?
   A) 190
   B) 380
   C) 760
   D) 6840
   E) 224

3. A school held a raffle to raise money. If a person who bought 3 tickets had a 0.0004 chance of winning, what is the total number of tickets sold for the raffle?
   A) 2,400 tickets
   B) 3,500 tickets
   C) 5,000 tickets
   D) 7,500 tickets
   E) 3,250 tickets

19. Which equation describes the linear relationship between x and y shown in the following table?

x	y
3	11
5	15
8	21

- A) $y = 2x + 5$
- B) $y = 5x + 5$
- C) $y = 4x + 5$
- D) $y = 3x + 5$
- E) None of the above

20. If a car uses 8 gallons of gas to travel 650 miles, how many miles can it travel using 12 gallons of gas?
- A) 870 miles
- B) 895 miles
- C) 915 miles
- D) 975 miles
- E) 875 miles

21. If $j = 4$, what is the value of $2(j - 4)^4 - j + \frac{1}{2}j$?
- A) −2
- B) 0
- C) 2
- D) 4
- E) 1

22. The formula for distance is $d = r \times t$, where r is the rate and t is the time. How long will it take a plane to fly 4,000 miles from Chicago to London if the plane flies at a constant rate of 500 mph?
- A) 3.5 hours
- B) 8 hours
- C) 20 hours
- D) 45 hours
- E) 12 hours

23. How much water is needed to fill 24 bottles that each hold 0.75 liters?
- A) 6 L
- B) 18 L
- C) 24 L
- D) 32 L
- E) 12 L

24. Yanni bought a used car. He made a down payment of $3,000 and then made monthly payments of $216 for three years. How much did Yanni pay for the car?
- A) $10,776
- B) $7,806
- C) $7,776
- D) $3,678
- E) $5,725

Practice Test #2

13. Simplify:

$$\frac{7.2 \times 10^6}{1.6 \times 10^{-3}}$$

   A) 4.5×10^{-9}
   B) 4.5×10^{-3}
   C) 4.5×10^3
   D) 4.5×10^9
   E) 4.5×10^2

14. A high school cross-country team sent 25% of its runners to a regional competition. Of these runners, 10% won medals. If two runners earned medals, how many members does the cross-country team have?
   A) 8
   B) 80
   C) 125
   D) 1250
   E) 50

15. A teacher has 50 notebooks to hand out to students. If she has 16 students in her class, and each student receives two notebooks, how many notebooks will she have left over?
   A) 2
   B) 16
   C) 18
   D) 32
   E) 22

16. 40% of what number is equal to 17?
   A) 2.35
   B) 6.8
   C) 35
   D) 680
   E) 42.5

17. An ice chest contains 24 sodas, some regular and some diet. The ratio of diet soda to regular soda is 1:3. How many regular sodas are there in the ice chest?
   A) 1
   B) 4
   C) 18
   D) 24
   E) 15

18. Which expression is equivalent to $6x + 5 \geq -15 + 8x$?
   A) $x \leq -5$
   B) $x \leq 5$
   C) $x \leq 10$
   D) $x \leq 20$
   E) $x < 0$

9. Which one of the following numbers is equivalent to 2.61?
   A) $\frac{261}{10}$
   B) 2.061
   C) $2\frac{610}{100}$
   D) $2\frac{61}{1000}$
   E) $2\frac{61}{100}$

10. At a party, 6 girls and 9 boys each order a hot dog for $2 apiece. Which of the following equations correctly represents how much money was spent in total for hot dogs?
    A) $2 \times 6 + 9 = \$21$
    B) $2 + 6 + 9 = \$17$
    C) $2 \times (6 + 9) = \$30$
    D) $2 \times 6 \times 9 = \$108$
    E) $(2 \times 6) + 9 = \$21$

11. Which inequality is represented by the following graph?

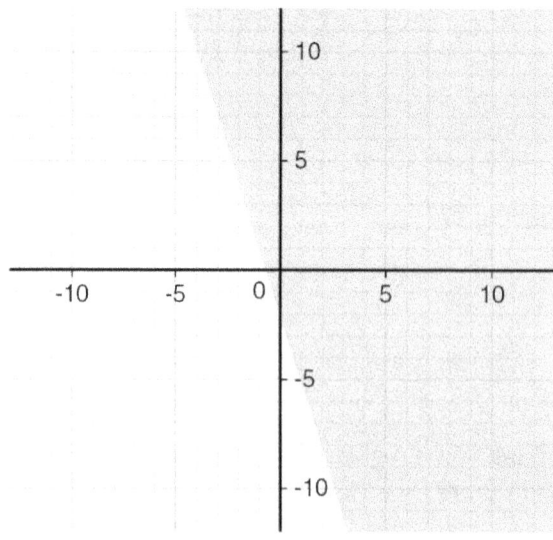

   A) $y \geq -3x - 2$
   B) $y \geq 3x - 2$
   C) $y > -3x - 2$
   D) $y \leq -3x - 2$
   E) $y \leq -2x + 3$

12. What number is equal to $(5^2 + 1)^2 + 3^3$?
    A) 703
    B) 694
    C) 53
    D) 30
    E) 20

Practice Test #2

4. A whole number is divided by 3. Which of the following CANNOT be the remainder?
   A) 0
   B) 1
   C) 2
   D) 3
   E) -2

5. Which expression has only prime factors of 3, 5, and 11?
   A) 66×108
   B) 15×99
   C) 42×29
   D) 28×350
   E) None of the above

6. The following pie graph shows how a state's government plans to spend its annual budget of $3 billion. How much more money does the state plan to spend on infrastructure than on education?

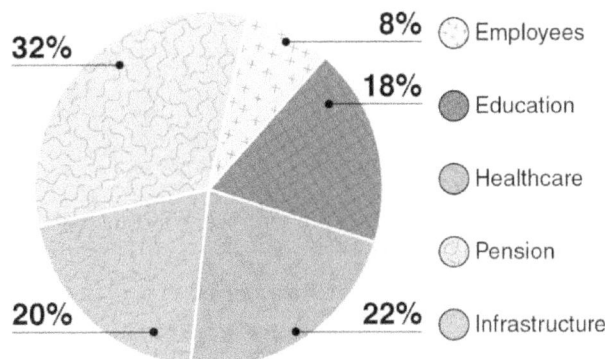

   A) $60,000,000
   B) $120,000,000
   C) $300,000,000
   D) $540,000,000
   E) $100,000,000

7. A company interviewed 21 applicants for a recent opening. Of these applicants, 7 wore blue, 6 wore white, and 5 applicants wore both blue and white. How many applicants wore neither blue nor white?
   A) 6
   B) 8
   C) 12
   D) 13
   E) 10

8. If $x = 5$, what is the value of the algebraic expression $2x - x$?
   A) 5
   B) 10
   C) 15
   D) 20
   E) -5

Practice Test #2

Quantitative Section #1

1. If $4x = 3$, what is the value of $8x$?
   A) 0.75
   B) 6
   C) 12
   D) 24
   E) 3

2. If $x + y$ is an odd number, which of the following must be true?
   A) Both x and y must be odd numbers.
   B) Neither x nor y can equal 0.
   C) Either x or y is odd, while the other is even.
   D) The product of x and y is odd.
   E) There is not enough information to determine the answer.

3. The table below shows the number of hours employees worked during the week. What is the median number of hours the employees worked per week?

Employee	Number of Hours Worked
Suzanne	42
Joe	38
Mark	26
Ellen	50
Jill	45
Rob	46
Nicole	17
Sean	41
Maria	46

   A) 39
   B) 41
   C) 42
   D) 46
   E) 50

24. **C)** Shovels are tools used to dig a hole; pumps are tools used for a well.
25. **A)** A clock chimes; a watch ticks.
26. **B)** Shoes have soles; boots have heels.
27. **C)** You read a book; you make a recipe.
28. **C)** Play and frolic are synonyms; incredible and implausible are synonyms.
29. **C)** A diamond goes on a ring; syrup goes on a pancake.
30. **C)** Wallets hold money; purses hold keys.

26. A) *Discreet* means "considerate" or "careful to avoid causing offense or injury."

27. E) When something *recurs*, it "returns" or "appears again." *Recurrence* is the noun form of the verb *recur*.

28. C) *Latent* means "hidden or dormant."

29. C) An *anomaly* is "a deviation from the norm or an irregularity."

30. D) *Imminent* means "about to happen."

Analogies

1. E) Combining "milk" with "shake" creates something new: *milkshake*. By combining "French" with "fry," we make "French fry."

2. B) Running is fast; walking is slow.

3. D) A stop sign and a traffic light are both tools put in place for drivers.

4. C) Frantic and desperate are synonyms; angry and irate are synonyms.

5. B) A cup and a mug are synonyms; a trophy and a prize are synonyms.

6. C) Cookie is a whole; chocolate chips are a part of that whole. Pizza is a whole; pepperoni is a part of that whole.

7. D) Combining sun and shine equals a new word—"sunshine"; combining star and light becomes a new word—"starlight."

8. B) A piece is a part of the puzzle; a player is part of a team.

9. B) Feathers protect a bird; fur protects a dog.

10. A) A tree is part of a forest; a bird is part of a flock.

11. C) A train rides on rails; a car rides on roads.

12. B) A string is part of a guitar; a lace is part of a shoe.

13. A) A lighthouse uses a foghorn; a firetruck uses a siren.

14. E) A log is used in a fireplace; a shovel is used in a garden.

15. B) A houseplant goes into a flowerpot; brownies go into a pan.

16. B) A landscaper works directly with a lawn; a teacher works directly with a class.

17. C) A library contains books; an ocean contains fish.

18. C) A photo comes from a camera; an apple comes from a tree.

19. D) An inch is a part of a foot; an ounce is part of a pound.

20. B) Jump and hop are similar actions; run and jog are similar actions.

21. D) A bear hibernates; a man snores.

22. A) Oil and water are opposites; alkaline and acid are opposites.

23. B) Bricks make walls; sand makes sandcastles.

cause physical separation, the idea of *pride* being used to describe a feeling or trait can rule out the other answer options. In the third paragraph, the author mentions that "Kion caught the briefest trace of his pride's scent." Since the feeling or trait of being proud or having pride is an intangible quality, it does not have a smell. A group of lions would, however, have a smell, especially for other members of the pride, or group of lions.

Verbal

Synonyms

1. A) *Amalgam* means "a mixture or blend."

2. C) *Succumb* means "to yield or stop resisting."

3. A) *Potent* means "wielding power; strong; effective."

4. B) *Prone* means "lying flat."

5. E) *Ambulatory* means "able to walk."

6. A) *Superficial* means "shallow in character or attitude; on the surface."

7. C) *Regress* means "to move backward, often to a worse state."

8. A) *Respiration* means "breathing."

9. A) *Pragmatic* means "concerned with practical matters and results."

10. E) *Retain* means "to hold or keep in possession."

11. D) *Dysfunctional* means "not functioning properly."

12. A) *Accountability* means "to be responsible for something" or "to be held to account."

13. B) *Diminish* means "become less in amount or intensity."

14. C) *Benign* means "not harmful; not malignant."

15. C) *Abstain* means "to refrain; choose to avoid or not participate."

16. E) *Vital* means "related to life; essential to existence or well-being."

17. A) *Adhere* means "to follow devotedly; to hold closely to an idea or course."

18. C) *Cohort* means "a group of people with something in common."

19. B) *Deleterious* means "harmful or deadly to living things."

20. C) *Malaise* means "a general feeling of illness and discomfort."

21. E) *Transient* means "lasting for only a short period of time."

22. C) *Incompatible* means "mismatched" or "unable to work together."

23. C) To *transmit* something is to send it or pass it on.

24. C) *Void* can be a noun or a verb, meaning "emptiness" or "to empty or evacuate."

25. A) *Therapeutic* means "having a beneficial or healing effect."

address the winning/losing aspect. Option *E* is incorrect because assistance implies helping, not winning against someone.

34. E) Option *E* is correct because the rulebook is continually undergoing adjustments and additions, so it makes sense that this will continue in the future. Option *A* is incorrect, as nothing indicates that Zoe gives up easily. Option *B* is incorrect as the competition is a family-only event. Option *C* is incorrect because no hint is given that the dish will change. Option *D* is incorrect because the family clearly enjoys the tradition, with no implication of conflict.

35. B) Option *B* is correct because the passage follows Kion's transition from total helplessness to budding independence evidenced by his survival over three days. Option *A* is incorrect because no survival instructions are provided—the protagonist is figuring it out as he goes. Option *C* is incorrect because the savannah is just the setting, not the focus. Option *D* is incorrect because the supernatural elements of mythology are not present. Option *E* is incorrect because the writing style is literary rather than scientific.

36. A) Option *A* is correct because Kion's inner struggle revolves around his lack of confidence and hunting skills. Option *B* is incorrect because his separation from his pride is external. Option *C* is incorrect because the environmental challenges are secondary to his internal challenges. Option *D* is incorrect because his desire to be like his father is only mentioned briefly and not the main focus. Option *E* is incorrect because navigation difficulties are not presented as internal struggles but practical ones.

37. E) Option *E* is correct because Kion simply watches the other animals without interacting with them. Option *A* is incorrect because Kion actively avoids hunting behavior. Option *B* is incorrect because Kion does not compete with other animals. Option *C* is incorrect because no hostility erupts between Kion and the other animals. Option *D* is incorrect because Kion shows caution—not fear—when encountering other animals.

38. D) Option *D* is correct because Kion's developing mane indicates immaturity. Option *A* is incorrect because hunting inability could indicate something other than age, like inexperience or developmental issues. Option *B* is incorrect because fear is not specifically mentioned regarding his development. Option *C* is incorrect because even adults can get lost sometimes. Option *E* is incorrect because being ignored can also happen regardless of age.

39. D) Option *D* is correct because Kion's inexperience is portrayed in a way that evokes compassion from the reader. Option *A* is incorrect because the emphasis of the story is on personal struggles rather than survival skills. Option *B* is incorrect because future potential is only implied and not explicitly contrasted against Kion's predicament. Option *C* is incorrect because familial or social bonds are not directly tied to references of inexperience. Option *E* is incorrect because the passage contains no critiques of lion social structures.

40. C) In the context of this passage, a pride is used to describe a group of lions. There are two clues to help determine the meaning of this term as it is used: In the first paragraph, the author writes " . . . since he was swept up in the flash flood that separated him from his pride." Knowing that a flash flood can

26. E) Option *E* is correct because Maya specifically tries to think of what life was like in past generations. Option *A* is incorrect because Maya does not try to learn Spanish in the story. Option *B* is incorrect because Maya appears to willingly participate in the tamale preparation. Option *C* is incorrect because it is evident that Maya values her heritage rather than feels embarrassed. Option *D* is incorrect because Maya is choosing to be with her Abuela instead of elsewhere.

27. A) Option *A* is correct because the sentence signals that Maya's challenges at school disappear when she is in Abuela's kitchen. Option *B* is incorrect because heat is used as a metaphor, not literally. Option *C* is incorrect because the passage shows Maya connecting with her heritage, not losing it. Option *D* is incorrect because the sentence refers to worries disappearing, not the passage of time. Option *E* is incorrect because there is no mention of adjusting cooking methods.

28. B) Option *B* is correct because Maya's cousins speak Spanish knowing she will be excluded, implying distance. Option *A* is incorrect because Maya is intentionally excluded by her cousins. Option *C* is incorrect because competition is not mentioned. Option *D* is incorrect because interaction is clearly happening. Option *E* is incorrect because their relationship does not indicate conflict, just distance.

29. C) Option *C* is correct because Abuela's words directly address their Mexican-American identity as a gift. Option *A* is incorrect, as the paragraph does not explain the move to Chicago. Option *B* is incorrect because no contrast is mentioned between the old and new countries. Option *D* is incorrect because the activity in the kitchen goes beyond a simple cooking lesson. Option *E* is incorrect because Abuela does not explicitly praise Maya's progress.

30. C) Option *C* is correct because the passage traces the event from the past to the present. Option *A* is incorrect because the passage does not provide any pie-baking instructions. Option *B* is incorrect since the passage mentions rules but does not treat them as the main focus. Option *D* is incorrect since the emphasis is on the tradition itself, not the skills. Option *E* is incorrect because pie-baking strategies are only briefly mentioned.

31. B) Option *B* is correct because the first sentence states that the competition originates from a rivalry between Grandma Josephine and her sister. Option *A* is incorrect because Grandpa Joe is only mentioned as a former participant. Option *C* is incorrect because nothing is mentioned about a professional contest. Option *D* is incorrect because no cooking shows are mentioned. Option *E* is incorrect since Zoe's skills came after the competition's inception.

32. A) Option *A* is correct because the additions to the rulebook show formalized rules developing through trial and error. Option *B* is incorrect because nothing special is suggested by the timer—it is just standard cooking equipment. Option *C* is incorrect, as the photos only document each contest. Option *D* is incorrect since leadership does not imply seriousness beyond a basic level. Option *E* is incorrect because variety alone does not indicate seriousness.

33. C) Option *C* is correct because *dethroned* implies Zoe's removal and Devin's installation as champion. Option *A* is incorrect since losing a title is not a cause for celebration. Option *B* is incorrect because Zoe is not simply challenged but eventually defeated. Option *D* is incorrect because replacement does not

12. E) The passage discusses the large number of women in political positions in Latin America.

13. C) The passage explains that a legislated candidate quota requires parties to place women on at least 30 percent of their candidate lists in an effort to increase women's presence in government.

14. B) The passage states that 25 percent of legislators in Latin America are now women.

15. C) The passage explains that while one of these works of art was sold, the other three are not for sale and are instead housed in a museum or gallery in Oslo.

16. E) Because three of the four versions of his most famous piece of art are housed in Oslo, we can assume that Munch was likely from Oslo. One of the locations with his work is also named after him.

17. D) The author writes, "*The Scream of Nature* by Edvard Munch is one of the world's best known and most desirable artworks."

18. A) The passage explains how valuable *The Scream of Nature* is by providing the amount one of the paintings sold for and describing the theft of two others.

19. B) Two versions of this work of art were paintings and two were pastels.

20. B) The author writes that "jazz music was played by and for a more expressive and freed populace than the United States had previously seen." In addition to "the emergence of the flapper," the 1920s saw "the explosion of African American art and culture now known as the Harlem Renaissance.

21. A) The author writes, "Jazz music was played by and for a more expressive and freed populace than the United States had previously seen." In addition to "the emergence of the flapper," the 1920s saw "the explosion of African American art and culture now known as the Harlem Renaissance."

22. C) The author opens the passage saying, "In recent decades, jazz has been associated with New Orleans and festivals like Mardi Gras, but in the 1920s, jazz was a booming trend whose influence reached into many aspects of American culture." The author then elaborates on these movements.

23. B) At the end of the first paragraph, the author writes, "Ella Fitzgerald, for example, moved from Virginia to New York City to begin her much-lauded singing career, and jazz pioneer Louis Armstrong got his big break in Chicago."

24. C) The author writes that "jazz music was played by and for a more expressive and freed populace than the United States had previously seen." In addition to "the emergence of the flapper," the 1920s saw "the explosion of African American art and culture now known as the Harlem Renaissance."

25. D) Option *D* is correct because the passage explores the character's experience being sandwiched between Mexican heritage and American life. Option *A* is incorrect because traditional Mexican food is not the focus but a means to deliver the larger theme. Option *B* is incorrect because the generation gap is not meaningfully portrayed. Option *C* is incorrect since the immigration story is only briefly mentioned. Option *E* is incorrect because maintaining traditions is just one part of Maya's journey.

25. A) Convert each value to a decimal.

$$(a): 0.6$$
$$(b): 3/5 = 0.6$$
$$(c): 1/2 \text{ of } 1.2 = 0.6$$

Therefore, a, b, and c are equal.

Reading

1. A) The passage explains how a baby's senses develop and allow it to interact with the world.

2. D) The passage explains that infants rely mostly on hearing because vision does not become a dominant sense until around the age of twelve months.

3. C) The passage states that babies' senses are much like those of adults except for their vision, which develops later.

4. D) The passage describes human studies as the study of "the relationship between human activity and the environment." That would include farmers interacting with river systems.

5. A) The passage explains what the study of geography involves and outlines its main subdisciplines.

6. E) Only this option summarizes the two main points of the passage: the definition of geography and the breakdown of its subdisciplines.

7. B) The author writes, "All other explanations for the war are either a direct consequence of the South's desire for wealth at the expense of her fellow man or a *fanciful* invention to cover up this sad portion of our nation's history."

8. E) The author writes, "But people who try to sell you this narrative are wrong. The Civil War was not a battle of cultural identities—it was a battle about slavery."

9. B) The author writes, "The Civil War was not a battle of cultural identities—it was a battle about slavery. All other explanations for the war are either a direct consequence of the South's desire for wealth at the expense of her fellow man or a fanciful invention to cover up this sad portion of our nation's history."

10. D) The author writes this passage to correct misinformation on the topic of the causes of the Civil War. He writes with an assertive, or self-confident tone, insisting that his interpretation of this historical event is accurate while the others are wrong. For example, he says, "People who try to sell you this narrative are wrong," showing his confidence in his position and his disdain for others' opinions on this topic.

11. E) The passage explains that Latin America has the second highest percentage of female members of parliament after Nordic Europe, meaning Nordic Europe has the highest percentage.

21. B) Simplify each expression.

$$(a): 8 + (3 - 2) = 8 + 1 = 9$$

$$(b): (8 + 3) - 2 = 11 - 2 = 9$$

$$(c): 8 - (3 - 2) = 8 - 1 = 7$$

$$(a) = (b) > (c)$$

22. D) The average of 5 numbers is equal to the sum of those numbers divided by 5. If the smallest value is x, the next values are $x + 1, x + 2, x + 3,$ and $x + 4$. Therefore, we have:

$$\frac{x + x + 1 + x + 2 + x + 3 + x + 4}{5} = 20$$

$$\frac{5x + 10}{5} = 20$$

$$5x + 10 = 100$$

$$5x = 90$$

$$x = 18$$

Substitute x to find the largest value:

$$x + 4 = 22$$

23. A) The numbers in the series are increasing by 5.

$$-8, -3, \_\_, 7, 12$$

$$-3 - (-8) = 5$$

$$12 - 7 = 5$$

To find the missing number, add 5 to the previous number.

$$-3 + 5 = 2$$

24. C) Add the values and divide by 5:

$$4.6 + 4.8 + 5.3 + 5.2 + 6 = 25.9$$

$$25.9 \div 5 = 5.18 \text{ mi}$$

14. B) The numbers in the series are decreasing by 2.

$$-14 - (-12) = -2$$
$$-16 - (-14) = -2$$
$$-18 - (-16) = -2$$

To find the first number, subtract -2 from the second number.

$$-12 - (-2) = -10$$

15. C) Write 12 more than $\frac{2}{3}$ of 33 as an equation and solve using the order of operations:

$$12 + \frac{2}{3} \times 33$$
$$12 + 22 = 34$$

16. A) The prime factors of 54 are 9, 3, and 2. Therefore, any two of these values are prime factors. The other values are either not prime or not factors.

17. D) Find each value. The formula for the circumference of a circle is $C = 2\pi r$, and $d = 2r$ (where r is the radius and d is the diameter).

$$(a): C = 2\pi r = 2\pi(4) = 8\pi$$
$$(b): C = 2\pi r = \pi d = 4\pi$$
$$(c): C = 2\pi r = 2\pi(2) = 4\pi$$
$$(a) > (b) = (c)$$

18. D) Use the formula for an arithmetic sum.

$$S_n = \frac{n}{2}(2a_1 + (n-1)d)$$

$$\frac{25}{2}(2(14) + (25-1)2) = 950$$

19. A) Simplify each expression.

$$(a): 30\% \text{ of } 50 = 0.3 \times 50 = 15$$
$$(b): 50\% \text{ of } 30 = 0.5 \times 30 = 15$$
$$(c): 3\% \text{ of } 500 = 0.03 \times 500 = 15$$
$$(a) = (b) = (c)$$

20. C) A rectangular prism has four sides that are congruent. The diagonals of those four rectangles are all congruent.

7. C) To find the number for which $\frac{2}{3}$ equals 150, create an equation where a is the number being solved for.

$$\frac{2}{3} \times a = 150$$

$$a = \frac{3}{2} \times 150 = 225$$

8. C) Create an equation to find what number (a) added to 4 equals 10.

$$(a + 4) = 10$$

$$a = 6$$

9. A) The area of a circle is πr^2. The area is given as 900π. Use these values to solve for the radius, r.

$$900\pi = \pi r^2$$

$$r^2 = 900$$

$$r = \sqrt{900} = 30 \text{ feet}$$

The question is asking for the circumference. The equation for the circumference is $2\pi r$.

$$C = 2\pi(30)$$

$$C = 60\pi$$

10. D) Choose two consecutive odd integers (e.g., 7 and 9, 13 and 15) and subtract the lower one from the higher. The difference is always 2.

11. D) Simplify each expression.

$$(a): 0 + (3 - 2) = 0 + 1 = 1$$

$$(b): 0 \times (3 - 2) = 0 \times 1 = 0$$

$$(c): 0 - (3 - 2) = 0 - 1 = -1$$

$$(a) > (b) > (c)$$

12. A) To find 20% of 25% of 80, multiply.

$$0.2(0.25)(80) = 4$$

13. B) First write $\frac{2}{3}$ of 60 divided by 8 as an equation, then solve.

$$\frac{2}{3} \times 60 \div 8 = 40 \div 8 = 5$$

Quantitative Section #2

1. C) Carla's age is c; Megan's age is m, so $c = 3m$.

$$c - 8 = m - 8 + 18$$

Substitute $3m$ for c in the equation:

$$3m - 8 = m + 10$$

$$m = 9$$

2. B) Let j be John's age and s be Sally's age:

$$j + 4 = 2(s + 4)$$

$$s - 8 = 10$$

$$s = 18$$

$$j + 4 = 2(18 + 4)$$

$$j = 40$$

3. C) To find $\frac{1}{3}$ of 36, multiply.

$$\frac{1}{3} \times 36 = 12$$

4. B) To find the solution to 11 less than 6 squared, first write it as a numerical equation.

$$6^2 - 11$$

$$36 - 11 = 25$$

5. A) One pen sells for $12, so on the sale of a pen, the profit is $12 - 6 = 6$. To make $60, 10 pens need to be sold.

6. B) The numbers in the series are decreasing by 3.5:

$$83.5, 80, \underline{\quad}, 73, 69.5$$

$$80 - 83.5 = -3.5$$

$$69.5 - 73 = -3.5$$

To find the missing number, subtract 3.5 from the previous number.

$$80 - 3.5 = 76.5$$

22. A) Rewrite each value as a decimal.

$$(a): 30\% = 0.3$$

$$(b): 0.3$$

$$(c): \frac{3}{100} = 0.03$$

$$(a) = (b) > (c)$$

23. E) To find the mean, add all of the scores and divide by the total number of scores.

$$\frac{90 + 78 + 45 + 98 + 84 + 79 + 66 + 87 + 78 + 94}{10} = 79.9$$

To find the median: Sort the scores in ascending order, and find the middle number. Since it is an even number of scores, the middle will be the average between the two middle numbers. There are 10 scores, which is an even number, so the median will be the average of the fifth and sixth scores once the list of numbers is put in ascending order.

$$45, 66, 78, 78, \mathbf{79}, \mathbf{84}, 87, 90, 94, 98$$

$$\frac{79 + 84}{2} = 81.5$$

Mode is the most frequent value. Since the number 78 appears twice in the list, and no other numbers are repeated, 78 is the mode.

24. E) To find the solution, first write it as an equation. 21 more than 4 squared means to add 21 to 4 squared.

$$21 + 4^2 = 21 + 16 = 37$$

25. B) Simplify each expression.

$$(a): \frac{2}{3} \times 42 = 28$$

$$(b): \frac{7}{10} \times 40 = 28$$

$$(c): \frac{5}{4} \times 24 = 30$$

$$(c) > (a) = (b)$$

16. B) The circumference of a circle is $C = 2\pi r$. Since $d = 2r$, then $C = \pi d$.

$$50 \text{ ft} = \pi d$$

$$d = \frac{50}{\pi}$$

17. B) There are 15 minutes between 7:45 a.m. and 8:00 a.m. and 20 minutes between 8:00 a.m. and 8:20 a.m.

$$15 \text{ minutes} + 20 \text{ minutes} = 35 \text{ minutes}$$

18. D) The numbers in the series are increasing by 1.3.

$$1.3, 2.6, 3.9, 5.2, \ldots$$

$$2.6 - 1.3 = 1.3$$

$$3.9 - 2.6 = 1.3$$

$$5.2 - 3.9 = 1.3$$

To find the next number, add 1.3 to the previous number.

$$5.2 + 1.3 = 6.5$$

19. D) In 2005, the value was 1.8 times its value in 1995. So, $1.8x = 7{,}200 \rightarrow x = 4000$.

20. A) The numbers in the series are increasing. The difference between each value is increasing by 1.

$$567, 579, 592, 606, 621, \underline{}$$

$$579 - 567 = 12$$

$$592 - 579 = 13$$

$$606 - 592 = 14$$

$$621 - 606 = 15$$

To find the next number, add 16 to the previous number.

$$621 + 16 = 637$$

21. C) Simplify each expression.

$$(a): 3.48 \times 10^{-3} = 0.00348$$

$$(b): -3 \times -48 = 144$$

$$(c): -2 - (-4) = 2$$

Therefore, (a), (b), and (c) are positive.

12. D) The series is geometric with a common ratio of $\frac{1}{2}$ (meaning each number is multiplied by $\frac{1}{2}$ or divided by 2 to find the next number).

$$4848, 2424, 1212, 606, \ldots$$

$$\frac{2424}{4848} = \frac{1}{2}$$

$$\frac{2424}{2424} = \frac{1}{2}$$

$$\frac{606}{1212} = \frac{1}{2}$$

To find the next number, multiply the previous number by $\frac{1}{2}$:

$$606 \times \frac{1}{2} = 303$$

13. C) (a): 7 circles

(b): 8 circles

(c): 7 circles

$$(b) > (a) = (c)$$

14. D) A counterexample is an exception to a proposed general rule. The statement $17 + 15 = 32$ is a counterexample because it shows that the sum of two odd numbers can be an even number.

15. B) The numbers in the series are increasing. The difference between the values increases by 1 with each number.

$$13, 14, 16, 19, \ldots$$

$$14 - 13 = 1$$

$$16 - 14 = 2$$

$$19 - 16 = 3$$

To find the next number, add 4 to the previous number.

$$19 + 4 = 23$$

To find the number after that, add 5 to the previous number.

$$23 + 5 = 28$$

To find the next number, multiply the previous number by 2:

$$0.32 \times 2 = 0.64$$

7. D) Simplify each expression and find the expression that equals 25.

$$400 \div 16 = 25$$

$$2(200 - 8) = 2(192) = 384$$

$$(400 \div 4) \div 12 = 100 \div 12 = 8.\overline{3}$$

$$(216 \div 8) + (184 \div 8) = 27 + 23 = 50$$

$$(216 \div 16) + (184 \div 16) = 13.5 + 11.5 = 25$$

$$(216 \div 16) + (184 \div 16)$$

8. C) To find the number that $\frac{3}{5}$ of is 300, create an equation where a is the number being solved for.

$$\frac{3}{5} \times a = 300$$

$$a = \frac{5}{3}(300) = 500$$

9. C) Find the area of each figure.

$$(a): A_{square} = s^2 = 10^2 = 100$$

$$(b): A_{rectangle} = lw = 5(2) = 10$$

$$(c): A_{triangle} = \frac{1}{2}bh = \frac{1}{2}(12)(3) = 18$$

$$(a) > (c) > (b)$$

10. D) To find $\frac{3}{5}$ of 500, multiply:

$$\frac{3}{5} \times 500 = 300$$

11. D) Find the perimeter of each figure. In an equilateral shape, all the sides have the same lengths.

$$(a): P_{square} = 4s = 4(6) = 24$$

$$(b): P_{triangle} = 3s = 3(8) = 24$$

$$(c): P_{hexagon} = 6s = 6(3) = 18$$

$$(a) = (b) > (c)$$

Answer Explanations #1

Quantitative Section #1

1. E) The numbers in the series are decreasing by 6.

$$67 - 73 = -6$$
$$61 - 67 = -6$$
$$43 - 49 = -6$$

Find the missing number by subtracting 6 from the previous number.

$$61 - 6 = 55$$

2. A) The diagonal of a rectangle equally divides the rectangle's area, so the shaded areas of (a) and (b) are equal. Figure (c) shows less than half of the rectangle shaded, so (c) is less shaded than (a) and (b).

$$(a) = (b) > (c)$$

3. C) To find 75% of 24, simply multiply:

$$0.75(24) = 18$$

4. C) Round each number and multiply.

$$16,000 \times 200 = 3,200,000 \approx 3,300,000$$

5. C) To find the number for which $\frac{2}{3}$ of it is equal to 12, create a proportion where *a* is the number being solved for.

$$\frac{2}{3} \times a = 12$$

$$a = \frac{3}{2} \times 12 = 18$$

6. E) The series is geometric with a common ratio of 2 (meaning each number is multiplied by 2 to find the next number).

$$0.04, 0.08, 0.16, 0.32, \ldots$$

$$\frac{0.08}{0.04} = 2$$

$$\frac{0.16}{0.08} = 2$$

27. Read is to book as make is to
    A) Laugh
    B) Restaurant
    C) Recipe
    D) Water
    E) Boil

28. Play is to frolic as incredible is to
    A) Unremarkable
    B) Believable
    C) Implausible
    D) Mediocre
    E) Credible

29. Diamond is to ring as syrup is to
    A) Sap
    B) Tree
    C) Pancake
    D) Old-fashioned
    E) Sticky

30. Money is to wallet as keys are to
    A) Locksmith
    B) Doorway
    C) Purse
    D) Detective
    E) Travel

13. Foghorn is to lighthouse as siren is to
    A) Firetruck
    B) School
    C) Alarm
    D) Weather
    E) Alert

14. Log is to fireplace as shovel is to
    A) Pitchfork
    B) Tool
    C) Dirt
    D) Snow
    E) Garden

15. Flowerpot is to houseplant as pan is to
    A) Sink
    B) Brownies
    C) Stove
    D) Cabinet
    E) Water

16. Landscaper is to lawn as teacher is to
    A) School
    B) Class
    C) Community
    D) Principal
    E) Lesson

17. Library is to books as ocean is to
    A) Lake
    B) Sun
    C) Fish
    D) Sailor
    E) Island

18. Photo is to camera as apple is to
    A) Pie
    B) Sauce
    C) Tree
    D) Forest
    E) Food

19. Inch is to foot as ounce is to
    A) Gallon
    B) Liquid
    C) Orange juice
    D) Pound
    E) Weight

20. Jump is to hop as run is to
    A) Walk
    B) Jog
    C) Saunter
    D) Gallop
    E) Skip

21. Hibernating is to bear as snoring is to
    A) Cat
    B) Cave
    C) Bed
    D) Man
    E) Sleep

22. Oil is to water as alkaline is to
    A) Acid
    B) Salt
    C) Sugar
    D) Water
    E) Sodium

23. Brick is to wall as sand is to
    A) Clay
    B) Castle
    C) Ocean
    D) Clams
    E) Fish

24. Shovel is to hole as pump is to
    A) Pool
    B) Dirt
    C) Well
    D) Bucket
    E) Water

25. Clock is to chime as watch is to
    A) Tick
    B) Explode
    C) Time
    D) See
    E) Minute

26. Sole is to shoe as heel is to
    A) Sandal
    B) Boot
    C) Slipper
    D) Bandage
    E) Sock

Practice Test #1

Analogies

Directions: The first two words in each question have a relationship. Choose the response that recreates that same relationship in the second set of words.

1. Milk is to shake as French is to
   - A) Eggs
   - B) Oil
   - C) Omelet
   - D) Hat
   - E) Fry

2. Run is to walk as fast is to
   - A) Quick
   - B) Slow
   - C) Hurry
   - D) Turtle
   - E) Jaunt

3. Stop is to sign as traffic is to
   - A) Slow
   - B) Stop
   - C) Yield
   - D) Light
   - E) Police

4. Frantic is to desperate as angry is to
   - A) Happy
   - B) Energetic
   - C) Irate
   - D) Cool
   - E) Mystical

5. Cup is to mug as trophy is to
   - A) Beaker
   - B) Prize
   - C) Demitasse
   - D) Weight
   - E) Coffee

6. Cookie is to chocolate chips as pizza is to
   - A) Oven
   - B) Yeast
   - C) Pepperoni
   - D) Delicious
   - E) Place

7. Sun is to shine as star is to
   - A) Moon
   - B) Comet
   - C) Black hole
   - D) Light
   - E) Meteor

8. Puzzle is to piece as team is to
   - A) Referee
   - B) Player
   - C) Soccer
   - D) Base
   - E) Goal

9. Feather is to bird as fur is to
   - A) Frog
   - B) Dog
   - C) Penguin
   - D) Turkey
   - E) Coat

10. Tree is to forest as bird is to
    - A) Flock
    - B) Nest
    - C) Feather
    - D) Flight
    - E) Egg

11. Train is to rail as car is to
    - A) Path
    - B) Sidewalk
    - C) Road
    - D) Parking
    - E) Lot

12. String is to guitar as lace is to
    - A) Coat
    - B) Shoe
    - C) Plant
    - D) Rug
    - E) Paper

17. ADHERE
    A) Follow
    B) Reject
    C) Uphold
    D) Interpret
    E) Classify

18. COHORT
    A) Colleague
    B) Acquaintance
    C) Group
    D) Associate
    E) Colony

19. DELETERIOUS
    A) Helpful
    B) Harmful
    C) Gentle
    D) Constructive
    E) Unfortunate

20. MALAISE
    A) Nausea
    B) Headache
    C) Unease
    D) Vomiting
    E) Humidity

21. TRANSIENT
    A) Repetitive
    B) Severe
    C) Extreme
    D) Transparent
    E) Temporary

22. INCOMPATIBLE
    A) Friendly
    B) Cooperative
    C) Mismatched
    D) Talkative
    E) Uncomfortable

23. TRANSMIT
    A) Treat
    B) Study
    C) Pass on
    D) Eliminate
    E) Hide

24. VOID
    A) Ease
    B) Strengthen
    C) Empty
    D) Feel
    E) Exhaust

25. THERAPEUTIC
    A) Healing
    B) Prescribed
    C) Systemic
    D) Targeted
    E) Careful

26. DISCREET
    A) Careful
    B) Accurate
    C) Loud
    D) Exact
    E) Discomfort

27. RECURRENCE
    A) Cure
    B) Upset
    C) Resolution
    D) Suppression
    E) Return

28. LATENT
    A) Obvious
    B) Lasting
    C) Hidden
    D) Misunderstood
    E) Behind

29. ANOMALY
    A) Crime
    B) Mistake
    C) Irregularity
    D) Improvement
    E) Normal

30. IMMINENT
    A) Delayed
    B) Avoidable
    C) Fatal
    D) Impending
    E) Extra

3. POTENT
   A) Powerful
   B) Weak
   C) Detrimental
   D) Nutritional
   E) Appropriate

4. PRONE
   A) Excited
   B) Flat
   C) Unconscious
   D) Uncomfortable
   E) Upside down

5. AMBULATORY
   A) Healthy
   B) Recovered
   C) Symptomatic
   D) Broken
   E) Walking

6. SUPERFICIAL
   A) Shallow
   B) Impressive
   C) Gruesome
   D) Jagged
   E) Sharp

7. REGRESS
   A) Get better
   B) Strengthen
   C) Worsen
   D) Fail
   E) Exit

8. RESPIRATION
   A) Breathing
   B) Sleeping
   C) Digestion
   D) Heartbeat
   E) Sweating

9. PRAGMATIC
   A) Practical
   B) Logical
   C) Emotional
   D) Aloof
   E) Attractive

10. RETAIN
    A) Forget
    B) Shed
    C) Filter
    D) Train
    E) Hold

11. DYSFUNCTIONAL
    A) Vast
    B) Expensive
    C) Intricate
    D) Flawed
    E) Precious

12. ACCOUNTABILITY
    A) Responsibility
    B) Accuracy
    C) Compliance
    D) Confidence
    E) Numerous

13. DIMINISH
    A) Identify
    B) Decrease
    C) Stop
    D) Intensify
    E) Confuse

14. BENIGN
    A) Problematic
    B) Worrisome
    C) Harmless
    D) Unattractive
    E) Colorless

15. ABSTAIN
    A) Ingest
    B) Resist
    C) Refrain
    D) Intake
    E) Connect

16. VITAL
    A) Contrary
    B) Bloody
    C) Unrelated
    D) Secondary
    E) Necessary

36. Kion's internal conflict is most closely related to which one of the following?
    A) His inexperience and self-doubt
    B) His separation from his pride
    C) The harsh environment of the savannah
    D) His desire to be like his father
    E) Navigating unfamiliar surroundings

37. Which one of the following best describes Kion's interaction with other animals?
    A) Predatory
    B) Competitive
    C) Antagonistic
    D) Fearful
    E) Observational

38. Which detail most clearly shows Kion is not yet an adult lion?
    A) He cannot hunt.
    B) He is afraid of other animals.
    C) He is lost.
    D) His mane is just starting to grow.
    E) He is ignored by other animals.

39. The repeated references to Kion's inexperience serve to do which one of the following?
    A) Emphasize the harsh nature of survival
    B) Contrast his current abilities with his future potential
    C) Highlight the importance of close kinship
    D) Build sympathy for the protagonist
    E) Criticize the failures of lion social structures

40. What does the word *pride* mean as it is used in the final sentence of the first paragraph?
    A) A description of how Kion feels about being a lion, despite his youth compared to other lions
    B) The feeling Kion's father has as he watches Kion grow
    C) The group of lions of which he used to be a member
    D) Kion's disappointment that he is smaller than the other lions
    E) A trait Kion hopes to develop as he matures

Verbal

Synonyms

Directions: Find the synonym or the word closest in meaning.

1. AMALGAM
    A) Blend
    B) Process
    C) Schedule
    D) Conference
    E) Rhythm

2. SUCCUMB
    A) Ignore
    B) Fight
    C) Surrender
    D) Enjoy
    E) Cornucopia

33. What does the word *dethroned* in the second paragraph most likely mean?
    A) Celebrated
    B) Challenged
    C) Defeated
    D) Replaced
    E) Assisted

34. Based on the passage, which one of the following is most likely to happen during next year's competition?
    A) Zoe will sit out next year if she loses again this year.
    B) Judges from other families will be chosen to keep things fair.
    C) The family will switch to a different dessert.
    D) The competition will be canceled due to disagreements.
    E) A new rule will be added to the official rulebook.

Passage 9

Kion was a young male lion. No longer a cub, he was starting to grow his golden mane. He wanted to be powerful like his father. Crouching in the savannah grass, Kion felt helpless and small. The sun had set and risen three times since he was swept up in the flash flood that separated him from his pride.

He knew how vulnerable he was. He was hungry and salivated at the scent of a nearby zebra herd. Kion tried to listen for his mother's familiar call or his uncle's roar. Instead, the distant squawking of birds taunted the young lion. He had never hunted on his own, and the strong musk of hyena territory markings meant he wouldn't begin anytime soon.

Kion caught the briefest trace of his pride's scent, indicating their presence beyond a ridge to the south. The trumpeting of a nearby elephant herd spurred him on.

He came upon three adult lions patrolling the edges of their territory and hid until they passed. His heart beat rapidly under his ribs. His breathing was shallow. Would they see him as a lost child or a potential rival?

Kion approached a watering hole, wary of the other animals that emerged from the brush to have a drink—gazelles, warthogs, giraffes. They all had their turn. None of the animals noticed Kion, but it wasn't like they would be scared anyway. He couldn't hunt, and he was unsure of himself—traits absent in an experienced predator. Kion drank and followed a nearby streambed until he arrived at a familiar rocky ridge. This was where his mother had taught him how to stalk and pounce.

A deep roar penetrated the twilight. Kion's ears perked up at the sound of his uncle's call. He answered. His voice was not yet fully developed, but it was clear: I am here. I am coming home.

35. How can the passage MOST accurately be described?
    A) As a survival manual
    B) As a coming-of-age story
    C) As a detailed description of savannah life
    D) As a mythological journey
    E) As a scientific observation

Passage 8

It began as a sisterly rivalry between Grandma Josephine and her sister, Great-Aunt Esther. Back in their youth, they would regularly challenge each other to make the best apple pie. Their 40-year rivalry had transformed into the Simmons household's annual pie-baking competition. It became the event of the year. The festivities grew more elaborate over time as each generation added its own quirks and rules.

Twelve-year-old Zoe woke early today, ready to begin preparations for her specialty: apple-blackberry pie. She used to hold the trophy for the junior division until her older cousin Devin dethroned her with his lemon meringue pie. This year would be different—it would be her first try at a lattice-top crust.

The kitchen had been transformed into a pie-baking extravaganza. The counters were unrecognizable, disappearing under containers and bags of flour, fruits, and more spices than necessary. Relatives-turned-competitors claimed their own baking zone and safeguarded their recipes from suspicious eyes.

Grandma Josephine was the ringleader of this circus. "Don't forget, presentation counts for 25 points!" she reminded them, turning the page over in the official rulebook. The three-ring binder looked huge and heavy—it had grown thick with amendments and addendums.

Zoe really enjoyed looking at the photos of each competition over the decades. She saw pictures of her aunts and uncles before they started their own families. There were pictures of cousins she hadn't seen in a while since they moved to other states. She looked at Cousin Phil's picture. He was banned from competing for a year. His crime: using store-bought crust. The most recent picture was of Grandpa Joe's last competition.

Zoe felt a mix of nervousness and satisfaction when the kitchen timer rang. The final countdown had begun. Whether or not she won, she knew she was part of something special.

30. What is the main purpose of the passage?
    A) To explain how to bake a pie
    B) To describe the rules of a pie-baking competition
    C) To show how a family tradition evolved
    D) To highlight a family's baking skills
    E) To compare different pie-baking strategies

31. According to the passage, how did the pie-baking competition originate?
    A) It was Grandpa Joe's favorite hobby.
    B) It started as a rivalry between siblings.
    C) Grandma Josephine wanted a professional baking contest.
    D) It was inspired by a cooking show.
    E) Zoe wanted to improve her baking skills.

32. Which detail suggests that the family takes this competition seriously?
    A) The thick rulebook with amendments
    B) The kitchen timer ringing
    C) Pictures of past competitions
    D) Grandma Josephine's role as ringleader
    E) The variety of pies being made

They would have conversations in their perfect Spanish knowing that Maya would be excluded. All of this melted away in Abuela's kitchen like lard on the stovetop.

Maya paid close attention to Abuela's stories as they spread masa on the corn husks. She learned how her grandfather had worked hard to bring the family to America. He had two jobs and never slept. Maya listened intently as Abuela described her hometown celebrations and how they shared food and music and life. As Maya formed her tamales, she could feel something else take shape.

"We are Mexican. And now, we're American, too. We are lucky to have this gift, mija," Abuela said as she handed Maya the last tamale.

25. What is the central theme of the passage?
    A) The importance of traditional cuisine
    B) The generation gap between Maya and her grandmother
    C) A family's journey from Mexico City to Chicago
    D) A girl's experience between two worlds
    E) The difficulties of maintaining traditions

26. Which one of the following is the best description of how Maya feels in Abuela's kitchen?
    A) Eager to learn Spanish
    B) Frustrated by the number of tamales to prepare
    C) Embarrassed by a lack of connection to her cultural heritage
    D) Anxious to join her friends at the mall later
    E) A sense of connection with the past

27. What does the sentence "All of this melted away in Abuela's kitchen like lard on the stovetop" suggest?
    A) Maya's worries went away when she was with her grandmother.
    B) The kitchen was too hot and made Maya uncomfortable.
    C) Maya's Mexican heritage was slowly disappearing.
    D) Time passes quickly when preparing food with loved ones.
    E) Abuela was trying to cut back on using lard in her cooking.

28. Which word best describes Maya's relationship with her cousins based on the passage?
    A) Supportive
    B) Distant
    C) Competitive
    D) Nonexistent
    E) Combative

29. What is the purpose of the final paragraph?
    A) To explain why the family moved to Chicago
    B) To juxtapose life in Mexico with life in America
    C) To reveal a perspective on dual identity
    D) To conclude Maya's cooking lesson
    E) To express Abuela's pride in Maya's growth

21. What is a reasonable inference that can be drawn from this passage?
    A) Jazz music was important to minority groups struggling for social equality in the 1920s.
    B) Duke Ellington, Fats Waller, and Bessie Smith were the most important jazz musicians of the Harlem Renaissance.
    C) Women gained the right to vote with the help of jazz musicians.
    D) Duke Ellington, Fats Waller, and Bessie Smith all supported women's right to vote.
    E) The success of jazz music contributed to a spike in America's economic wealth.

22. What is the author's primary purpose in writing this essay?
    A) To explain the role jazz musicians played in the Harlem Renaissance
    B) To inform the reader about the many important musicians playing jazz in the 1920s
    C) To discuss how jazz influenced important cultural movements in the 1920s
    D) To provide a history of jazz music in the 20th century
    E) To describe how jazz music and the Roaring Twenties are depicted in modern popular culture

23. Which of the following is NOT a fact stated in the passage?
    A) The years between World War I and the Great Depression were known as the Jazz Age.
    B) Ella Fitzgerald and Louis Armstrong both moved to New York City to start their music careers.
    C) Women danced to jazz music during the 1920s to make a statement about their role in society.
    D) Jazz music was an integral part of the emerging African American culture of the 1920s.
    E) In modern day popular culture, jazz music is most often associated with New Orleans and Mardi Gras.

24. What can the reader conclude from the passage above?
    A) F. Scott Fitzgerald supported jazz musicians in New York and Chicago.
    B) Jazz music is no longer as popular as it once was.
    C) Both women and African Americans used jazz music as a way of expressing their newfound freedom.
    D) Flappers and African American musicians worked together to produce jazz music.
    E) The Jazz Age took place during the Great Depression.

Passage 7

Abuela's kitchen always smelled like fresh masa dough. On Saturdays, Maya would join in the fun. It was a ritual that happened on the weekends, and she could sense the memories handed down through the generations—recollections of kneaded masa and roasted chiles and corn. Maya stood in the doorway, a portal connecting her present to her past. She closed her eyes and thought about what it must have been like back then—back when their family came to Chicago from Mexico City.

"Want to know the secret, mija?" Abuela asked. "You have to know what the masa should feel like—not too dry, not too wet." Maya tried to emulate Abuela's precision, but she obviously needed more practice.

"I was just like you, mija," Abuela continued. "I remember mixing and kneading masa with my abuela. There were no recipes, only our hands. Sometimes the mind is quick to forget."

At school, Maya felt like a walking contradiction. Her friends would talk about spending weekends at the mall. They didn't understand why she wouldn't join them instead of making tamales with her grandmother. Her cousins who grew up in Mexico City also went to her school.

17. What is the primary purpose of the passage?
    A) To describe the image depicted in *The Scream in Nature*
    B) To explain the origin of the painting *The Scream in Nature*
    C) To clarify the number of versions of *The Scream in Nature* that exist
    D) To prove the high value of *The Scream in Nature*
    E) To outline the different ownerships of *The Scream in Nature*

18. What is the topic of this passage?
    A) The value of The Scream of Nature
    B) The theft of The Scream of Nature
    C) Edvard Munch's life as an artist
    D) The danger associated with owning art
    E) Edvard Munch's childhood

19. According to the passage, what is true about two of the versions of Munch's *The Scream of Nature*?
    A) They have been sold.
    B) They are pastels.
    C) They are still missing.
    D) They were in the National Gallery.
    E) They are not authentic.

Passage 6

In recent decades, jazz has been associated with New Orleans and festivals like Mardi Gras, but in the 1920s, jazz was a booming trend whose influence reached into many aspects of American culture. In fact, the years between World War I and the Great Depression were known as the Jazz Age, a term coined by F. Scott Fitzgerald in his famous novel The Great Gatsby. Sometimes also called the "Roaring Twenties," this time period saw major urban centers experiencing new economic, cultural, and artistic vitality. In the United States, musicians flocked to cities like New York and Chicago, which would become famous hubs for jazz musicians. Ella Fitzgerald, for example, moved from Virginia to New York City to begin her much-lauded singing career, and jazz pioneer Louis Armstrong got his big break in Chicago.

Jazz music was played by and for a more expressive and freed populace than the United States had previously seen. Women gained the right to vote and were openly seen drinking and dancing to jazz music. This period marked the emergence of the flapper, a woman determined to make a statement about her new role in society. Jazz music also provided the soundtrack for the explosion of African American art and culture now known as the Harlem Renaissance. In addition to Fitzgerald and Armstrong, numerous musicians, including Duke Ellington, Fats Waller, and Bessie Smith, promoted their distinctive and complex music as an integral part of the emerging African American culture.

20. What is the main idea of the passage?
    A) People should associate jazz music with the 1920s, not modern New Orleans.
    B) Jazz music played an important role in many cultural movements of the 1920s.
    C) Many famous jazz musicians began their careers in New York City and Chicago.
    D) African Americans were instrumental in launching jazz into mainstream culture.
    E) The Jazz Age was culturally important but had little economic or political significance.

12. What is the main idea of the passage?
    A) Few women in Latin America are selected as CEOs of public companies.
    B) In Latin America, political parties must nominate women for office.
    C) Latin America is the region with the greatest gender equality.
    D) Women in Latin America have greater economic influence than political influence.
    E) Women have a significant presence in Latin American politics.

13. For which reason were legislated candidate quotas implemented in many Latin American countries?
    A) So that men could win back the government seats they had recently lost to women
    B) So that Nordic Europe would have the highest percentage of female members of parliament
    C) So that more women could serve in elected government positions
    D) So that citizens would be forced to elect women during every election
    E) So that the ratio of male to female candidates would be equal

14. According to the passage, what is true about women in Latin America?
    A) They must hold 30 percent of the government positions.
    B) They make up 25 percent of the legislators.
    C) They are more likely to be elected than men.
    D) They are increasingly becoming leaders in business.
    E) They are better educated in politics.

Passage 5

The Scream of Nature by Edvard Munch is one of the world's best known and most desirable artworks. While most people think of it as a single painting, the iconic creation actually has four different versions: two paintings and two pastels. In 2012, one of the pastels earned the fourth-highest price paid for a painting at auction when it was sold for almost $120 million. The three others are not for sale; the Munch Museum in Oslo holds a painted version and a pastel version, while the National Gallery in Oslo holds the other painting. However, the desire to acquire the artworks has been strong: in 1994 the National Gallery's version was stolen, and in 2004 the painting at the Munch Museum was stolen at gunpoint in the middle of the day. Both paintings were eventually recovered.

15. Why are three versions of Munch's *The Scream of Nature* in museums or galleries?
    A) They are too expensive.
    B) Selling art for profit is illegal.
    C) They are not for sale.
    D) They were once stolen.
    E) They increase ticket sales.

16. What can most likely be concluded about Edvard Munch, based on this passage?
    A) He was poor.
    B) He was a criminal.
    C) He was an orphan.
    D) He was scared.
    E) He was from Oslo.

7. What is the meaning of the word *fanciful* in the passage?
   A) Complicated
   B) Imaginative
   C) Successful
   D) Unfortunate
   E) Opulent

8. What is the author's primary purpose in writing this essay?
   A) To describe the various causes of the American Civil War
   B) To illustrate the cultural differences between the North and the South before the Civil War
   C) To persuade readers that the North deserved to win the Civil War
   D) To demonstrate that the history of the Civil War is too complicated to be understood clearly
   E) To convince readers that slavery was the main cause of the Civil War

9. What is the main idea of the passage?
   A) The Civil War was the result of cultural differences between the North and South.
   B) The Civil War was caused by the South's reliance on labor from enslaved persons.
   C) The North's use of commerce and manufacturing allowed it to win the war.
   D) The South's belief in the rights of man and state cost the war.
   E) America's reliance on slave labor in the centuries before the Civil War is a sad and shameful part of the country's history.

10. What is the tone of this passage?
    A) Hopeful
    B) Humorous
    C) Cautious
    D) Assertive
    E) Despairing

Passage 4

In an effort to increase women's presence in government, several countries in Latin America, including Argentina, Brazil, and Mexico, have implemented legislated candidate quotas. These quotas require that at least 30 percent of a party's candidate list in any election cycle consists of women who have a legitimate chance at election. As a result, Latin America has the greatest number of female heads of government in the world, and the second highest percentage of female members of parliament after Nordic Europe. These trends, however, do not carry over outside of politics. While 25 percent of legislators in Latin America are now women, less than 2 percent of CEOs in the region are women.

11. According to the passage, what is true about Nordic Europe?
    A) It has more female heads of government than Latin America does.
    B) It recently implemented legislated candidate quotas.
    C) It saw an increase in female CEOs.
    D) It has the highest population of women.
    E) It has the highest percentage of female members of parliament.

"Where?" For geographers, where any interaction, event, or development happens is the key to understanding it.

There are many subdisciplines of geography. These can be organized into four main categories. Regional Studies looks at the characteristics of a particular place. Topical Studies looks at a single physical or human feature that impacts the whole world. Physical Studies focuses on the physical features of Earth. Human Studies examine the relationship between human activity and the environment.

4. A researcher studying the relationship between farming and river systems would be engaged in which one of the following geographical subdisciplines?
    A) Regional studies
    B) Topical studies
    C) Physical studies
    D) Human studies
    E) Physical and human studies

5. Which type of passage is this?
    A) Expository
    B) Narrative
    C) Persuasive
    D) Descriptive
    E) Rhetorical

6. Which one of the following is a concise summary of the passage?
    A) The most important questions in geography are where an event or development took place.
    B) The relationship between humans and their physical space is an important one.
    C) Regional Studies is the study of a single region or area.
    D) Geography can be broken down into four subdisciplines: Regional Studies, Topical Studies, Physical Studies, and Human Studies.
    E) Geography, which is the study of the physical space on Earth, can be broken down into four subdisciplines.

Passage 3

It could be said that the great battle between the North and South we call the Civil War was a battle for individual identity. The states of the South had their own culture, one based on farming, independence, and the right of both man and state to determine their own paths. Similarly, the North had forged its own identity as a center of centralized commerce and manufacturing. This clash of lifestyles was bound to create tension, and this tension was bound to lead to war. But people who try to sell you this narrative are wrong. The Civil War was not a battle of cultural identities—it was a battle about slavery. All other explanations for the war are either a direct consequence of the South's desire for wealth at the expense of her fellow man or a <u>fanciful</u> invention to cover up this sad portion of our nation's history. And it cannot be denied that this time in our past was very sad indeed.

Reading

Directions: For each passage, read the excerpt and answer the questions that follow.

Passage 1

The greatest changes in sensory, motor, and perceptual development happen in the first two years of life. When babies are born, most of their senses operate like those of adults. For example, babies are able to hear before they are born; studies show that babies turn toward the sound of their mothers' voices just minutes after being born, indicating they recognize the mother's voice from their time in the womb.

The exception to this rule is vision. A baby's vision changes significantly in the first year of life; initially a baby has a vision range of only 8 - 12 inches and no depth perception. As a result, infants rely primarily on hearing; vision does not become the dominant sense until around the age of twelve months. Babies also prefer faces to other objects. This preference, along with their limited vision range, means that their sight is initially focused on their caregivers.

1. Which one of the following best describes this passage type?
    A) Expository
    B) Narrative
    C) Persuasive
    D) Descriptive
    E) Rhetorical

2. According to the passage, newborns mostly rely on which one of the following?
    A) Vision
    B) Touch
    C) Taste
    D) Hearing
    E) Smell

3. Which one of the following is a concise summary of the passage?
    A) Babies have no depth perception until 12 months, which is why they focus only on their caregivers' faces.
    B) When babies are born, they can recognize their mothers' voices; therefore, they initially rely primarily on their sense of hearing.
    C) Babies have senses similar to those of adults except for their sense of sight, which does not fully develop until 12 months.
    D) Babies' senses go through many changes in the first year of their lives.
    E) Babies are especially focused on their caregivers during the first 12 months of life.

Passage 2

Geography is the study of space. More specifically, it studies the physical space of Earth and how the planet interacts with, shapes, and is shaped by people and animals. Geographers look at the world from a spatial perspective. In other words, geographers are always asking the question,

21. Examine (a), (b), and (c) to determine the correct answer.
    (a) $8 + (3 - 2)$

    (b) $(8 + 3) - 2$

    (c) $8 - (3 - 2)$

    A) (b) and (c) are equal
    B) (b) is greater than (c)
    C) (c) is greater than (a)
    D) (a), (b), and (c) are equal
    E) There is not enough information to determine the answer.

22. The average of 5 consecutive digits is 20. What is the largest value of those digits?
    A) 19
    B) 20
    C) 21
    D) 22
    E) 23

23. Which number should fill in the blank in the series?

    $$-8, -3, \_\_, 7, 12$$

    A) 2
    B) 3
    C) -2
    D) 0
    E) 1

24. Yvonne ran 4.6 miles, 4.8 miles, 5.3 miles, 5.2 miles, and 6 miles on five consecutive days. What was her average distance over the five days?
    A) 4.1 mi
    B) 25.9 mi
    C) 5.18 mi
    D) 4.975 mi
    E) 6.2 mi

25. Examine (a), (b), and (c) to determine the correct answer.
    (a) 0.6

    (b) $\frac{3}{5}$

    (c) $\frac{1}{2}$ of 1.2

    A) (a), (b), and (c) are equal
    B) (a) is greater than (b)
    C) (b) is greater than (c)
    D) (c) is greater than (a)
    E) None of the above

Practice Test #1

17. Examine (a), (b), and (c), and then choose the best answer.
    (a) The circumference of a circle with a radius of 4

    (b) The circumference of a circle with a diameter of 4

    (c) The circumference of a circle with a radius of 2

    A) (a) is less than (b)
    B) (a), (b), and (c) are all equal
    C) (c) is greater than (b)
    D) (b) and (c) are equal
    E) There is not enough information to determine the answer.

18. The number of chairs in the front row of a movie theater is 14. Each subsequent row contains 2 more seats than the row in front of it. If the theater has 25 rows, what is the total number of seats in the theater?
    A) 336
    B) 350
    C) 888
    D) 950
    E) 546

19. Examine (a), (b), and (c) to determine the correct answer.
    (a) 30% of 50

    (b) 50% of 30

    (c) 3% of 500

    A) $(a) = (b) = (c)$
    B) $(a) = (b) > (c)$
    C) $(b) > (a) > (c)$
    D) $(a) > (b) = (c)$
    E) There is not enough information to determine the answer.

20. Examine the rectangular prism below and choose the best answer.

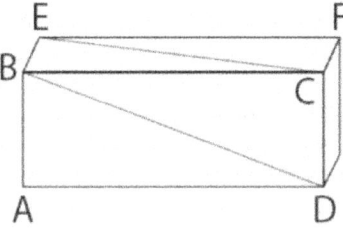

    A) AD is equal to BD.
    B) AB is greater than AD.
    C) BD is equal to CE.
    D) CF is less than AB.
    E) All of the sides are equal.

- A) (a) is equal to 0
- B) both (a) and (b) are positive
- C) (a), (b), and (c) are equal
- D) (a) is greater than (c)
- E) None of the above

12. What number is 20% of 25% of 80?
    - A) 4
    - B) 5
    - C) 36
    - D) 16
    - E) 6

13. What number is $\frac{2}{3}$ of 60 divided by 8?
    - A) 60
    - B) 5
    - C) 25
    - D) 4
    - E) 10

14. Which number should fill in the blank in the series?

    $$\_\_\_, -12, -14, -16, -18$$

    - A) −8
    - B) −10
    - C) 10
    - D) −9
    - E) 12

15. What number is 12 more than $\frac{2}{3}$ of 33?
    - A) 10
    - B) 33
    - C) 34
    - D) 30
    - E) 42

16. What are two different prime factors of 54?
    - A) 9 and 3
    - B) 27 and 2
    - C) 7 and 3
    - D) 7 and 2
    - E) 6 and 9

5. It costs $6 to make a pen that sells for $12. How many pens need to be sold to make a profit of $60?
   A) 10
   B) 6
   C) 72
   D) 30
   E) 12

6. Which number should fill in the blank in the series?

   $$83.5, 80, \_\_\_, 73, 69.5$$

   A) 76
   B) 76.5
   C) 77
   D) 75.5
   E) 74

7. $\frac{2}{3}$ of what number is equal to 150?
   A) 100
   B) 200
   C) 225
   D) 250
   E) 185

8. The sum of what number and 4 is equal to 10?
   A) 10
   B) 14
   C) 6
   D) 156
   E) 8

9. Find the circumference of a circle with an area of 900π square feet.
   A) 60π ft
   B) 9π ft
   C) 100π ft
   D) 30π ft
   E) 90π ft

10. What number is the difference between two consecutive odd integers?
    A) 8
    B) 7
    C) 1
    D) 2
    E) There is not information to determine the answer.

11. Examine (a), (b), and (c) to determine the correct answer.
    (a) $0 + (3 - 2)$

    (b) $0 \times (3 - 2)$

    (c) $0 - (3 - 2)$

25. Examine (a), (b), and (c) to determine the correct answer.

(a) $\frac{2}{3} \times 42$

(b) $\frac{7}{10} \times 40$

(c) $\frac{5}{4} \times 24$

- A) (a) is greater than (c)
- B) (c) is greater than (a) and (b)
- C) (b) is greater than (c)
- D) (c) is less than (a) but not (b)
- E) There is not enough information to determine the answer.

Quantitative Section #2

1. Carla is 3 times older than her sister Megan. Eight years ago, Carla was 18 years older than her sister. What is Megan's age?
    - A) 10
    - B) 8
    - C) 9
    - D) 6
    - E) 5

2. Four years from now, John will be twice as old as Sally will be. If Sally was 10 eight years ago, how old is John right now?
    - A) 35
    - B) 40
    - C) 45
    - D) 50
    - E) 55

3. What number is $\frac{1}{3}$ of 36?
    - A) 18
    - B) 6
    - C) 12
    - D) 24
    - E) 16

4. What number is 11 less than 6 squared?
    - A) 47
    - B) 25
    - C) 1
    - D) −25
    - E) 26

20. Which number should come next in the series?

$$567, 579, 592, 606, 621, \_\_\_$$

- A) 637
- B) 636
- C) 638
- D) 635
- E) 641

21. Examine (a), (b), and (c) to determine the correct answer.
    (a) 3.48×10^{-3}

    (b) -3×-48

    (c) $-2 - (-4)$

- A) (a), (b), and (c) are all negative
- B) only (c) is negative
- C) (a), (b), and (c) are positive
- D) (a) and (b) are negative
- E) only (a) is negative

22. Twelve teams competed in a mathematics test. The scores recorded for each team are: 29, 30, 28, 27, 35, 43, 45, 50, 46, 37, 44, and 41. What is the median score?
- A) 37
- B) 41
- C) 39
- D) 44
- E) 45

23. A class of 10 students scores 90, 78, 45, 98, 84, 79, 66, 87, 78, and 94. What is the mean score? What is the median score? What is the mode?
- A) 69.9, 81.5, 78
- B) 79.9, 80, 78
- C) 79.9, 87, 76
- D) Not enough information is provided
- E) None of the above

24. What number is 21 more than 4 squared?
- A) 13
- B) 5
- C) 32
- D) 25
- E) 37

15. Which two numbers should come next in the series?

$$13, 14, 16, 19, ...$$

- A) 23, 27
- B) 23, 28
- C) 22, 25
- D) 24, 27
- E) 25, 29

16. A circular swimming pool has a circumference of 50 feet. What is the diameter of the pool in feet?
- A) $\frac{25}{\pi}$
- B) $\frac{50}{\pi}$
- C) 25π
- D) 50π
- E) $\frac{25\pi}{2}$

17. Students board a bus at 7:45 a.m. and arrive at school at 8:20 a.m. How long are the students on the bus?
- A) 30 minutes
- B) 35 minutes
- C) 45 minutes
- D) 60 minutes
- E) 20 minutes

18. Which number should come next in the series?

$$1.3, 2.6, 3.9, 5.2, ...$$

- A) 6.1
- B) 6.3
- C) 6.7
- D) 6.5
- E) 7.1

19. A painting by Van Gogh increased in value by 80% from 1995 to 2000. If the painting was worth $7,200 in 2000, what was its value in 1995?
- A) $1,500
- B) $2,500
- C) $3,000
- D) $4,000
- E) $5,000

11. Examine (a), (b), and (c), and then choose the best answer.
    (a) the perimeter of a square with a side of 6
    (b) the perimeter of an equilateral triangle with a side of 8
    (c) the perimeter of an equilateral hexagon with a side of 3

    A) (a) is less than (c)
    B) (c) and (b) are both less than (a)
    C) (b) is less than (a)
    D) (a) and (b) are each greater than (c)
    E) There is not enough information to determine the answer.

12. Which number should come next in the series?

    $$4848, 2424, 1212, 606, ...$$

    A) 353
    B) 202
    C) 909
    D) 303
    E) 217

13. Examine (a), (b), and (c), and then choose the best answer.

    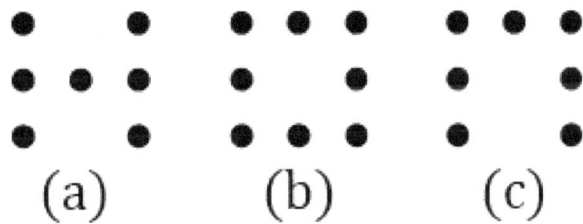

    A) (a) and (b) have the same number of circles
    B) (a) and (c) each have more circles than (b)
    C) (b) has more circles than (a)
    D) (c) has fewer circles than (a)
    E) There is not enough information to determine the correct answer.

14. If $a + b$ is an even number, then both a and b must be even. Which statement is a counterexample to the statement above?
    A) $6 + 9 = 15$
    B) $8 + 3 = 11$
    C) $10 + 14 = 24$
    D) $17 + 15 = 32$
    E) None of the above

5. $\frac{2}{3}$ of what number is equal to 12?
   A) 24
   B) 8
   C) 18
   D) 6
   E) 20

6. Which number should come next in the series?

$$0.04, 0.08, 0.16, 0.32, \ldots$$

   A) 0.48
   B) 0.6
   C) 0.46
   D) 0.36
   E) 0.64

7. Which expression is equivalent to dividing 400 by 16?
   A) $2(200 - 8)$
   B) $(400 \div 4) \div 12$
   C) $(216 \div 8) + (184 \div 8)$
   D) $(216 \div 16) + (184 \div 16)$
   E) $216(184 \div 16)$

8. $\frac{3}{5}$ of what number is 300?
   A) 180
   B) 120
   C) 500
   D) 300
   E) 450

9. Examine (a), (b), and (c), and then choose the best answer.
   (a) The area of a square with a side length of 10
   (b) The area of a rectangle with a length of 5 and a width of 2
   (c) The area of a triangle with a base of 12 and a height of 3
   A) (c) is greater than (a)
   B) (c) is less than (b)
   C) (b) and (c) are each less than (a)
   D) (a) and (b) are equal
   E) There is not information to determine the answer.

10. What number is $\frac{3}{5}$ of 500?
    A) 180
    B) 120
    C) 500
    D) 300
    E) 275

Practice Test #1

Practice Test #1

Quantitative Section #1

1. Which number should fill in the blank in the series?

    73, 67, 61, ___, 49, 43

    A) 53
    B) 54
    C) 52
    D) 56
    E) 55

2. Examine (a), (b), and (c), and then choose the best answer.

    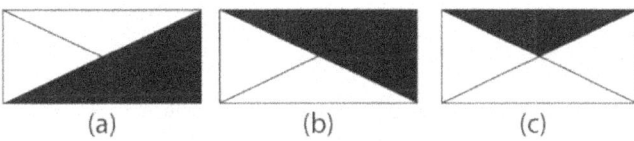

    (a) (b) (c)

    A) (a) is more shaded than (c)
    B) (a), (b), and (c) are equally shaded
    C) (b) is less shaded than (c)
    D) (c) is more shaded than (a)
    E) There is not enough information to determine the answer.

3. What number is 75% of 24?
    A) 6
    B) 30
    C) 18
    D) 75
    E) 20

4. Which of the following is closest to 15,886 × 210?
    A) 33,000
    B) 330,000
    C) 3,300,000
    D) 33,000,000
    E) 33,300

Answer Key

1. D) The prefix *belli–* means combative or warlike. It is also found in *belligerent*. The word choice closest in meaning to *combative* is *aggressive*.

2. B) The root *juven* means *young* and the prefix *re–* means *again*, so *rejuvenate* means *to be made young again*. *Invigorated* means *to give strength or energy to* or *revitalize*.

3. E) The word root *circum* means *around*, and the word root *specere* means *to look*, so a circumspect person looks cautiously around herself and is guarded.

4. D) The prefix *con–* means *with or together* and the word root *concurrere* means *to run together*. Two or more concurrent events happen at the same time, or simultaneously.

5. C) The word root *pater* means *father*, and the word root *arkhein* means to rule, so a patriarch is a man who leads his family.

6. A) *Advance* and *promote* both mean *to move something or someone forward*. Note the prefix *ad–* in *advance*. The prefix *ad–* means *toward*. Likewise, the prefix *pro–* in *promote* means *forward*. To advance something is to promote it, to push it forward.

7. B) *Rudimentary* means *basic or elementary*. For example, familiarity with the alphabet is a rudimentary reading skill that children learn at a young age.

8. C) The prefix *im–* means *not*, and the word root *parcial* means *biased*, so an impartial jury is one whose members are not biased and are therefore able to evaluate evidence in an objective, unprejudiced manner.

9. E) *Prudent* means *wise or judicious*. A prudent decision is a wise, sensible one.

10. A) The word root *ācer* in *acrid, acrimony,* and *acrimonious* means *sharp and sour*, and the suffix *–ous* means *possessing or full of*. An acrimonious relationship is full of bitterness.

11. C) This is an action analogy; dogs bark and cats meow.

12. D) This is an antonym analogy. *Ugly* and *pretty* are opposites; *hungry* and *full* are also opposites.

13. A) This is a synonym analogy. *Durable* is a synonym for *sturdy*; *arid* is a synonym for *parched*.

14. C) This is a member-to-group analogy. A *student* is one member of a *class*; a *teacher* is one member of a *faculty*.

15. B) Generosity causes gratitude; derision causes humiliation.

13. DURABLE is to STURDY as ARID is to
    A) Parched
    B) Fertile
    C) Gluttony
    D) Resilient
    E) Flimsy

14. STUDENT is to CLASS as TEACHER is to
    A) Kindergarten
    B) Instructor
    C) Faculty
    D) Classroom
    E) Principal

15. GENEROSITY is to GRATITUDE as
    A) Sympathy is to Compassion
    B) Derision is to Humiliation
    C) Negligence is to Cautiousness
    D) Thoughtfulness is to Consideration
    E) Malice is to Cruelty

In a **synonym analogy**, the two words in each pair are synonyms (words with similar meanings). *Confusing* and *perplexing* are synonyms (have the same or similar meaning); *intelligent* and *brainy* are also synonyms.

    CONFUSING is to PERPLEXING as INTELLIGENT is to BRAINY

In an **antonym analogy**, the two words in each pair are antonyms (words with opposite meanings). *Comprehensible* and *perplexing* are antonyms as are *sensible* and *foolish*.

    COMPREHENSIBLE is to PERPLEXING as SENSIBLE is to FOOLISH.

In an **action analogy**, each pair contains a noun (person, animal, or thing) and a verb that describes an action that person, animal, or thing commonly performs. A *horse gallops*, just as a *runner sprints*.

    HORSE is to GALLOPS as RUNNER is to SPRINTS

In a **function analogy**, each pair contains a noun and a verb that describes that person's, animal's, or thing's function (what it is supposed to do). A *microphone*'s function is to *amplify* sound, just as a *wheelbarrow*'s function is to *transport* things.

    MICROPHONE is to AMPLIFY as WHEELBARROW is to TRANSPORT

The word pair in an analogy can also have a relationship of **size**, **degree**, or **amount**. The following example is a degree analogy that shows increasing intensity. Someone who is extremely *sad* feels *despondent*; someone who is extremely *happy* feels *ecstatic*.

    SAD is to DESPONDENT as HAPPY is to ECSTATIC

In a **part-to-whole analogy**, the first word forms a part of the object described by the second word (or vice versa). A *step* is one part of a *staircase*, just as a *key* is one part of a *keyboard*.

    STEP is to STAIRCASE as KEY is to KEYBOARD

In a **member-to-group analogy**, the first word is a member of the group described by the second word (or vice versa). A *kitten* is one member of a *litter*, just as a *kindergartner* is one member of a *kindergarten*.

    KITTEN is to LITTER as KINDERGARTNER is to KINDERGARTEN

Practice Questions

11. DOG is to BARK as CAT is to
    - A) Kitten
    - B) Veterinarian
    - C) Meow
    - D) Chirp
    - E) Howl

12. UGLY is to PRETTY as HUNGRY is to
    - A) Thirsty
    - B) Starving
    - C) Empty
    - D) Full
    - E) Dry

Chapter 4 – Verbal Reasoning

Practice Questions

6. ADVANCE
    A) Promote
    B) Abduct
    C) Destroy
    D) Review
    E) Endanger

7. RUDIMENTARY
    A) Impolite
    B) Basic
    C) Juvenile
    D) Innovative
    E) Uncomfortable

8. IMPARTIAL
    A) Fond
    B) Incomplete
    C) Objective
    D) Mathematical
    E) Unnecessary

9. PRUDENT
    A) Lackluster
    B) Inquisitive
    C) Terrified
    D) Modest
    E) Sensible

10. ACRIMONIOUS
    A) Bitter
    B) Inedible
    C) Rotten
    D) Loud
    E) Flavorful

Analogies

An **analogy** presents two sets of words that share a relationship. The relationship is set up using the following format:

_____ is to _____ as _____ is to _____

Solving analogies requires you to determine the relationship between the first two words, and then use that relationship to fill in the missing words. The relationships between the words can vary.

Practice Questions

Select the answer that most closely matches the definition of the given word.

1. BELLICOSE
    A) Misbehaved
    B) Friendly
    C) Scared
    D) Aggressive
    E) Beautiful

2. REJUVENATED
    A) Established
    B) Invigorated
    C) Improved
    D) Motivated
    E) Embellished

3. CIRCUMSPECT
    A) Round
    B) Viewed
    C) Winding
    D) Dominant
    E) Guarded

4. CONCURRENT
    A) Billowing
    B) Sophisticated
    C) Ornate
    D) Simultaneous
    E) Disastrous

5. PATRIARCH
    A) Patriotic person
    B) Wise councilor
    C) Male leader
    D) Equal partner
    E) Harsh master

Synonyms

Different words with the same meanings are known as **synonyms**. While having a large vocabulary will help answer these question types, using root words and affixes will also help to determine the meaning of unfamiliar words. Check the prefixes: does the prefix on the word correspond to the meaning of any of the answer options? If so, that is a hint that the words might have a related meaning.

Chapter 4 – Verbal Reasoning

Word Structure

It's not necessary to memorize long lists of words to do well on the Verbal Reasoning portion of the SSAT. Instead, learning word structures can help determine the definitions of words. Many words can be broken down into three main parts to help determine their meaning: prefixes, roots, and suffixes.

Prefixes are elements added to the beginning of a word, and **suffixes** are elements added to the end of the word; together they are known as **affixes**. They carry assigned meanings and can be attached to a word to completely change the word's meaning or to enhance the word's original meaning. To understand prefixes, let's use the word *prefix* itself as an example:

> *Fix* means *to place something securely*, and *pre–* means *before*; therefore, *prefix* means *to place something before or in front of*.

Now let's look at a suffix:

> In the word *fearful*, *fear* is the root word. The suffix *–ful* means *full of*; therefore, *fearful* means *being full of fear* or *being afraid*.

The **root** is what is left when you take away the prefixes and suffixes from a word. For example, in the word *unclear*, if you take away the prefix *un–*, you have the root *clear*. Roots are not always recognizable words. They often come from Latin or Greek terms (e.h., *nat*, a Latin root meaning *born*). The word *native*, which means *a person born in a referenced place*, comes from this root.

Table 4.1. Common Affixes and Root Words		
Prefixes	**Root Words**	**Suffixes**
a–, an–, im–, in–, un– (without, not)	*ambi* (both)	*–able, –ible* (capable)
ab– (away from)	*aud* (to hear)	*–ian* (related to)
ante– (before)	*bell* (combative)	*–dom* (quality)
anti– (against)	*bene* (good)	*–en* (made of)
bi–, di– (two)	*contra* (against)	*–ful* (full of)
dis– (not, apart)	*dys* (bad, impaired)	*–ine* (nature of)
ex– (out)	*equ* (equal)	*–ment* (act of)
micro– (small)	*morph* (shape)	
omni– (all)		
over– (excessively)		
pre– (before)		
re– (again)		
sym– (with)		
uni– (single)		

16. B) This sentence is made up of two independent clauses joined by a conjunction (*but*), so it is compound.

17. B) In this sentence, the main independent clause—*this…students*—is held until the very end, so it is periodic. Furthermore, despite its length, the sentence is simple because it has only one subject (*dizzying array*) and verb (*proved*).

18. A) Here, the main clause *Jessica…test* begins the sentence; the other clauses modify the main clause, providing more information about the main idea and resulting in a cumulative sentence. In addition, the sentence is compound as it links two independent clauses together with a comma and the coordinating conjunction *for*.

19. B) Commas are only needed when joining three items in a series; this sentence only has two items (*milk* and *watermelon*).

20. B) When setting apart nonessential words and phrases, use either dashes or commas, but not both.

21. B) Prepositional phrases are usually essential to the meaning of the sentence, so they do not need to be set apart with commas. Here, the prepositional phrase *with extra cheese* helps the reader understand that the speaker wants a particularly unhealthy meal; however, the friend is encouraging a healthier option. Removing the prepositional phrase would limit the contrast between the burger and the salad. Note that the second comma remains because it is separating two independent clauses.

22. B) In the first sentence, the person shifts from third (*someone*) to second (*you*). It needs to be rewritten to be consistent.

23. C) *Spring* is the name of a season and should not be capitalized unless it is the first word in a sentence.

24. B) *Tomatos* should be spelled *tomatoes*.

25. C) *Patients* is the correct spelling and the correct homophone. *Patients* are people being treated in a hospital; *patience* is the ability to avoid getting upset in negative situations.

26. D) You can exclude answer option C because the author provides no root cause or a list of effects. From there this question gets tricky, because the passage contains structures similar to those described above. For example, it compares two things (*cities in the North and South*) and describes a place (*a sprawling city*); however, if you look at the overall organization of the passage, you can see that it starts by presenting a problem (*transportation*) and then presents a solution (*trains and buses*), making answer D the only option that encompasses the entire passage.

Answer Key

1. B) *Student* is a singular noun, but *their* is a plural pronoun, making the first sentence grammatically incorrect. To correct it, replace *their* with the singular pronoun *his* or *her*.

2. B) *Everybody* is a singular noun, but *their* is a plural pronoun; the first sentence is grammatically incorrect. To correct it, replace *their* with the singular pronoun *his* or *her*.

3. B) Option A begins in third-person perspective and finishes in second-person perspective. To correct it, ensure the sentence finishes with third-person perspective.

4. B) This sentence refers to a teacher and a student. But to whom does *she* refer: the teacher or the student? To improve clarity, use specific names or state more clearly who spotted the mistake.

5. B) *Cat* is singular, so it takes a singular verb (which confusingly ends with an *s*); *dogs* is plural, so it needs a plural verb.

6. B) Sometimes the subject and verb are separated by clauses or phrases. Here, the subject *cars* is separated from the verb phrase *were returned*, making it more difficult to conjugate the verb correctly; this results in a number error.

7. A) *Deer* is a collective noun, which describes a group of people or things, and can also be singular if it is referring to the group as a whole or plural if it refers to each item in the group as a separate entity. *Deers* is incorrect.

8. A) When the subject contains two or more nouns connected by *and*, that subject is plural and requires a plural verb. Singular subjects joined by *or*, *either/or*, *neither/nor*, or *not only/but also* remain singular; when these words join plural and singular subjects, the verb should match the closest subject.

9. B) All the verb tenses in a sentence need to agree both with each other and with the other information in the sentence. In the first sentence, the tense does not match the other information in the sentence: last night indicates the past (*rained*) not the future (*will rain*).

10. B) The phrase *running through the hall* should be placed next to *student*, the noun it modifies.

11. B) While the lion may indeed be terrifying, the word *terrifyingly* is an adverb and can therefore only modify a verb, an adjective or another adverb, not the noun *lion*. In the second sentence, *terrifyingly* is modifying the adjective *loud*, telling us more about the loudness of the lion's roar—so loud, it was terrifying.

12. A) is an independent clause—it has a subject (*I*) and a verb (*have wanted*) and has no subordinating conjunction. **B)** is a phrase made up of a preposition (*under*), its object (*sky*), and words that modify sky (*bright*, *filled with stars*), but it lacks a conjugated verb. **C)** is a dependent clause—it has a subject (*sister*), a verb (*is running*), and a subordinating conjunction (*because*).

13. A) Although the sentence is lengthy, it is simple because it contains only one subject and verb (*San Francisco . . . is*) modified by additional phrases.

14. C) The sentence has one independent clause (*I love...*) and one dependent (*because I...*), so it is complex.

15. D) This sentence has three clauses: two independent (*I wanted...* and *I got a fish*) and one dependent (*because my roommate...*), so it is compound-complex.

I wished I was able to visit those far-off lands in the books and make friends with the knights and astronauts of my favorite stories. At the library, I could visit the past, the future, kingdoms, planets, and ordinary places, too. I could slip into the minds of people just like me and people I could never imagine being friends with. I found a lot of answers there. Questions, too.

There's an unspoken agreement between myself and other visitors: Of the two oversized armchairs in the back left corner of the library, the left one is mine. From there, I can look out the window to the courtyard. The chairs are green, and mine fades into a softer shade of green on the armrests. I can sense the presence of countless readers who found comfort there before me. I can also see most of the library from there while still feeling unexposed. It feels like I'm invisible but still present. There's got to be a word for that. Unnoticed. Hidden.

My parents had been arguing for a while, almost two years. It was a tense time in my life. It felt loud in my head, but there was a sense of emptiness at the same time. Our house was small, so the shouting would boom everywhere. It would find me no matter where I hid. It would bounce off the walls to the ceiling and crash to the floor. The silence between the yelling wasn't any better. It hung heavy as rain. It meant a storm was likely. This was when the library was most important to me. During that time, I would just head straight there after school.

Now that I'm almost done with eighth grade, it's really dawned on me how much the library meant to me back then. It's where I found my mentors. It's where I learned how to do my research projects. It's where I learned that I had all this anxiety bubbling up inside me and how much I needed the comfort of knowing I was seen and that I mattered. It was where I first felt like I truly belonged.

Susie was a corporate lawyer who was now running writing workshops at the library. We met a young couple who came from the city to start an organic beet farm on cheap land.

By dinnertime, we were invited to a potluck in the town square—the same one that was empty hours earlier. Like magic, tables were set, food appeared, and the bluegrass club even came out to play some tunes. We hadn't noticed the string lights when we first came into town, but they came on, and the town suddenly felt energized.

Instead of heading out the next day, we stayed the weekend. During that time, my parents helped the local history society transfer their records onto computers, my brother played soccer with kids his age, and I helped wherever I could. We left with a changed perspective—the town was smaller than before but much livelier.

My friends asked how my vacation was, but I didn't mention any of the famous cities. I told them about the ghost town that suddenly came to life like an old car with a fussy engine. I told them about how I learned to look past first impressions. I told them that beauty can be found where you least expect it.

Personal Essay Example

My special place is just four blocks away from home. It doesn't really look special; it is just a regular, one-story brick building with normal-looking windows and an unimpressive garden that could use some work. It has a sign out front that might have looked nice in the past, but it's just sun-faded now and hard to read. The newest additions just might be the painted lines in the parking lot. Other people pass by it daily without giving it a second thought, but to me, this place is a sanctuary. My small-town library is the place where I discovered books—and myself.

The first thing that hit me was always the smell. I find the combined smell of paper, book glue, and old furniture to be very calming. And then there's Ms. Kim. She made sure to greet me from behind the desk when she worked the weekday afternoons. She's quiet, but I'm pretty sure she knows my name by now. She knows what I like to read since she was always setting aside books I might like. I didn't get to receive these small gestures anywhere else. They made me feel seen.

I still look over at the children's section sometimes. I know I am too old for those books, but the memories comfort me. Mom used to bring me there when things got complicated at home. I'd sit in the red bean bag chair next to the little bookshelves. They replaced the bean bag chairs with a yellow table and upright chairs last month. I don't know why that made me sad. I still glance over at the kids during their story time. I remember being just like them, captivated by enchanting stories of make-believe and magical creatures.

Back then, I wasn't sure why the library felt like home. Maybe because it was the opposite of my actual home. The rules were different at the library. You had to stay quiet or else use your whisper voice. My movements were always my own—I was in control. I never had to sit on the edge of my seat, bracing myself to react to whatever might happen to me. The library had silence, and it had respect—even the way the inside was set up, everything in order and purposeful. Everything had its place, and it made sense. I wished my home was like this.

Rockfield was supposed to be charming, with the usual small-town attractions. Our travel guide said so—"a hidden gem with friendly faces." Those photographs were colorful and vivid, unlike this place. We walked about half a mile from where we parked our minivan when we realized our expectations were off.

Mom suggested, "Maybe everyone's at lunch?"

Dad drove down the street and parked in front of the only place with an open sign, one of those neon ones, except the "P" and "E" were broken so that we were greeted with a backward "NO."

The place was called Rusty's. Nice. Once inside, we were greeted by a waitress who must have been older than the town. She looked up, startled. Two locals turned on their stools to stare at us.

After a loud sneeze, she greeted us. "Welcome to Rockfield, name's Dot, what can I get for you?" she said, wiping her hands on her apron.

We picked a booth and noticed the pictures on the wall. They showed a much nicer Rockfield—crowded streets, parades, and smiling people. The pictures were faded and discolored.

Dot noticed us looking at the wall and back down at our guidebook. "That's got to be out of date." She came over to check it out. "That was back when the factory and mill were running. Half the town found work way out in the big cities now."

The food was delicious—real, homemade comfort food. We ate while Dot shared more of the town's past. Most people here were retired or just too poor to move. The nearest town that had work was about an hour and a half up north.

One of the locals chimed in. Fred seemed unimpressive at first, until he mentioned he was a former mayor of the town. "If you all are interested, I'll show you around the real Rockfield past this dusty counter." Dot didn't like that.

Fred led us through the diner's alleyway, behind the main street, to a small community quietly fighting to save itself. We arrived at a beautiful garden. A nice old man handed Mom a handwoven basket with an assortment of vegetables and herbs as if he had been expecting us.

We entered a converted warehouse that felt more like a town than what we had seen up until this point—artisanal studios were set up along the back wall, with pottery, furniture, and beautifully woven textiles on display. The space was small, but the energy was undeniable.

We learned that the local high school suffered from under-enrollment. Its curriculum, though, promoted entrepreneurial skills and something called "sustainable development." Students helped in the warehouse. I asked one of them what they were doing. He said, "We're helping fix up that old church; you guys must've seen it. I'm supposed to join my uncle later and help clear that wild area so the tourists can come back."

Fred proudly told us, "See, the town's not dead yet."

Word had spread that visitors were in town. People greeted us, eager to share their stories. Walt, a retired engineer, had started a small technology repair business about 25 years ago, and it's still going.

- o **Specific**: Teens often think they are hidden behind their computer screens. If teenagers give out personal information such as age or location on a website, it can lead to dangerous strangers seeking them out.
- **General**: Schools can teach students how to use technology appropriately and offer them new tools.
  - o **Specific**: Schools can help students learn to use technology to work on class projects, communicate with classmates and teachers, and carry out research for classwork.
  - o **Specific**: Providing students with laptops or tablets will allow them to get lots of practice using technology and programs at home, and only school districts can ensure that these tools are distributed widely, especially to students who may not have them at home.

Creative and Personal Knowledge Starter Examples

The following are examples of the types of creative starters you may see on the exam:

- Grandma knew I couldn't keep her secret for long.
- I finally broke the lock open to dad's old briefcase, revealing…
- We didn't expect this town to be so empty.

Examples of the types of personal knowledge starters you may see on the writing portion of the SSAT include the following:

- Think back to a difficult situation you went through. In what ways were you changed by this experience?
- Consider a place that is special to you. Describe it in detail and explain why it holds such importance in your life.
- Write about a time when you had to stand up for someone you care about. Discuss what this experience has taught you.

The following sections provide one example each of a creative and personal knowledge essay. Note that for each sample, one of the prompts listed above is used as the first sentence. In the case of the personal knowledge starter, the prompt is slightly revised so that it can function more appropriately as a first sentence.

Creative Essay Example

We didn't expect this town to be so empty. The small storefronts looked like something out of a magazine. It was touristy looking, except there were no tourists. We trudged along the town square. The only signs of life were dirty pigeons squawking for food we didn't have. They pecked the dusty ground in hunger.

Creative Story prompts will require you to create a narrative with original characters and a clear plot. The narrative must have a beginning, middle, and end. Think of what the conflict might be:

How does it happen?

What might the results be?

Stick to one point of view—first person ("I, me, we, our"), third person ("he, she, it, they"), etc. Use the same tense throughout your writing—past (I saw, they went) or present (I see, they go). The latter is often challenging to maintain, which is why proofreading is so important.

Personal Knowledge prompts will require you to elaborate on your own thoughts and opinions. It will help to be authentic, so draw on events from your own experiences. Make sure your ideas are connected and lead to a personal insight. Pay close attention to how much time remains so that you can double-check for potential spelling, punctuation, and grammar errors when you have finished.

The Body Paragraphs and Conclusion

The **body** of an essay consists of a series of structured paragraphs that describe or support the thesis. For the creative starter prompt, the body paragraphs can be used to tell a story that supports the chosen prompt. Be sure that each body paragraph consists of related ideas. For the personal knowledge prompt, the body paragraphs can be used to compare and contrast the merits of two opposing sides of an issue. Make sure to draw a conclusion about which is better at the end of the essay if the prompt requires it.

Each paragraph must be well-organized and begin with a topic sentence to introduce the main idea, followed by supporting ideas and examples. No extra ideas unrelated to the paragraph's focus should appear. Use transition words and phrases to connect body paragraphs and improve the flow and readability of your essay.

To end your essay, write a **conclusion** that reminds the reader why you were talking about these topics in the first place. Go back to the ideas in the prompt used in the first sentence of the introduction. Do not simply restate your ideas; instead, remind the reader of your point of view or the story you are trying to convey. Remember that the writing sample is designed to showcase who you are as an individual.

Providing Supporting Evidence

Evidence is needed to support a point of view or convey specific ideas. Whenever you make a general statement, follow it with specific examples to convince the reader that you are right. These specific examples do not bring new ideas to the paragraph; instead, they explain or defend the general ideas that have already been stated. The following are some examples of general statements and specific statements that provide more detailed support:

- **General**: Students may get distracted online or access harmful websites.
  - **Specific**: Some students spend too much time using chat features, social media, or online games. Others spend time reading websites that have nothing to do with an assignment.

26. How can the organization of this passage best be described?
   A) As a comparison of two similar ideas
   B) As a description of a place
   C) As a discussion of several effects all related to the same cause
   D) As a discussion of a problem followed by a suggested solution
   E) As a chronological retelling of a story

Writing a Thesis Statement

The thesis, or **thesis statement**, is a sentence that sums up the main idea of an essay; it presents the writer's point of view on an issue. A thesis statement tells readers specifically what the author thinks and what the author will discuss.

Writing a good thesis statement is as simple as stating an idea and why the author thinks that idea is true or correct. Below is a sample similar to one that may appear on the exam.

Take a position on the following topic. You can choose to write about either of the two viewpoints discussed in the prompt, or you may argue for a third point of view.

Many high schools have begun to adopt 1:1 technology programs, meaning that each school provides every student with a device such as a laptop or tablet. Teachers who support these initiatives say that the technology improves the classroom experience and that students need to learn technology skills. On the other hand, opponents worry about distractions and dangers like cyber-bullying or unsupervised internet use as reasons not to provide students with such devices.

The following are examples of possible thesis statements for this prompt:

- Providing technology to every student is good for education because it allows students to learn important skills such as typing, web design, and video editing; it also gives students more opportunities to work cooperatively with their classmates and teachers.

- I disagree with the idea that schools should provide technology to students because most students will simply be distracted by games and websites when they should be studying or doing homework.

- Schools have a responsibility to teach students how to use technology safely; providing each student with a laptop or tablet is one way to help them do that.

Structuring the Writing Sample

Introductory Content

The introduction of a piece of writing is a paragraph that introduces the topic and clearly states the author's thesis statement which sets forth the position or point the essay will prove. The two types of prompts for the writing portion of the SSAT will require using one of a few provided sentence options as the opening line; test takers will then be expected to build their narrative off of that sentence.

Practice Questions

24. Find the sentence that has an error in spelling.
    A) It was unusually warm that winter, so we didn't need to use our fireplace.
    B) Our garden includes tomatos, squash, and carrots.
    C) The local zoo will be opening a new exhibit that includes African elephants.
    D) My sister is learning to speak a foreign language so she can travel abroad.
    E) The event will continue whether or not it rains.

25. Choose the word that best completes the sentence.

The nurse has three ____ to see before lunch.
    A) patents
    B) patience
    C) patients
    D) patient's
    E) portents

Text Organization

Authors can organize their writing in many ways. These distinct organizational patterns, called **text structure**, use the logical relationships between ideas to improve the readability and coherence of a text. The most common ways in which passages are organized are:

- **Problem-solution:** The author outlines a problem and then discusses a solution.
- **Comparison-contrast:** The author presents two situations and then discusses the similarities and differences.
- **Cause-effect:** The author recounts an action and then discusses the resulting effects.
- **Descriptive:** The author describes an idea, object, person, or other item in detail.

Practice Question

The issue of public transportation has begun to haunt the fast-growing cities of the southern United States. Unlike their northern counterparts, cities like Atlanta, Dallas, and Houston have long promoted growth out and not up. These cities are full of sprawling suburbs and single-family homes, not densely concentrated skyscrapers and apartment buildings. What to do, then, when all those suburbanites need to get downtown for work? For a long time it seemed highways were the answer: twenty-lane-wide expanses of concrete that would allow commuters to move from home to work and back again. But these modern miracles have become time-sucking, pollution-spewing nightmares. The residents of these cities may not like it, but it's time for them to turn toward public transport like trains and buses if they want their cities to remain livable.

Generally, the types of words that are exceptions to this rule fall into one of the following categories:

- The words have a long *a* sound (e.g., *eight*).
- The words have a long *i* sound (e.g., *science*).

Regular nouns are made plural by adding the letter *s*. Irregular nouns can follow many different rules for pluralization, which are summarized below.

Table 3.6. Irregular Plural Nouns

Ends with...	Make it plural by...	Example
-y	changing *y* to *i* and adding –*es*	baby → babies
-f	changing *f* to *v* and adding –*es*	leaf → leaves
-fe	changing *f* to *v* and adding –*s*	knife → knives
-o	adding –*es*	potato → potatoes
-us	changing –*us* to –*i*	nucleus → nuclei
Words that are Always the Same sheep deer fish moose pants binoculars	**Words that Do Not Follow the Rules** man → men child → children person → people tooth → teeth goose → geese mouse → mice	

Reading regularly—and reading a variety of texts—can help you become more familiar with how different words are spelled, which will make it easier for you to recognize spelling exceptions.

Commonly Misspelled Words

Accommodate	Intelligence	Possession
Across	Judgment	Receive
Argument	Knowledge	Separate
Believe	License	Successful
Committee	Lightning	Technique
Completely	Lose	Tendency
Conscious	Maneuver	Unanimous
Discipline	Misspell	Until
Experience	Noticeable	Usually
Foreign	Occasionally	Vacuum
Government	Occurred	Whether
Guarantee	Opinion	Which
Height	Personnel	
Immediately	Piece	

Practice Question

23. Find the sentence that has an error in capitalization.
    A) My two brothers are going to New Orleans for Mardi Gras.
    B) On Friday, we voted to elect a new class president.
    C) Janet wants to go to Mexico this Spring.
    D) Peter complimented the chef on his cooking.

Homophones and Spelling

Be careful to not confuse homophones when writing. **Homophones** are words that are pronounced the same but have different spellings and meanings. *Bawl* and *ball*, for example, are homophones: they sound the same, but *bawl* means to cry, and *ball* is a round toy. Common homophones include the following:

Bare/bear	Insure/ensure	Stair/stare
Brake/break	Morning/mourning	Suite/sweet
Die/dye	Peace/piece	Their/there/they're
Effect/affect	Poor/pour	Wear/where
Flour/flower	Principal/principle	
Heal/heel	Sole/soul	

Special Spelling Rules

The English language contains a variety of special spelling rules. While there are exceptions to these rules, knowing the following basics can help you avoid spelling errors.

- Double a final consonant when adding suffixes if the consonant is preceded by a single vowel:
    - *Run* becomes *running*
    - *Admit* becomes *admittance*
- Drop the final vowel when adding a suffix:
    - *Sue* becomes *suing*
    - *Observe* becomes *observance*
- Change the final *y* to an *i* when adding a suffix.
    - *Lazy* becomes *laziest*
    - *Tidy* becomes *tidily*

Another important rule is "*i* comes before *e* except after *c*." This is used in words like *belief*, *thief*, *receive*, and *ceiling*. However, this rule has exceptions. For example:

Your foreign neighbors weighed the iciest beige glaciers!

Chapter 3 – Writing and the Writing Sample

Editing, Revising, and Proofreading

It's important to look over your essay and check for spelling and grammar mistakes that may interfere with a reader's understanding. Some common mistakes to look out for include:

- Subject/verb disagreement
- Pronoun/antecedent disagreement
- Comma splices and run-on sentences
- Sentence fragments (phrases or dependent clauses unconnected to an independent clause)

Capitalization

It is important to use proper capitalization when writing. The first word of a sentence is always capitalized:

<u>W</u>e will be having dinner at a new restaurant tonight.

The first letter of a proper noun is always capitalized:

We're going to <u>C</u>hicago on <u>W</u>ednesday.

Titles are capitalized if they precede the name they modify:

Harry Truman, the vice president, met with <u>P</u>resident Roosevelt.

Months are capitalized, but not the names of the seasons:

Snow fell in <u>M</u>arch even though winter was over.

The names of major holidays should be capitalized. The word *day* is only capitalized if it is part of the holiday's name:

We always go to a parade on <u>M</u>emorial <u>D</u>ay, but <u>C</u>hristmas day we stay home.

The names of specific places should always be capitalized. General location terms are not capitalized:

We're going to <u>S</u>an <u>F</u>rancisco next weekend so I can see the ocean.

Titles for relatives should be capitalized when they precede a name, but not when they stand alone:

Fred, my uncle, will make fried chicken, and <u>A</u>unt Wanda is going to make spaghetti.

Paying attention to the following details will make the perspective clear and help readers understand the writing.

- **First-person perspective** appears when the writer's personal experiences, feelings, and opinions are important elements of the text.
- **Second-person perspective** is used when the author directly addresses the reader.
- **Third-person perspective** is most common in formal and academic writing; it creates distance between the writer and the reader.

Practice Question

22. Which sentence below is correct?
    A) If someone wants to be a professional athlete, you have to practice often.
    B) If you want to be a professional athlete, you have to practice often.

Transitions

Transitions are words, phrases, and ideas that help connect ideas throughout a text. They can be used between sentences and between paragraphs. Some common transitions include *then*, *next*, *in other words*, *as well*, and *in addition to*. Be creative with your transitions, and make sure you understand what the transition you are using shows about the relationship between the ideas. For instance, the transition *although* implies that there is some contradiction between the first idea and the second idea.

Syntax

Syntax—the way in which the structure of a sentence is organized—is an important component of maintaining the reader's interest; readers appreciate variety. For example, each sentence should begin differently. Some sentences should be long, and some sentences should be short. Write simple sentences as well complex sentences that have complex ideas in them. Be sure, however, that your sentences make sense: it is better to have clear and simple writing that a reader can understand than to have complex, confusing syntax that does not clearly express an idea.

Word Choice and Tone

The words you choose influence the impression you make on readers. Use words that are specific, direct, and appropriate to the task. A formal text may benefit from complex sentences and impressive vocabulary, while simple vocabulary and sentences may be more appropriate to use when writing for a young audience.

Use strong vocabulary; avoid using vague, general words such as *good*, *bad*, *very*, or *a lot* if you can think of a better way to express yourself. It is critical, however, to be sure that you are comfortable with the vocabulary you choose: if you are unsure about a word's meaning or its use in the context of your essay, do not use it.

Table 3.4. Basic Rules of Punctuation		
Punctuation	Usage	Example
Quotation marks	Indicating a direct quote	I said to her, "Tell me more about parentheses."
Em dash	Setting apart nonessential words and phrases (must use either two em dashes or two commas, but not both)	Punctuation—with its many rules—is an important part of writing.

Practice Questions

19. Which sentence below is correct?
    A) Her roommate asked her to pick up milk, and a watermelon from the grocery store.
    B) Her roommate asked her to pick up milk and a watermelon from the grocery store.

20. Which sentence below is correct?
    A) The softball coach—who had been in the job for only a year, quit unexpectedly on Friday.
    B) The softball coach—who had been in the job for only a year—quit unexpectedly on Friday.

21. Which sentence below is correct?
    A) I'd like to order a hamburger, with extra cheese, but my friend says I should get a fruit salad instead.
    B) I'd like to order a hamburger with extra cheese, but my friend says I should get a fruit salad instead.

Point of View

A **point of view** is the perspective from which it is written. Point of view is described as either first, second, or third person. A sentence's point of view must remain consistent.

Table 3.5. Point of View			
Person	Pronouns	Who's acting?	Example
First	I, we	The writer	I take my time when shopping for shoes.
Second	You	The reader	You prefer to shop online.
Third	He, she, it, they	The subject	She buys shoes from her cousin's store.

Practice Questions

17. Classify the following sentence: *The GED, the SSAT, the SAT, the ACT—this dizzying array of exams proved no match for the determined students.*
    A) Cumulative sentence
    B) Periodic sentence

18. Classify the following sentence: *Jessica was well prepared for the test, for she had studied for weeks, taken practice exams, and reviewed the material with other students.*
    A) Cumulative sentence
    B) Periodic sentence

Punctuation

The basic rules for using the major punctuation marks are given in Table 3.4.

Table 3.4. Basic Rules of Punctuation

Punctuation	Usage	Example
Period	Ending sentences	Periods go at the end of complete sentences.
Question mark	Ending questions	What's the best way to end a sentence?
Exclamation point	Ending sentences that show extreme emotion	I'll never understand how to use commas!
Comma	Joining two independent clauses (always with a coordinating conjunction)	Commas can be used to join clauses, but they must always be followed by a coordinating conjunction.
Comma	Setting apart introductory and nonessential words and phrases	Commas, when used properly, set apart extra information in a sentence
Comma	Separating items in a list	My favorite punctuation marks include the colon, semicolon, and period.
Semicolon	Joining together two independent clauses (never used with a conjunction)	I love exclamation points; they make sentences seem so exciting!
Colon	Introducing a list, explanation, or definition	When I see a colon I know what to expect: more information.
Apostrophe	Forming contractions / Showing possession	Parentheses are my sister's favorite punctuation; she finds commas' rules confusing.

In the sentence above, *City traffic frustrates David* is an independent clause, as is *he is seeking an alternate route home*; however, the subordinating conjunction *because* indicates that *because the streets are so congested* is a dependent clause.

When two independent clauses are joined with only a comma and no coordinating conjunction, it is a punctuation error known as a **comma splice**. When drafting your writing sample, be sure to avoid sentences with comma splices.

Practice Questions

13. Classify the following sentence: *San Francisco is one of my favorite places in the United States.*
    A) Simple sentence
    B) Compound sentence
    C) Complex sentence
    D) Compound-complex sentence
    E) None of the above

14. Classify the following sentence: *I love listening to the radio in the car because I enjoy loud music on the open road.*
    A) Simple sentence
    B) Compound sentence
    C) Complex sentence
    D) Compound-complex sentence
    E) None of the above

15. Classify the following sentence: *I wanted to get a dog, but I got a fish because my roommate is allergic to pet dander.*
    A) Simple sentence
    B) Compound sentence
    C) Complex sentence
    D) Compound-complex sentence
    E) None of the above

16. Classify the following sentence: *The game was canceled, but we will still practice on Saturday.*
    A) Simple sentence
    B) Compound sentence
    C) Complex sentence
    D) Compound-complex sentence
    E) None of the above

Clause Placement

Sentences can also be defined by the location of the main clause. In a **periodic sentence**, the main idea of the sentence is held until the end. In a **cumulative sentence**, the independent clause comes first, and any modifying words or clauses follow it.

This type of classification—periodic or cumulative—is not used in place of the simple, compound, complex, or compound-complex classifications. A sentence can be both cumulative and complex, for example.

Practice Question

12. Classify each of the following as a phrase, independent clause, or dependent clause:
    A) I have always wanted to drive a bright red sports car
    B) Under the bright sky filled with stars
    C) Because my sister is running late

Types of Sentences

A sentence can be classified as simple, compound, complex, or compound-complex based on the type and number of clauses it has. Table 3.3. describes the various sentence classifications.

Table 3.3. Sentence Classifications		
Sentence Type	Number of Independent Clauses	Number of Dependent Clauses
Simple	1	0
Compound	2+	0
Complex	1	1+
Compound-complex	2+	1+

A **simple sentence** consists of only one independent clause. Because there are no dependent clauses in a simple sentence, it can be as short as two words: a subject and a verb (e.g., *I ran.*). However, a simple sentence may also contain prepositions, adjectives, and adverbs. Even though these additions can extend the length of a simple sentence, it is still a simple sentence as long as it does not contain any dependent clauses.

Compound sentences have two or more independent clauses and no dependent clauses. Usually, a comma and a coordinating conjunction (*for, and, nor, but, or, yet,* and *so*) join the independent clauses, though semicolons can be used as well:

> *My computer broke, so I took it to be repaired.*
>
> *My computer broke; I took it to be repaired.*

Complex sentences have one independent clause and *at least* one dependent clause:

> *<u>If you lie down with dogs</u>, you'll wake up with fleas.*

In the complex sentence above, the first clause (underlined) is dependent because of the subordinating conjunction *if*, and the second clause is independent.

Compound-complex sentences have two or more independent clauses and at least one dependent clause:

> *City traffic frustrates David because the streets are congested, so he is seeking an alternate route home.*

Did You Know?

A **run-on sentence** is similar to a comma splice, except that no conjunctions or proper punctuation marks are used to join two independent clauses:

INCORRECT: *I took my SSAT today it was not as difficult as I thought it would be.*

CORRECT: *I took my SSAT today, and it was not as difficult as I thought it would be.*

11. Which sentence below is correct?
    A) The terrifyingly lion's loud roar scared the zoo's visitors.
    B) The lion's terrifyingly loud roar scared the zoo's visitors.

Other Parts of Speech

Prepositions generally help describe relationships in space and time; they may express the location of a noun or pronoun in relation to other words and phrases in a sentence:

The nurse parked her car in a parking garage.

The preposition *in* describes the position of the car in relation to the garage. The noun that follows the preposition is called its **object**. In the example above, the object of the preposition *in* is the noun *parking garage*. Other prepositions include *after*, *between*, *by*, *during*, *of*, *on*, *to*, and *with*.

Conjunctions connect words, phrases, and clauses. The conjunctions summarized in the acronym **FANBOYS—For, And, Nor, But, Or, Yet, So**—are called **coordinating conjunctions** and are used to join independent clauses. In the following sentence, the conjunction *and* joins the two independent clauses together:

The nurse prepared the patient for surgery, and the doctor performed the surgery.

Subordinating conjunctions join independent and dependent clauses. Subordinating conjunctions include *although*, *because*, and *if*. In the following sentence, the conjunction *because* joins together the two clauses:

She had to ride the subway because her car was broken.

Interjections (e.g., *wow* and *hey*) express emotion and are most commonly used in conversation and casual writing. They are often followed by exclamation points.

Constructing Sentences

Phrases and Clauses

A **phrase** is a group of words that contains either a subject or a verb, but not both; it cannot stand alone as a sentence. Phrases can be constructed from several different parts of speech. A prepositional phrase includes a preposition and the object of that preposition (e.g., under the table). A verb phrase includes the main verb and any helping verbs (e.g., had been running).

A **clause** is a group of words that contains both a subject and a verb. There are two types of clauses: independent and dependent clauses. Independent clauses can stand alone as sentences, while dependent clauses cannot. Dependent clauses are recognizable because they begin with subordinating conjunctions.

Practice Questions

5. Which sentence below is correct?
    A) The cat chase the ball while the dogs runs in the yard.
    B) The cat chases the ball while the dogs run in the yard.

6. Which sentence below is correct?
    A) The cars that had been recalled by the manufacturer was returned within a few months.
    B) The cars that had been recalled by the manufacturer were returned within a few months.

7. Which sentence below is correct?
    A) The deer hid in the trees.
    B) The deers are not all the same size.

8. Which sentence below is correct?
    A) The doctor and nurse work in the hospital.
    B) Neither the nurse nor her boss were scheduled to take a vacation.

9. Which sentence below is correct?
    A) Because it will rain during the party last night, we had to move the tables inside.
    B) Because it rained during the party last night, we had to move the tables inside.

Adjectives and Adverbs

Adjectives are words that describe nouns. Look at the following sentence:

> The boy hit the ball.

If you want to know more about the noun *ball*, then you could use an adjective to describe it:

> The boy hit the red ball.

> **Did You Know?**
>
> Remember that adverbs can never describe nouns—only adjectives can.

Like adjectives, **adverbs** provide more information about a part of a sentence. Adverbs can describe verbs, adjectives, and even other adverbs. For example, look at the word *recently* in the following sentence:

> The doctor had recently hired a new employee.

The adverb *recently* tells us more about how the action *hired* took place. Often—but not always—adverbs end in *–ly*. Adjectives, adverbs, and modifying phrases should always be placed as close as possible to the words they modify. Separating words from their modifiers can result in incorrect or confusing sentences.

> **Helpful Hint:**
>
> If the subject is separated from the verb, cross out the phrases between them to make conjugation easier.

Practice Questions

10. Which sentence below is correct?
    A) Running through the hall, the bell rang and the student knew she was late.
    B) Running through the hall, the student heard the bell ring and knew she was late.

2. Which sentence below is correct?
    A)   Everybody will receive their paychecks promptly.
    B)   Everybody will receive his or her paycheck promptly.

3. Which sentence below is correct?
    A)   When a nurse begins work at a hospital, you should wash your hands.
    B)   When a nurse begins work at a hospital, he or she should wash his or her hands.

4. Which sentence below is correct?
    A)   After the teacher spoke to the student, she realized her mistake.
    B)   After Mr. White spoke to his student, she realized her mistake. (*she* and *her* referring to *student*)

Verbs

A **verb** is the action of a sentence; verbs do things. A verb must be conjugated to match the context of the sentence, which can sometimes be a tricky achievement because English has many irregular verbs. For example, *run* is an action verb in the present tense that becomes *ran* in the past tense; the linking verb *is* (which describes a state of being) becomes *was* in the past tense.

Table 3.2. Conjugation of the Verb *To Be*			
	Past	Present	Future
Singular	was	is	will be
Plural	were	are	will be

Verb tense must make sense in the context of the sentence. For example, compare the following sentences:

   Sentence 1: I was baking cookies and eat some dough.

   Sentence 2: I was baking cookies and ate some dough.

The first sentence sounds strange, especially if you read it aloud. This is because the two verbs *was baking* and *eat* are in different tenses: *was baking* takes place in the past, while *eat* occurs in the present. To correct this, *eat* needs to be conjugated in the past tense, as seen in sentence 2.

> **Quick Review:**
>
> Think of the subject and the verb as sharing a single *s*. If the noun ends with an *s*, the verb should not end with an *s* and vice versa.

Like pronouns, verbs must agree in number with the nouns to which they refer. In the examples above, the verb *was* refers back to the singular *I*. If the subject of the sentence was plural, it would need to be modified to read as follows. Note that the verb *ate* does not change form; this is common for verbs in the past tense.

   They were baking cookies and ate some dough.

Chapter 3 – Writing and the Writing Sample

A strong writing sample will be organized and have clearly states thoughts about a particular topic. Using strong vocabulary and varied sentence structure will also help your essay stand out. The following sections are designed to reinforce basic concepts of writing and improve your confidence as a writer.

Grammar

Nouns and Pronouns

Nouns are people, places, or things. In the following sentence, the noun is *hospital*; it is a place:

The hospital was very clean.

Pronouns replace nouns and make sentences sound less repetitive:

Sentence 1: Sam stayed home from school because Sam was not feeling well.

Sentence 2: Sam stayed at home because he did not feel well.

In sentence 1, the word *Sam* appears twice. By using the pronoun *he* in place of *Sam* in the second sentence, the writer avoids repetition and improves the sentence. Because pronouns take the place of nouns, they need to agree both in number and gender with the nouns they replace. For example, a plural noun needs a plural pronoun, and a feminine noun needs a feminine pronoun. It is good practice to try to spot pronouns in texts you are reading and become familiar with incorporating them in your own writing.

Table 3.1. Singular and Plural Pronouns	
Singular Pronouns	**Plural Pronouns**
I, me, mine, my you, your, yours he, him, his she, her, hers it, its	we, us, our, ours they, them, their, theirs

Practice Questions

1. Which sentence below is correct?
    A) If a student forgets their homework, it is considered incomplete.
    B) If a student forgets his or her homework, it is considered incomplete.

Answer Key

1. C) Alyssa has a messy drawer. The paragraph begins by indicating Alyssa's gratitude that her coworkers do not know about her drawer. The drawer is described as an organizational nightmare; it's messy to the point that it doesn't function properly. The writer reveals that the drawer even has an odor, with old candy inside. Alyssa is clearly ashamed of her drawer and fearful of being judged by her coworkers about it.

2. D) The passage describes several technologies that are used to study the surfaces of other planets, such as space probes and powerful telescopes. Option A directly contradicts the rest of the passage. Options B, C, and E can also be eliminated because, while they state details from the passage, they are used to support the main idea.

3. B) The authors states that children who have a poor diet and don't exercise will face further illnesses in adulthood. Choices A, C, and E are incorrect because they contradict information in the passage. The passage does not mention taking children to doctors, Option D.

4. E) The crowd's support for Alfie and their collective roar after the shot implies that Alfie scored the goal and won the championship.

5. B) The purpose of the passage is to persuade the reader of the author's opinion of the novel *Mockingjay,* specifically that the ending did not do the main character justice. The passage's use of the verb "argue" tells us that the passage is presenting a case to the reader. The passage follows this statement with evidence—that the main character had a powerful personality.

6. C) The author states that exercise "is proven to decrease the likelihood of developmental diabetes, obesity, and a multitude of other health problems."

7. A) The passage is written in a neutral, professional tone. It does not include any informal, emotional, or first-person language.

8. A) The context implies that the fighting was intense and tiring. The author describes the fight as lasting "a month" in the "bitter cold."

Positive/negative clues tell you whether a word has a positive or negative meaning. In the following example, the positive descriptions *stunning* and *nominated for several awards* suggest that *lauded* has a positive meaning:

The film was lauded by critics as stunning, and it was nominated for several awards.

Practice Question

8. Read the passage and answer the question which follows it.

In December of 1945, Germany launched its last major offensive campaign of World War II, pushing through the dense forests of the Ardennes region of Belgium, France, and Luxembourg. The attack, designed to block the Allies from the Belgian port of Antwerp and to split their lines, caught the Allied forces by surprise. Due to troop positioning, the Americans bore the brunt of the attack, incurring 100,000 deaths, the highest number of casualties of any battle during the war. However, after a month of grueling fighting in the bitter cold, a lack of fuel and a masterful American military strategy resulted in an Allied victory that sealed Germany's fate.

In the last sentence, the word *grueling* most nearly means
- A) Exhausting
- B) Expensive
- C) Intermittent
- D) Ineffective
- E) Spontaneous

Practice Question

7. Read the passage and answer the question which follows it.

East River High School has released its graduation summary for the class of 2024. Out of a total of 558 senior students, 525 (94 percent) successfully completed their degree program and graduated. Of these, 402 (representing 72 percent of the total class) went on to attend a two- or four-year college or university. The distribution of students among the four main types of colleges and universities—small or large private and small or large public—is shown in the figure below. As the data shows, the majority of East River High School's college-attending graduates chose a large, public institution.

Which of the following best describes the tone of the passage?
- A) Professional
- B) Casual
- C) Concerned
- D) Congratulatory
- E) Pessimistic

Using Context to Determine Word Definitions

Questions on the Reading Comprehension section may also ask you to determine the meanings of words within passages. Although you may have never encountered some of these words before the exam, you can use context clues to help you figure out a word's definition.

There are two types of contexts that can help you understand unfamiliar words: situational context and sentence context. **Situational context** helps you determine the meaning of a word through the setting or circumstances in which that word or phrase occurs. **Sentence context** requires analyzing only the sentence in which the new word appears in order to understand it.

To figure out words using sentence context clues, you should first identify the most important words in the sentence. There are four types of clues that can help you understand the context, and therefore the meaning of a word.

Restatement clues state the definition of the word in the sentence. The definition is often set apart from the rest of the sentence by a comma, parentheses, or a colon. In the following example, the meaning of *intrinsic* is restated as *internal*.

> *Teachers often prefer teaching students with intrinsic motivation: these students have an internal desire to learn.*

Contrast clues include the opposite meaning of a word. Words like *but*, *on the other hand*, and *however* are tip-offs that a sentence contains a contrast clue. In the following example, *destitute* is contrasted with *wealthy*, so the definition of destitute is *poor*.

> *Janet was destitute after she lost her job, but her wealthy sister helped her get back on her feet.*

Table 2.1. Words to Describe Tone and Mood		
Positive	**Neutral**	**Negative**
humorous	unconcerned	depressed
optimistic		disrespectful
playful		fearful
proud		gloomy
respectful		melancholy
sentimental		pessimistic
silly		skeptical
sympathetic		unsympathetic

Diction, or **word choice**, helps determine mood and tone in a passage. Many readers make the mistake of using the author's ideas alone to determine tone; however, a much better practice is to look at specific words and try to identify a pattern in the emotions they evoke.

A writer who uses words like *ambitious* and *confident* might be described as having an admiring tone, whereas a writer who uses terms like *greedy* and *overbearing* might be described as having a disapproving tone.

When looking at tone, it is important to look beyond the dictionary definition of words. Many authors use **figurative language**, which uses words to imply something other than the word's literal definition. There are several common types of figurative language:

Simile: a comparison of two things using the words *like* or *as*

The movie was as exciting as watching grass grow.

Metaphor: a direct correlation between two things that are not actually alike; does not use the words *like* or *as*

The unruly child behaved like a bull in a china shop.

Hyperbole: exaggeration (e.g., *I'm so tired I could sleep for three days*.)

I love mac and cheese so much that I can smell it a mile away!

Verbal irony: when the narrator says something that is the opposite of what he or she means

"What balmy weather we're having," the teacher said as the winter winds stung her face.

Situational irony: when something happens that is the opposite of what the reader expected

After 100 days of drought and dusty winds, my mother finally went to the car wash—and then drove home in a torrential rain storm.

Personification: when human characteristics are attributed to objects, animals, or nature

The angry clouds unleashed a torrent of rain.

Practice Question

6. Read the passage carefully and choose the best answer to the question which follows it.

Exercise is critical for healthy development in children. Today in the United States, there is an epidemic of poor childhood health; many of these children will face further illnesses in adulthood that are due to poor diet and lack of exercise now. This is a problem for all Americans, especially with the rising cost of health care. It is vital that school systems and parents encourage children to engage in a minimum of thirty minutes of cardiovascular exercise each day, mildly increasing their heart rate for a sustained period. This is proven to decrease the likelihood of developmental diabetes, obesity, and a multitude of other health problems. Children also need a proper diet rich in fruits and vegetables so that they can develop physically and learn healthy eating habits early on.

Which of the following is a fact in the passage, not an opinion?
- A) Fruits and vegetables are the best way to help children be healthy.
- B) Children today are lazier than they were in previous generations.
- C) The risk of diabetes in children is reduced by physical activity.
- D) Children should engage in thirty minutes of exercise a day.
- E) If children do not learn healthy eating habits early on, they will never do so.

Literary Elements and Techniques

Tone and Point of View

Point of view is the perspective from which the author is writing. A reading passage may be in the first, second, or third person. In **first-person** point of view, the narrative is described from the writer's point of view. Words like *I, me, we, us* are used. In **second-person** point of view, the narrative addresses the reader directly as *you*. This point of view is typically used in instructional writing, such as recipes. In **third-person** point of view, the narrative is described by somebody who is not the writer. Third-person point of view uses *he, she, they, them*.

The **tone** of a passage describes the author's attitude toward the topic. The **mood** is the pervasive feeling or atmosphere in a passage that provokes specific emotions in the reader; it's how the reader feels about the text. Mood and tone can generally be categorized as positive, neutral, or negative. The table below describes words that are often used to describe tone and mood.

Table 2.1. Words to Describe Tone and Mood		
Positive	**Neutral**	**Negative**
admiring	casual	angry
approving	detached	annoyed
celebratory	formal	belligerent
encouraging	impartial	bitter
excited	informal	condescending
funny	objective	confused
hopeful	questioning	cynical

Author's Purpose

Authors typically write with a purpose. Sometimes referred to as **intention**, an **author's purpose** lets us know why the author is writing and what the author would like to accomplish. There are many reasons an author might write, but these reasons generally fall into four categories:

- **Narrative** writing tells a story to entertain. The writing may include vivid characters; exciting plot twists; or beautiful, figurative language.

- **Persuasive** writing attempts to persuade the reader to accept an idea. The passage may present an argument or contain convincing examples that support the author's point of view.

- **Informational** writing describes something, such as a person, place, thing, or event. It is characterized by detailed descriptions and a lack of persuasive elements (meaning it is written to *inform* the reader, not persuade the reader).

- **Instructional** writing explains a process or procedure. It may include step-by-step instructions or present information in a sequence.

Practice Question

5. Read the passage and answer the question which follows it.

One of my summer reading books was Mockingjay. *I was captivated by the adventures of the main character and the complicated plot of the book; however, I would argue that the ending didn't reflect the excitement of the story. Given what a powerful personality the main character has, I felt like the ending didn't do her justice.*

Which of the following best captures the author's purpose?
- A) To explain the plot of the novel *Mockingjay*
- B) To persuade the reader that the ending of *Mockingjay* is inferior
- C) To list the novels she read during the summer
- D) To explain why the ending of a novel is important
- E) To inform the reader where to find a copy of the novel *Mockingjay*

Reasoning

One type of question on the exam will ask the test taker to identify a statement from the passage as either a fact or an opinion. A **fact** is a statement or thought that can be proven to be true, while an **opinion** is an assumption that is not based in fact and cannot be proven to be true.

For example, saying that Wednesday comes after Tuesday is a fact because looking at a calendar will prove it. On the other hand, saying that watching television is more entertaining than watching a movie is an opinion. People will disagree about this, and there is no reference that can be used to prove or disprove this statement.

Making Inferences

In addition to understanding the main idea and factual content of a passage, you will also be asked to make inferences about the passage. An **inference** is a conclusion that is not directly stated in the passage but is based on information found within the passage. In an excerpt from a fictional work, for example, you might be asked to anticipate what the character would do next. In a nonfiction passage, you might be asked which statement the author of the passage would agree with.

Helpful Hint:

Just because an answer option is true, it does not make it correct. The correct answer needs to come from the passage, not from your own experience.

Did You Know?

Conclusions are drawn by thinking about how the author wants the reader to feel. A group of carefully selected facts can cause the reader to feel a certain way.

To answer such questions, you need a solid understanding of the topic and main idea of the passage. Armed with this information, you can figure out which of the answer options best fits the criteria (or, alternatively, which answer options do not). For example, if the author of the passage is advocating for safer working conditions in factories, any details that could be added to the passage should support that idea, such as sentences that contain information about the number of accidents that occur in factories or that outline a new plan for fire safety.

Practice Question

4. Read the passage carefully and choose the best answer to the question.

Alfie closed his eyes and took several deep breaths. He was trying to ignore the sounds of the crowd, but even he had to admit that it was hard not to notice the tension in the stadium. He could feel 50,000 sets of eyes burning through his skin—this crowd expected perfection from him. He took another breath and opened his eyes, setting his sights on the soccer ball resting peacefully in the grass. One shot, just one last shot, between his team and the championship. He didn't look up at the goalie, who was jumping nervously on the goal line just a few yards away. Afterward, he would swear he didn't remember anything between the referee's whistle and the thunderous roar of the crowd.

Which of the following conclusions is best supported by the passage?
A) Alfie passed out on the field and was unable to take the shot.
B) The goalie blocked Alfie's shot.
C) Alfie struggles with anxiety.
D) The referee declared the game a tie.
E) Alfie scored the goal and won his team the championship.

The authors of the reading comprehension passages that will appear on the SSAT will present similar details that support their main ideas or arguments. Let's look again at the passage about athlete Babe Zaharias.

> *Babe Didrikson Zaharias, one of the most decorated female athletes of the twentieth century, is an inspiration for everyone. Born in 1911 in Beaumont, Texas, Zaharias lived in a time when women were considered second class to men, but she never let that stop her from becoming a champion. Babe was one of seven children in a poor immigrant family and was competitive from an early age. As a child she excelled at most things she tried, especially sports, which continued into high school and beyond. After high school, Babe played amateur basketball for two years and soon after began training in track and field. Zaharias represented the United States in the 1932 Los Angeles Olympics. Even though women were only allowed to enter three events, she won two gold medals and one silver in track and field events.*

Remember that the main idea of the passage is that Zaharias is someone to admire—an idea introduced in the opening sentence. The remainder of the paragraph provides ideas or details that support this assertion. These details include the circumstances of her childhood, her childhood success at sports, and the medals she won at the Olympics.

When looking for supporting details, be alert for signal words. **Signal words** tell you that the author is about to introduce a supporting detail. Common signal words include *for example, specifically, in addition, furthermore, for instance, others, in particular,* and *some*.

Practice Question

3. Read the passage carefully and choose the best answer to each question.

Exercise is critical for healthy development in children. Today in the United States, there is an epidemic of poor childhood health; many of these children will face further illnesses in adulthood that are due to poor diet and lack of exercise now. This is a problem for all Americans, especially with the rising cost of health care. It is vital that school systems and parents encourage children to engage in a minimum of thirty minutes of cardiovascular exercise each day, mildly increasing their heart rate for a sustained period. This is proven to decrease the likelihood of developmental diabetes, obesity, and a multitude of other health problems. Also, children need a proper diet, rich in fruits and vegetables, so that they can develop physically and learn healthy eating habits early on.

The author states that many adulthood illnesses are the result of which one of the following?
- A) A diet rich in fruits and vegetables
- B) Poor diet and lack of exercise in childhood
- C) Excessive cardiovascular exercise during childhood
- D) Children not being taken to the doctor
- E) Poor parenting

Practice Questions

1. Read the passage and answer the question which follows it.

Fortunately, none of Alyssa's coworkers have ever seen inside the large filing drawer in her desk. Disguised by the meticulous neatness of the rest of her workspace, the drawer betrayed no sign of the chaos within. To even open it, she had to struggle for several minutes with the enormous pile of junk jamming the drawer, until it would suddenly give way, and papers, folders, and candy wrappers spilled out onto the floor. It was an organizational nightmare, with torn notes and spreadsheets haphazardly thrown on top of each other and melted candy smeared across pages. She was worried the odor would soon waft to her coworkers' desks, revealing her secret.

Which sentence best describes the main idea of the paragraph?
- A) Alyssa wishes she could move to a new desk.
- B) Alyssa wishes she had her own office.
- C) Alyssa is glad none of her coworkers know about her messy drawer.
- D) Alyssa is sad because she doesn't have any coworkers.
- E) Alyssa lacks self-confidence.

2. Read the passage and answer the question which follows it.

From far away it's easy to imagine the surface of our solar system's planets as enigmas—how could we ever know what those far-flung planets really look like? It turns out, however, that scientists have a number of tools that allow them to examine many planets' surfaces. The topography of Venus, for example, has been explored by several space probes, including the Russian Venera landers and NASA's Magellan orbiter. In addition to these long-range probes, NASA has also used its series of "great observatories" to study distant planets. These four massively powerful orbiting telescopes are the famous Hubble Space Telescope, the Compton Gamma Ray Observatory, the Chandra X-Ray Observatory, and the Spitzer Space Telescope. Such powerful telescopes aren't just found in space: NASA uses Earth-based telescopes as well. Scientists at the National Radio Astronomy Observatory in Charlottesville, Virginia, have spent decades using radio imaging to build an incredibly detailed portrait of Venus's surface.

Which sentence best describes the main idea of the passage?
- A) It's impossible to know what the surfaces of other planets are really like.
- B) Telescopes are an important tool for scientists studying planets in our solar system.
- C) Venus's surface has many of the same features as Earth's.
- D) Scientists use a variety of advanced technologies to study the surfaces of other planets.
- E) Russia's telescopes are more advanced than those of the US.

Supporting Details

Supporting details reinforce the author's main idea. Looking back at the previous example about convincing your family to order pizza for dinner, you might present supporting details to reinforce your main idea or argument:

- Everybody in the family likes pizza.
- If we order pizza, we will not have to wash a lot of dishes.

Look at this example paragraph:

> *One of my summer reading books was Mockingjay. Though it's several hundred pages long, I read it in just a few days. I was captivated by the adventures of the main character and the complicated plot of the book; however, I felt like the ending didn't reflect the excitement of the story. Given what a powerful personality the main character has, I felt like the ending didn't do her justice.*

Even without a clear topic sentence, this paragraph has a main idea. To help determine what the main idea is, ask yourselves the following questions:

- What is the writer's perspective on the book?
- What is the writer saying about the book?

Now consider some possible answer options to the question of "What is the main idea of this passage?":

- *Mockingjay is a terrific novel.*
- *Mockingjay is disappointing.*
- *Mockingjay is full of suspense.*
- *Mockingjay is a lousy novel.*
- *Mockingjay is a boring story.*

There are some clues in the passage to help determine the correct answer:

- *I was captivated by the adventures of the main character and the complicated plot of the book; <u>however</u>, I felt like the ending didn't reflect the excitement of the story.*
- *Given what a powerful personality the main character has, I felt like the ending didn't do her justice.*

Note the use of the transition word *however* in the third sentence of the passage. This transition, which follows a positive reflection about the book, serves as a clue that the main idea is not that the book is "terrific," allowing you to eliminate Option A. While the author does describe the book as containing *adventures, excitement,* and a *complicated plot*, it does not mention *suspense* or go into details that would support the main idea that the book is full of suspense, thereby allowing you to eliminate Option C. The second sentence and the first part of the third sentence eliminate Option D: if the author considers the book to be lousy, he or she would likely not have been captivated and able to read such a long book in a short period of time. Option B best describes the main idea of the passage: *Mockingjay* is disappointing. This main idea is implied in the following sentences from the passage:

- *I felt like the ending didn't reflect the excitement of the story.*
- *I felt like the ending didn't do her justice.*

Chapter 2 – Reading Comprehension

Chapter 2 – Reading Comprehension

Ideas and Details

The Main Idea and the Implied Main Idea

The **main idea** of a text is the argument the author is trying to make. Every sentence in a passage should support or address the main idea in some way. Another way to understand the concept of the main idea is to picture yourself presenting an argument during a conversation and trying to persuade your audience. For example, imagine you are hungry for dinner, and you want to order a pizza. You need to talk to your family and convince them to eat pizza for dinner:

- The topic of your conversation is dinner.
- The main idea is that the family should eat pizza for dinner.

Let's look at an example passage to see how to identify the topic and main idea:

> *Babe Didrikson Zaharias, one of the most decorated female athletes of the twentieth century, is an inspiration for everyone. Born in 1911 in Beaumont, Texas, Zaharias lived in a time when women were considered second class to men, but she never let that stop her from becoming a champion. Zaharias was one of seven children in a poor immigrant family and was competitive from an early age. As a child she excelled at most things she tried, especially sports, which continued into high school and beyond. After high school, Zaharias played amateur basketball for two years and soon after began training in track and field. Zaharias represented the United States in the 1932 Los Angeles Olympics. Even though women were only allowed to enter three events, she won two gold medals and one silver in track and field events.*

The topic of this paragraph is Babe Zaharias; the whole passage describes events from her life. To figure out the main idea, consider what the writer is saying *about* Zaharias. The passage describes Zaharias' life, but focuses mostly on her accomplishments and the difficulties she overcame. The writer is saying that Zaharias is someone who should be admired for her determination and skill; this is the main idea and what unites all of the information in the paragraph.

The topic (and sometimes the main idea of a paragraph) is introduced in the **topic sentence**. The topic sentence usually appears early in a passage. The first sentence in the example paragraph above states both the topic and the main idea: "Babe Didrikson Zaharias, one of the most decorated female athletes of the twentieth century, is an inspiration for everyone." A summary sentence may appear at the end of a passage. As its name suggests, a **summary sentence** sums up the passage, often by restating the main idea and the author's key evidence to support that idea.

A paragraph without a clear topic sentence still has a main idea. Rather than being clearly stated, the main idea is implied and is known as an **implied main idea**. Determining the implied main idea requires some detective work. You will need to look at the author's word choice and tone in addition to the content of the passage to find the main idea.

1140 possible teams

$$P(n,r) = \frac{n!}{(n-r)!}$$

$$P(6,5) = \frac{6!}{(6-5)!} = \frac{720}{1} = 720$$

83. B) Use the formula to determine probability.

$$P(\text{rolling event}) = \frac{\text{number of favorable outcomes}}{\text{total number of possible outcomes}} = \frac{3}{6} = \frac{1}{2}$$

84. D) Use the formula to determine probability

$$P = \frac{\text{number of favorable outcomes}}{\text{total number of possible outcomes}}$$

$$\frac{\text{number of 3} - \text{consonant combinations}}{\text{number of 3} - \text{tile combinations}}$$

$$\frac{_{21}C_3}{_{26}C_3}$$

$$\frac{1330}{2600} = 0.51 = 51\%$$

B) True. Find the ratio of total number of people who prefer comedy to total number of people:

$$\frac{23}{103} = 0.22$$

1 in 5 is 20%, so 22% is about the same.

C) False. The percentage of men who choose horror is less than the percentage of women who choose horror.

$$part = \text{number of men who prefer horror} = 21$$

$$whole = \text{number of men surveyed} = 60$$

$$percent = \frac{part}{whole} = \frac{21}{60} = 0.35 = 35\%$$

$$part = \text{number of women who prefer horror} = 17$$

$$whole = \text{number of women surveyed} = 43$$

$$percent = \frac{part}{whole} = \frac{17}{43} = 0.40 = 40\%$$

D) False. More people (38) chose horror films than people (23) who chose comedy films.

E) False. Men (15) are *nearly* twice as likely to choose comedy films than women (8)—not the other way around. Note that the statement mentions an approximate, *nearly*. $8 \times 2 = 16$, so 15 is therefore *nearly* twice as many as 8.

79. A) Although not perfectly symmetrical, the number of customers peaks in the middle and is therefore considered symmetrical.

80. C) Multiply the number of outcomes for each individual event:

$$(70)(2)(5) = 700 \text{ outfits}$$

81. E) The order of the items does not matter, so use the formula for combinations:

$$C(n, r) = \frac{n!}{(n-r)!\,r!}$$

$$C(20,3) = \frac{20!}{(20-3)!\,3!}$$

$$\frac{20!}{(17!\,3!)}$$

$$\frac{(20)(19)(18)}{3!}$$

3, 9, 49, 64, 81, 100, 121, 144, 169

$$Q1 = \frac{49 + 9}{2} = 29$$

$$Q3 = \frac{121 + 144}{2} = 132.5$$

Find the IQR by subtracting Q1 from Q3:

$$IQR = Q3 - Q1 = 132.5 - 29 = 103.5$$

73. D) Create a frequency table to find the percentages and angle measurement for each category:

Category	Frequency	Percent	Angle Measure
High School	30	24%	86.4
Associate	30	24%	86.4
Bachelor's	40	32%	115.2
Master's	20	16%	57.6
Doctorate	5	4%	14.4

74. C) There is a somewhat weak positive correlation. As the number of hours spent studying increases, the average percent grade also generally increases.

75. D) According to the graph, statements A, B, C, and E are true; however look closely at answer option D compared to what is displayed on the line graph. According to the graph, the inverse is true: fifteen year-olds actually report being only slightly *more* happy than sixty year-olds.

76. B) According to the graph, Company X earned $20,000 in profit during 2013, which is more than 2012 ($15,000), 2011 ($12,000), and 2010 ($10,000).

77. D) Find the mean using the equation for the population mean:

$$\mu = \frac{\Sigma x}{N} = \frac{5281}{15} = 353.1 \text{ lbs.}$$

Find the median and IQR by counting the leaves and identifying Q1, Q2, and Q3.

$$Q1 = 253$$

$$Q2 = 345$$

$$Q3 = 410$$

$$IQR = 410 - 253 = 157$$

The median is 345 lbs. The IQR is 157 lbs.

78. A) True. More people (42) chose action movies than comedy (23) or horror (38).

First determine the known variables and what will be solved for.

$$WZ = b_1 = 80$$
$$XU = h_1 = 70$$
$$XZ = b_2 = 100$$

Find the area of the triangle.

$$A_1 = \frac{1}{2}(80)(70) = 2{,}800$$

$$A_2 = \frac{1}{2}(100)(h_2)$$

Set the two equations equal to each other and solve for WY:

$$2{,}800 = \frac{1}{2}(100)(h_2)$$
$$h_2 = 56$$
$$WY = 56$$

68. D) Rearrange the equation into slope-intercept form by solving the equation for y:

$$6x - 2y - 8 = 0$$
$$-2y = -6x + 8$$
$$y = 3x - 4$$
$$m = 3$$

69. B) Starting at the origin, move 5 units to the left and then up 2 units. The point is located in the top left quadrant, which is quadrant II.

70. B) The mean is the average number of points per game. Divide the total number of points by the number of games played:

$$\frac{1954}{74} \approx 26.4$$

71. D) The mode occurs the most often. The mode is pepperoni.

72. B) Use the equation for range:

$$R = largest\ point - smallest\ point = 169 - 3 = 166$$

Place the terms in numerical order and identify Q1, Q2, and Q3.

Multiply the area by 6 (because the cube has six faces):

$$SA = 25(6) = 150 \text{ m}^2$$

63. A) Plug the given values into the formula for the cylinder:

$$V(cylinder) = \pi r^2 h = 300 \text{ cubic meters}$$

Because the radius and height are the same, $\pi r^2 h = 300$ cubic meters can be substituted into the formula for the volume of a cone.

$$V(cone) = \frac{1}{3}\pi r^2 h = \frac{1}{3}(300 \text{ m}^2) = 100 \text{ cubic meters}$$

64. B) First divide the diameter by two to find the radius:

$$r = 10 \text{ cm} \div 2 = 5 \text{ cm}$$

Now use the formula for intercepted arc length:

$$l = 2\pi r \frac{\theta}{360°}$$

$$l = 2\pi(5 \text{ cm})\frac{46°}{360°}$$

$$l = 4.0 \text{ cm}$$

65. E) Use the formula for chord length:

$$Chord\ length = 2\sqrt{r^2 - d^2}$$

The chord length and the radius are given. Solve for d:

$$6 \text{ cm} = 2\sqrt{(5\text{cm}^2) - d^2}$$

$$3 \text{ cm} = \sqrt{(5\text{cm}^2) - d^2}$$

$$9 \text{ cm}^2 = 25 \text{ cm}^2 = d^2$$

$$d^2 = 16 \text{ cm}^2$$

$$d = 4\ cm$$

66. A) The sum of two sides is 23 and their difference is 3. To connect the two other sides and enclose a space, x must be less than the sum and greater than the difference (that is, $3 < x < 23$). Therefore, x's minimum value to the nearest hundredth is 3.01, and its maximum value is 22.99.

67. D) The given values can be used to write two equations for the area of $\triangle WXZ$ with two sets of bases and heights:

$$WY = h_2$$

Chapter 1 - Quantitative (Math) Section

The fast hose takes 9 hours to water the field. The slow hose takes $1.25(9) = 11.25$ hours.

55. D) Calculate how many apples each person can pick per hour:

Ben: $\frac{500 \text{ apples}}{2 \text{ hr.}} = \frac{250 \text{ apples}}{\text{hr.}}$

Frank: $\frac{450 \text{ apples}}{3 \text{ hr.}} = \frac{150 \text{ apples}}{\text{hr.}}$

Together: $\frac{250+150 \text{ apples}}{\text{hr.}} = \frac{400 \text{ apples}}{\text{hr.}}$

Now set up an equation to find the time it takes to pick 1,000 apples:

$$\text{Total time} = \frac{1 \text{ hr.}}{400 \text{ apples}} \times 1{,}000$$

$$\text{apples} = \frac{1000}{400 \text{ hr.}} = 2.5 \text{ hours}$$

56. B) Supplementary angles have a sum of 180°. Subtract the measure of angle M from 180°:

$$180° - 36° = 144°$$

57. C) $\dot{A}, \dot{B}, \vec{D}$. Points A and B and line D all lie on plane M.

58. A) The perimeter of a rectangle is equal to twice its length plus twice its width:

$$P = 2(20) + 2(28) = 96 \text{ m}$$

The farmer has 100 meters of fencing, so he'll have $100 - 96 = 4$ meters left.

59. D) Each side of the square wall is 3.5 meters:

$$A = 3.5^2 = 12.25 \text{ m}^2$$

60. C) Add the lengths of all the sides:

$$2 \text{ in} + 2 \text{ in} + 2 \text{ in} + 2 \text{ in} + 2 \text{ in} = 10 \text{ in}$$

61. A) Calculate each value.

(a): $P(square) = 4s = 4(6) = 24$

(b): $P(rectangle) = 2w + 2l = 2(4) + 2(8) = 24$

(c): $P(triangle) = s_1 + s_2 + s_3 = 7 + 7 + 7 = 21$

Therefore, a and b are equal, and are greater than c.

62. D) A cube has six faces, each of which is a square. Find the area of each side using the formula for the area of a square:

$$A = s^2 = 5^2 = 25 \text{ m}^2$$

Now substitute and solve: $d = 14t$

$$45 - d = 16t \rightarrow 45 - 14t = 16t$$
$$45 = 30t$$
$$t = 1.5$$

They will meet 1.5 hr. after they begin.

53. A) Start by figuring out how much of a house each sibling can clean on his or her own. Bridget can clean the house in 12 hours, so she can clean $\frac{1}{12}$ of the house in an hour. Using the same logic, Tom can clean $\frac{1}{8}$ of a house in an hour. By adding these values together, you get the fraction of the house they can clean together in an hour:

$$\frac{1}{12} + \frac{1}{8} = \frac{5}{24}$$

They can do $\frac{5}{24}$ of the job per hour.

Now set up variables and an equation to solve:

t = time spent cleaning (in hours)

h = number of houses cleaned = 2

$$work = rate \times time$$
$$h = \frac{5}{24}t$$
$$2 = \frac{5}{24}t$$
$$t = \frac{48}{5} = 9\frac{3}{5} \text{ hr.}$$

54. E) The first hose completes the job in f hours, so it waters $\frac{1}{f}$ field per hour. The slow hose waters the field in $1.25f$, so it waters the field in $\frac{1}{1.25f}$ hours. Together, they take 5 hours to water the field, so they water $\frac{1}{5}$ of the field per hour. Now you can set up the equations and solve:

$$\frac{1}{f} + \frac{1}{1.25f} = \frac{1}{5}$$
$$1.25f \left(\frac{1}{f} + \frac{1}{1.25f}\right) = 1.25f \left(\frac{1}{5}\right)$$
$$1.25 + 1 = 0.25f$$
$$2.25 = 0.25f$$
$$f = 9$$

Chapter 1 - Quantitative (Math) Section

51. E) The first step is to set up a table and fill in a value for each variable:

	d	r	t
Driving	d	30	t
Flying	$150-d$	60	$3-t$

You can now set up equations for driving and flying. The first row gives the equation $d = 30t$, and the second row gives the equation $150 - d = 60(3 - t)$.

Next, solve this system of equations. Start by substituting for d in the second equation:

$$d = 30t$$

$$150 - d = 60(3 - t)$$

$$150 - 30t = 60(3 - t)$$

Now solve for t:

$$150 - 30t = 180 - 60t$$

$$-30 = -30t$$

$$1 = t$$

Although you've solved for t, you're not done yet. Notice that the problem asks for distance. So, you need to solve for d: what the problem asked for. It does not ask for time, but you need to calculate it to solve the problem.

Driving: $30t = 30$ miles

Flying: $150 - d = 120$ miles

The distance from the airport to the hospital is 120 miles.

52. B) First, set up the table. The variable for time will be the same for each, because they will have been on the field for the same amount of time when they meet:

	d	r	t
Horse #1	d	14	t
Horse #2	$45-d$	16	t

Next set up two equations:

Horse #1: $d = 14t$

Horse #2: $45 - d = 16t$

Set up the second equation. Remember to isolate the absolute value before multiplying by -1:

$$2|y + 4| = 10$$
$$|y + 4| = 5$$
$$y + 4 = -5$$
$$y = -9$$
$$y = 1 \text{ or } -9$$

49. B) Start by listing all the data and defining the variable:

$$\text{total number of backpacks} = 48$$
$$\text{cost of backpacks} = \$476.00$$
$$\text{backpacks sold in store at price of } \$18 = 17$$
$$\text{backpacks sold to school at a price of } \$15 = 48 - 17 = 31$$
$$\text{total profit} = x$$

Now set up an equation:

$$\text{income} - \text{cost} = \text{total profit}$$
$$(306 + 465) - 476 = 295$$

The store owner made a profit of $295.

50. D) Start by listing all the data and defining your variables. Note that the number of students, while given in the problem, is not needed to find the answer:

$$\text{time on first day} = \frac{3}{5} \text{ hours} = 36 \text{ min.}$$
$$\text{time on second day} = \frac{1}{2}(36) = 18 \text{ min.}$$
$$\text{total time} = x$$

Now set up the equation and solve:

$$\text{total time} = \text{time on first day} + \text{time on second day}$$
$$x = 36 + 18 = 54$$

The students had 54 minutes to work on the projects.

Divide by 4 to isolate x:

$$\frac{4x}{4} > \frac{48}{4}$$

$$x > 12$$

46. C) Identify the quantities.

$$\text{total cost of shirts} = 12t$$

$$\text{total cost of pants} = 15p$$

$$\text{total cost of shoes} = 45s$$

The cost of all the items must be less than $2,500.

$$12t + 15p + 45s \leq 2,500$$

47. C) Set up the first equation by removing the absolute value symbol then solve for

$$x: |2x - 3| = x + 1$$

$$2x - 3 = x + 1$$

$$x = 4$$

For the second equation, remove the absolute value and multiply by -1:

$$|2x - 3| = x + 1$$

$$2x - 3 = -(x + 1)$$

$$2x - 3 = -x - 1$$

$$3x = 2$$

$$x = \frac{2}{3}$$

Both answers are correct, so the complete answer is $x = 4$ or $\frac{2}{3}$.

48. C) Set up the first equation:

$$2(y + 4) = 10$$

$$y + 4 = 5$$

$$y = 1$$

$$\text{Entry fee} = 3$$

Set up equations. The total cost for x tickets will be equal to the cost for x tickets plus the $3 flat fee:

$$5x + 3 = 28$$

Solve the equation for x:

$$5x + 3 = 28$$
$$5x = 25$$
$$x = 5$$

The student bought 5 tickets.

44. B) Assign variables.

$$\text{Student price} = s$$
$$\text{Nonstudent price} = n$$

Create two equations using the number of shirts Kelly sold and the money she earned:

$$10s + 4n = 84$$
$$20s + 10n = 185$$

Solve the system of equations using substitution. Solve one equation for one variable, then substitute into the other equation.

$$10s + 4n = 84$$
$$10n = -20s + 185$$
$$n = -2s + 18.5$$
$$10s + 4(-2s + 18.5) = 84$$
$$10s - 8s + 74 = 84$$
$$2s + 74 = 84$$
$$2s = 10$$
$$s = 5$$

The student cost for shirts is $5.

45. D) Inequalities can be solved just like equations.

$$4x + 10 > 58$$

Subtract 10 from both sides:

$$4x > 48$$

Combine like terms:

$$9g + 10r$$

39. B) Distribute the term $5x$ by multiplying by each of the three terms inside the parentheses:

$$5x(x^2 - 2c + 10)$$

$$(5x)(x^2) + (5x)(-2c) + (5x)(10)$$

$$5x^3 - 10xc + 50x$$

40. E) Substitute $b = -2$ and $c = -3$ into the expression $-3(b + 8c)$ and simplify.

$$-3(b + 8c)$$

$$-3(-2 + 8(-3))$$

$$-3(-2 + (-24))$$

$$-3(-26)$$

$$78$$

41. D) Distribute the 5 and combine like terms:

$$5(x + 3) - 12 = 43$$

$$5x + 15 - 12 = 43$$

$$5x + 3 = 43$$

Subtract 3 from both sides:

$$5x = 40$$

Divide both sides by 5:

$$\frac{5x}{5} = \frac{40}{5}$$

$$x = 8$$

42. D) Determine the amount per hour Mandy will charge this family. Charges: $8 for one child plus $3 each for additional children. 4 children would be $8 + 3 \times 3 = \$17$ per hour. If she babysits for 5 hours, then she should expect to earn $17 \times 5 = \$85$.

43. E) Identify the quantities.

$$\text{Number of tickets} = x$$

$$\text{Cost per ticket} = 5$$

$$\text{Cost for x tickets} = 5x$$

$$\text{Total cost} = 28$$

$$\left(\frac{2^7 5^4}{2^{-1} 5^2}\right)^3 = \left(2^{7-(-1)} 5^{4-2}\right)^3 = (2^8 5^2)^3$$

Then, we use the law of power of a product along with the law of power of a power to rewrite it:

$$2^{8 \cdot 3} 5^{2 \cdot 3} = 2^{24} 5^6$$

33. C) First, we use the law of product to simplify the expression in the parentheses by adding the exponents:

$$(10^2 10^5)^{-2} = (10^{2+5})^{-2} = (10^7)^{-2}$$

Then, we use the law of power of a power to multiply the exponents to obtain the answer:

$$10^{-14}$$

34. A) When using the associative property, the answer will remain the same in an addition problem regardless of where the parentheses are placed, making $2 + (1 + 5) = (2 + 1) + 5$ the correct answer.

35. A) Substitute the value -10 for a in the expression.

$$\frac{a^2}{4} - 3a + 4$$

$$\frac{(-10)^2}{4} - 3(-10) + 4$$

Simplify.

$$\frac{100}{4} + 30 + 4$$

$$25 + 30 + 4 = 59$$

36. A) Substitute the given terms for a and b.

$$2a + 3b = 2(xy) + 3(x^2) = 2xy + 3x^2$$

37. A) Combine like terms.

$$4x - 3y + 12z + 2x - 7y - 10z$$

$$(4x + 2x) + (-3y - 7y) + (12z - 10z)$$

$$6x - 10y + 2z$$

38. C) Write an expression for each person's tickets and then combine like terms. Paul has 3 boxes of green tickets and 8 boxes of red tickets: $3g + 8r$. Paula has 6 boxes of green tickets and 2 boxes of red tickets: $6g + 2r$.

$$3g + 8r + 6g + 2r$$

27. C) Set up a proportion and solve.

$$\frac{part}{whole} = \frac{\%}{100}$$

$$\frac{16}{x} = \frac{80}{100}$$

$$16(100) = 80(x)$$

$$x = 20$$

28. B) Identify the known values, and then substitute in the percentage equation.

$$original\ amount = \$1500$$

$$percent\ change = 45\% = 0.45$$

$$amount\ of\ change = ?$$

$$amount\ of\ change = original\ amount \times percent\ change$$

$$\$1500 \times 0.45 = \$675$$

$$original\ price - amount\ of\ change = new\ price$$

$$\$1500 - \$675 = \$825$$

29. C) Kevin can only have 120 people attend. More than 120 people can be invited if he expects 30% to decline his invitation. Convert the percentage to a decimal. He expects 70% of the people he invites to accept the invitation: 0.7, and x is the number of people he can invite.

$$x = \frac{120}{0.7}$$

$$x = 171$$

30. C) These numbers are already in the same format, so the decimal values just need to be compared. Remember that zeros can be added after the decimal without changing the value, so the three numbers can be rewritten as: 104.56, 104.50, 104.60. From this list, 104.60 is the greatest because 0.60 is larger than 0.50 and 0.56.

31. C) The first step is to convert the numbers into the same format. 65% is the same as $\frac{65}{100}$. Next, the fractions need to be converted to have the same denominator because it is difficult to compare fractions with different denominators. Using a factor of $\frac{5}{5}$ on the second fraction will give common denominators: $\frac{13}{20} \times \frac{5}{5} = \frac{65}{100}$. Now it is easy to see that the numbers are equivalent.

32. B) First, we use the law of quotient to simplify the expression in parentheses. Because there is a division of exponents with the same base, we just need to subtract the exponents:

22. A) Rewrite the numbers vertically, lining up the decimal points. Add:

$$\begin{array}{r} 2.20 \\ 32.54 \\ +\ 4.00 \\ \hline 38.74 \end{array}$$

The total bill was $38.74.

23. A) Convert each value to a decimal value.

$$(a)\ 0.79$$
$$(b)\ 0.0122 + 0.7778 = 0.79$$
$$(c)\ 0.3 \times 0.4 = 0.08$$

Therefore, a is equal to b, and both are greater than c.

24. D) The common denominator is 12. Convert each fraction to the common denominator:

$$\frac{1}{4}\frac{(3)}{(3)} = \frac{3}{12}$$

$$\frac{1}{3}\frac{(4)}{(4)} = \frac{4}{12}$$

Add the numerators and keep the denominator the same.

$$\frac{3}{12} + \frac{4}{12} = \frac{7}{12}\ \text{pizza}$$

25. C) Multiply 24 by $\frac{1}{4}$ to find the number of students who failed the test.

$$24 \times \frac{1}{4} = \frac{24}{4} = 6$$

Subtract to find the number of students who passed the test.

$$24 - 6 = 18\ \text{students}$$

26. D) Start by setting up the proportion:

$$\frac{120\ \text{miles}}{3\ \text{hours}} = \frac{180\ \text{miles}}{x\ \text{hours}}$$

Solve for the missing quantity through cross-multiplication:

$$120\ \text{miles} \times x\ \text{hours} = 3\ \text{hours} \times 180\ \text{miles}$$

Now solve the equation:

$$x\ \text{hours} = \frac{3\ \text{hours} \times 180\ \text{miles}}{120\ \text{miles}}$$

$$x = 4.5\ hours$$

Chapter 1 - Quantitative (Math) Section

Then complete the exponents, then multiplication.

$$-9 + 4(5) + 1 - 8$$

Then complete the addition and subtraction in order from left to right.

$$-9 + 20 + 1 - 8$$

$$4$$

17. C) Use the order of operation to simplify each expression.

(a): Simplify the expression in the parentheses, $2 \times 3 = 6$. Solve by subtracting, $6 - 6 = 0$.

(b): Simplify the parentheses, $6 - 2 = 4$. Solve by multiplying, $4 \times 3 = 12$.

(c): Multiply first and then subtract: $6 - 2 \times 3 = 6 - 6 = 0$.

Therefore, b (12) is greater than c (0).

18. C) Multiply the number of boxes by the number of pencils in each box to find the total number of pencils.

$$10 \times 150 = 1{,}500 \text{ pencils}$$

19. E) Use order of operations (PEMDAS) to solve the equation. First, complete the operations in the parentheses.

$$(12 - 8 \div 4)^2$$

Divide, and then subtract

$$8 \div 4 = 2$$

$$12 - 2 = 10$$

Complete the exponents outside the parentheses.

$$10^2 = 100$$

20. B) Because the temperature went down, add a negative number.

$$-3 + (-5) = -8°F$$

21. C) Simplify each expression:

$$(a) -5 + 25 = 20$$

$$(b) \, 13 - (-10) = 23$$

$$(c) \, 2 \times 14 = 28$$

The options in order from greatest to least is c, b, a.

The next number is:

$$77 - 11 = 66$$

12. C) The series is geometric with a common ratio of $\frac{1}{5}$.

$$\frac{1}{5}, \frac{1}{25}, \frac{1}{125}, \frac{1}{625}, \ldots$$

$$\frac{1}{5} \times \frac{1}{5} = \frac{1}{25}$$

$$\frac{1}{25} \times \frac{1}{5} = \frac{1}{125}$$

$$\frac{1}{125} \times \frac{1}{5} = \frac{1}{625}$$

The next number is:

$$\frac{1}{625} \times \frac{1}{5} = \frac{1}{3125}$$

13. E) The series is arithmetic with a difference of 4.

$$74, 78, 82, \_\_\_, 90, 94$$

$$78 - 74 = 4$$

$$82 - 78 = 4$$

To find the missing number, add 4 to the previous term.

$$82 + 4 = 86$$

14. B) Use a conversion factor to convert centimeters to meters.

$$2.5 \text{ m} \times \frac{100 \text{ cm}}{1 \text{ m}} = \frac{2.5 \text{ m} \times 100 \text{cm}}{1 \text{ m}} = 250 \text{ cm}$$

15. A) Convert each value to a common unit:

$$(a)\ 2\ c \times \frac{8\ oz}{1\ c} = 16 \text{ ounces}$$

$$(b)\ 0.5\ qt \times \frac{4\ c}{1\ qt} \times \frac{8\ oz}{1\ c} = 16 \text{ ounces}$$

$$(c)\ 16\ ounces$$

Therefore, a, b, and c are equal.

16. C) To simplify this expression, use PEMDAS. First complete the operations within the parenthesis.

$$-(3^2) + 4(5) + (5 - 6)^2 - 8$$

$$-(3^2) + 4(5) + (-1)^2 - 8$$

6. B) Calculate each value.

$$(a)\ 2^0 = 1$$

$$(b)\ 2^{-1} = \frac{1}{2^1} = \frac{1}{2}$$

$$(c)\ 2^1 = 2$$

From greatest to least, the options ared c, a, then b. Option B is correct because a is greater than b.

7. D) Hank earned 40% or 4,000 of the vote. Write and solve the proportion.

$$\frac{4{,}000}{x} = \frac{40}{100} \rightarrow x = 10{,}500$$

If voter turnout was 80%, then the number of registered voters is equivalent to:

$$\frac{10{,}000}{x} = \frac{80}{100} \rightarrow x = 12{,}500$$

8. B) Round each town population to the nearest thousand.

$$12{,}341 \approx 12{,}000$$

$$8{,}975 \approx 9{,}000$$

$$9{,}431 \approx 9{,}000$$

$$10{,}521 \approx 11{,}000$$

$$11{,}627 \approx 12{,}000$$

Add to find the total population.

$$12{,}000 + 9{,}000 + 9{,}000 + 11{,}000 + 12{,}000 = 53{,}000$$

9. C) Set up the appropriate equation and solve. Don't forget to change 15% to a decimal value:

$$whole = \frac{part}{percent} = \frac{45}{0.15} = 300$$

10. B) Set up the equation and solve:

$$percent = \frac{part}{whole} = \frac{39}{65} = 0.6 \text{ or } 60\%$$

11. B) The series is arithmetic with a difference of −11.

$$110, 99, 88, 77, \ldots$$

$$99 - 110 = -11$$

$$88 - 99 = -11$$

Answer Key

1. A) $\sqrt{5}$ is an irrational number because it cannot be written as a fraction of two integers. It is a decimal that goes on forever without repeating.

2. B) The last number in the decimal is in the hundredths place, so we can easily set up a fraction: $0.45 = \frac{45}{100}$. The next step is simply to reduce the fraction down to the lowest common denominator. Here, both 45 and 100 are divisible by 5: 45 divided by 5 is 9, and 100 divided by 5 is 20. You are therefore left with: $\frac{45}{100} = \frac{9}{20}$.

3. E) Divide the denominator into the numerator using long division.

$$\begin{array}{r} 0.875 \\ 8\overline{)7000} \\ -64 \\ \hline 60 \\ -56 \\ \hline 40 \end{array}$$

4. B) Dividing using long division yields a repeating decimal.

$$\begin{array}{r} 0.\overline{4545} \\ 11\overline{)50000} \\ -44 \\ \hline 60 \\ -55 \\ \hline 50 \\ -44 \\ \hline 60 \end{array}$$

5. A) Determine the largest square number that is a factor of the radicand, 48. Write the radicand as a product using that square number as a factor:

$$\sqrt{48} = \sqrt{(16 \times 3)} = \sqrt{16}\sqrt{3} = \mathbf{4\sqrt{3}}$$

Practice Questions

83. What is the probability that an even number results when a six-sided die is rolled?
    A) $\frac{1}{4}$
    B) $\frac{1}{2}$
    C) $\frac{1}{3}$
    D) $\frac{1}{4}$
    E) $\frac{1}{6}$

84. A bag contains 26 tiles representing the 26 letters of the English alphabet. If 3 tiles are drawn from the bag without replacement, what is the probability that all 3 will be consonants?
    A) 27%
    B) 18%
    C) 62%
    D) 51%
    E) 47%

Practice Questions

80. A personal assistant is struggling to pick a shirt, tie, and cufflink set that go together. If his client has 70 shirts, 2 ties, and 5 cufflinks, how many possible combinations does he have to consider?
    A) 500
    B) 650
    C) 700
    D) 750
    E) 425

81. If there are 20 applicants for 3 open positions, how many different combinations of teams can be made with the 3 people hired?
    A) 1250
    B) 704
    C) 987
    D) 1340
    E) 1140

82. Calculate the number of unique permutations that can be made with five of the letters in the word *pickle*.
    A) 720
    B) 640
    C) 575
    D) 804
    E) 89

Probability of a Single Event

The **probability of a single event** occurring is the number of outcomes in which that event occurs (called **favorable events**) divided by the number of items in the sample space (total possible outcomes):

$$P \text{ (an event)} = \frac{\text{number of favorable outcomes}}{\text{total number of possible outcomes}}$$

The probability of any event occurring will always be a fraction or decimal between 0 and 1. It may also be expressed as a percent. An event with 0 probability will never occur while an event with a probability of 1 is certain to occur. The probability of an event not occurring is referred to as that event's **complement**. The sum of an event's probability and the probability of that event's complement will always be 1.

a die is rolled (6 possible outcomes) and a coin is tossed (2 possible outcomes), there are $6 \times 2 = 12$ total possible outcomes.

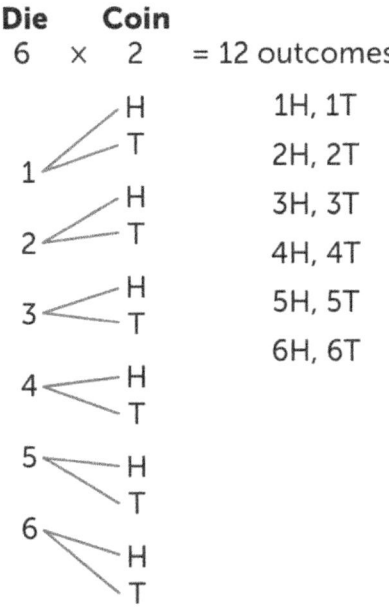

Figure 1.32. Fundamental Counting Principle

Combinations and permutations describe how many ways a number of objects taken from a group can be arranged. The number of objects in the group is written n, and the number of objects to be arranged is represented by r (or k). In a **combination**, the order of the selections does not matter because every available slot to be filled is the same. Examples of combinations include the following:

- Picking 3 people from a group of 12 to form a committee (220 possible committees)
- Picking 3 pizza toppings from 10 options (120 possible pizzas)

In a **permutation**, the order of the selection matters, meaning each available slot is different. Examples of permutations include the following:

- Handing out gold, silver, and bronze medals in a race with 100 participants (970,200 possible combinations)
- Selecting a president, vice-president, secretary, and treasurer from among a committee of 12 people (11,880 possible combinations)

The formulas for the both calculations are similar. The only difference, the $r! - n$ the denominator of a combination, accounts for redundant outcomes. Note that both permutations and combinations can be written in several different shortened notations:

$$\text{Permuation: } P(n,r) = {}_nP_r = \frac{n!}{(n-r)!}$$

$$\text{Combination: } C(n,r) = {}_nC_r = \left(\frac{n}{r}\right) = \frac{n!}{(n-r)!\,r!}$$

Determine whether each of the following statements is true or false:
A) Action films are the most popular type of movie.
B) About 1 in 5 moviegoers prefers comedy films.
C) Men choose the horror genre more frequently than women do.
D) Comedies are more popular than horror films.
E) Females are almost twice as likely to choose comedy films as men are.

79. A café owner tracked the number of customers he had over a twelve-hour period; the data is displayed in the following histogram. What kind of distribution does the data show?

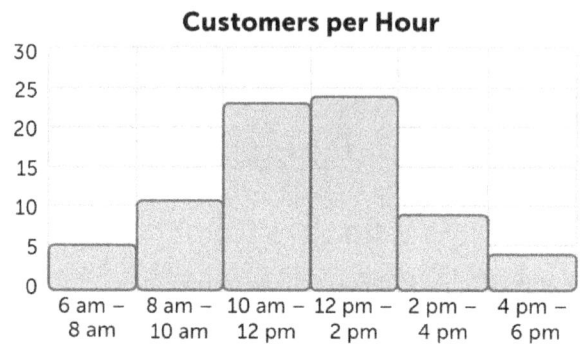

A) symmetrical
B) skewed right
C) multimodal
D) skewed left
E) There is not information to make a determination.

Probability and Counting Principles

Probability describes how likely something is to happen. In probability, an **event** is the single result of a trial, and an **outcome** is a possible event that results from a trial. The collection of all possible outcomes for a particular trial is called the **sample space**. For example, when rolling a die, the sample space is the numbers 1 through 6. Rolling a single number, such as 4, would be a single event.

Counting principles are methods used to find the number of possible outcomes for a given situation. The **fundamental counting principle** states that, for a series of independent events, the number of outcomes can be found by multiplying the number of possible outcomes for each event. For example, if

Histograms can be symmetrical, skewed left or right, or **multimodal** (i.e., data spread around). Note that **skewed left** means the peak of the data is on the right, with a tail to the left, while **skewed right** means the peak is on the left, with a tail to the right. While this seems counterintuitive, the "left" or "right" always refers to the *tail* of the data. This is because a long tail to the right, for example, means there are high outlier values that are skewing the data to the right.

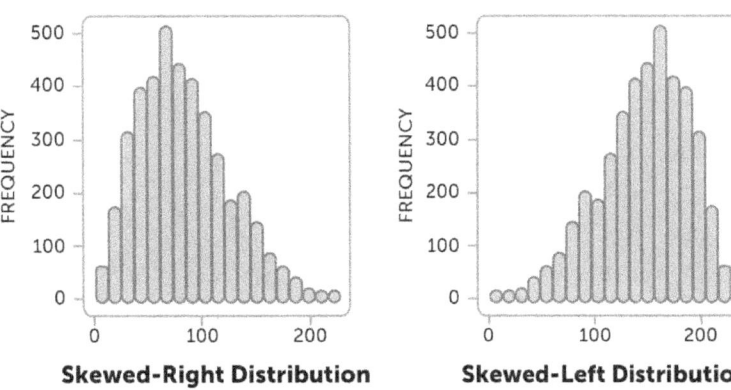

Figure 1.30. Histograms

A **two-way frequency table** compares categorical data (i.e., data in more than one category) of two related variables (bivariate data). Two-way frequency tables are also called **contingency tables** and are often used to analyze survey results. One category is displayed along the top of the table and the other category is displayed down along the side. Rows and columns are added and the sums appear at the end of the row or column. The sum of all the row data must equal the sum of all the column data.

From a two-way frequency table, the **joint relative frequency** of a particular category can be calculated by taking the number in the row and column of the categories in question and dividing by the total number surveyed. This gives the percent of the total in that particular category. Sometimes the conditional relative frequency is of interest. In this case, calculate the relative frequency confined to a single row or column.

Students by Grade and Gender					
Male	57	63	75	61	256
Female	54	42	71	60	227
Total	111	105	146	121	483

Figure 1.31. Two-Way Frequency Table

Practice Questions

78. Cineflix movie theater polled its moviegoers on a weeknight to determine their favorite type of movie. The results are in the two-way frequency table below.

Moviegoers	Comedy	Action	Horror	Totals
Male	15	24	21	60
Female	8	18	17	43
Totals	23	42	38	103

Practice Question

77. The following table gives the weights of wrestlers (in pounds) for a certain competition. What is the mean, median, and IQR of the data?

Stem	Leaf
2	05, 22, 53, 40
3	07, 22, 29, 45, 89, 96, 98
4	10, 25, 34
6	21

Key: 2|05 = 205 pounds
- A) 353.1 lbs (mean), 350 lbs (median), 150 lbs (IQR)
- B) 351.3 lbs (mean), 345 lbs (median), 157 lbs (IQR)
- C) 352 lbs (mean), 350 lbs (median), 15 lbs (IQR)
- D) 353.1 lbs (mean), 345 lbs (median), 157 lbs (IQR)
- E) 353 lbs (mean), 354 lbs (median), 105 lbs (IQR)

Frequency Tables and Histograms

The **frequency** of a data point is the number of times that data point occurs. Constructing a **frequency table** requires that the data or data classes be arranged in ascending order in one column and the frequency in another column.

A **histogram** is a graphical representation of a frequency table used to compare frequencies. A histogram is constructed in quadrant I of the xy-plane, with data in each equal-width class presented as a bar and the height of each bar representing the frequency of that class. Unlike bar graphs, histograms cannot have gaps between bars.

A histogram is used to determine the distribution of data among the classes.

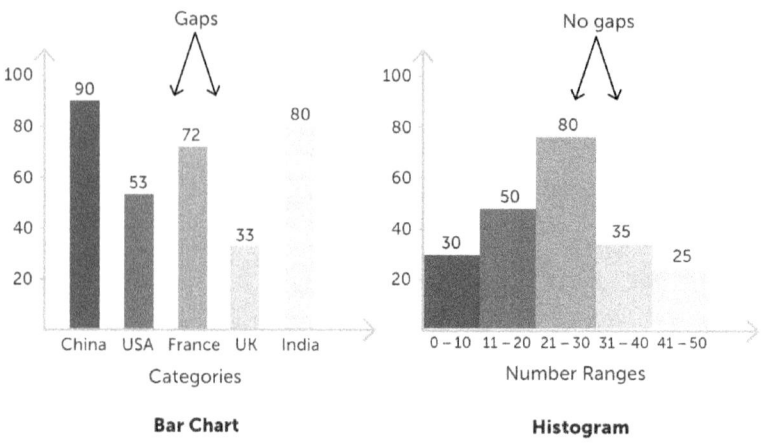

Figure 1.29. Bar Chart vs. Histogram

Practice Question

76. According to the bar graph below, in which year did Company X earn the most profit?

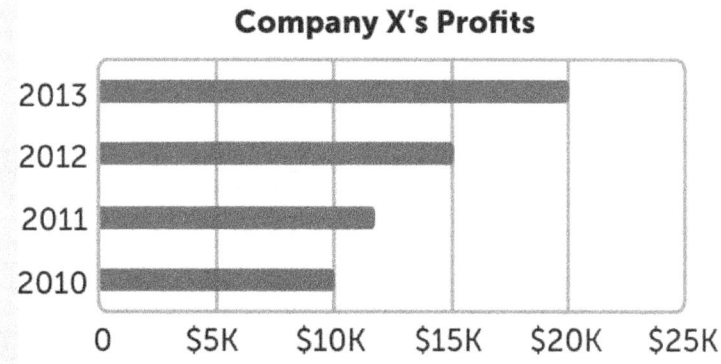

A) 2011
B) 2013
C) 2010
D) 2012
E) 2010 and 2011

Stem-and-Leaf Plots

Stem-and-leaf plots are ways of organizing large amounts of data by grouping them into classes. All data points are broken into two parts: a stem and a leaf. The number 512 might be broken into a stem of 5 and a leaf of 12. All data in the 500 range would appear in the same row (this group of data is a class). Usually a simple key is provided to explain how the data is being represented:

$$5|12 = 512$$

This shows that the stems are representing hundreds.

The advantage of this display is that it shows general density and shape of the data in a compact display, yet all original data points are preserved and available. It is also easy to find medians and quartiles from this display.

Stem	Leaf
0	5
1	6, 7
2	8, 3, 6
3	4, 5, 9, 5, 5, 8, 5
4	7, 7, 7, 8
5	5, 4
6	0

Figure 1.28. Stem-and-Leaf Plot

Practice Question

75. Individuals of various ages were asked to report their happiness level on a 20-point scale (0 being the least happy that person has been and 20 being the happiest). The data was then put into the following line graph, where the x-axis represents the ages of the respondents and the y-axis represents their levels of happiness. Based on the data presented in the graph, which of the following statements is NOT true?

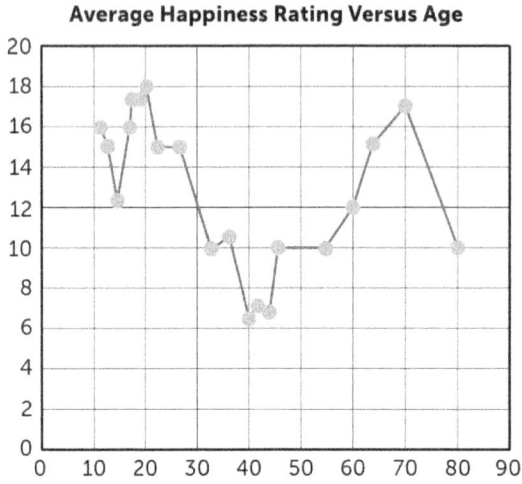

A) People in their late teens and early twenties are happier than people in their eighties.
B) On average, middle-aged people are less happy than young or older people are.
C) Happiness declines sharply between the ages of 70 and 80.
D) Fifteen-year-olds report being only slightly less happy than sixty-year-olds.
E) Happiness appears to remain at steady levels for people who are in their mid-twenties.

Bar Graphs

Bar graphs compare differences between categories or changes over a time. The data is grouped into categories or ranges and represented by rectangles. A bar graph's rectangles can be vertical or horizontal, depending on whether the dependent variable is placed on the x- or y-axis. Instead of the xy-plane, however, one axis is made up of categories (or ranges) instead of a numeric scale.

Bar graphs are useful because the differences between categories are easy to see: the height or length of each bar shows the value for each category.

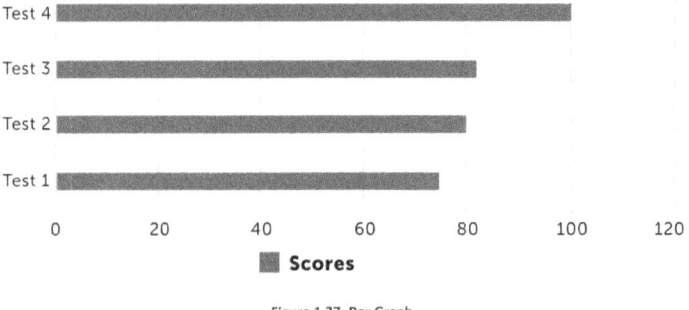

Figure 1.27. Bar Graph

Practice Question

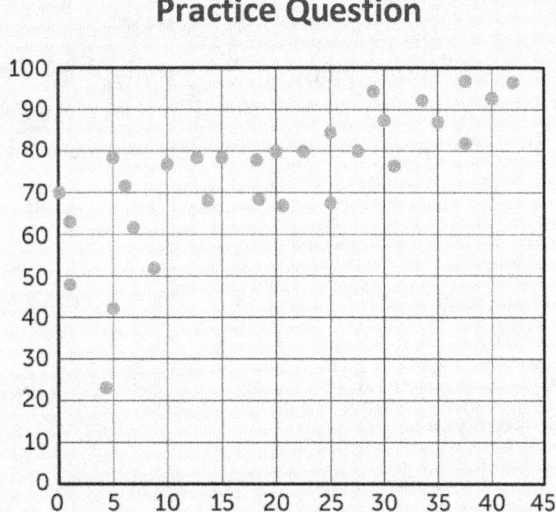

74. Based on the scatter plot on the following page, where the x-axis represents hours spent studying per week and the y-axis represents the average percent grade on exams during the school year, which type of correlation exists between the amount of studying for a test and test results?
    A) A strong positive correlation
    B) A strong negative correlation
    C) A somewhat weak positive correlation
    D) A somewhat weak negative correlation
    E) There is not enough information to determine the answer.

Line Graphs

Line graphs are used to display a relationship between two variables, such as change over time. Like scatter plots, line graphs exist in quadrant I of the xy-plane. Line graphs are constructed by graphing each point and connecting each point to the next consecutive point by a line. To create a line graph, it may be necessary to consolidate data into single bivariate data points.

A line graph is a function, with each x-value having exactly one y-value, whereas a scatter plot may have multiple y-values for one x-value.

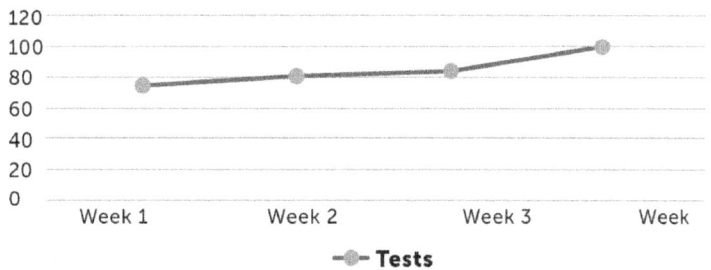

Figure 1.26. Line Graph

Scatter Plots

A **scatter plot** is displayed in the first quadrant of the xy-plane where all numbers are positive. Data points are plotted as ordered pairs, with one variable along the horizontal axis and the other along the vertical axis. Scatter plots can show if there is a correlation between two variables:

- There is a **positive correlation** (expressed as a positive slope) if increasing one variable appears to result in an increase in the other variable.
- A **negative correlation** (expressed as a negative slope) occurs when an increase in one variable causes a decrease in the other.
- If the scatter plot shows no discernible pattern, then there is **no correlation** (a zero, mixed, or indiscernible slope).

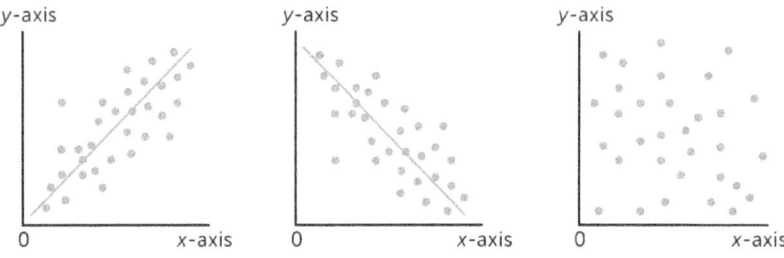

Figure 1.25. Scatter Plots and Correlation

It is important to note that just because two variables have a strong positive or negative correlation, it cannot necessarily be inferred that those two quantities have a causal relationship. In other words, it does not necessarily mean that having one variable change will cause the other quantity to change. There are often other factors that play into their relationship.

For example, a positive correlation can be found between the number of ice cream sales and the number of shark attacks at a beach. It would be incorrect to say that selling more ice cream causes an increase in shark attacks. It is much more likely that on hot days more ice cream is sold, and many more people are swimming, so one of them is more likely to get attacked by a shark. Confusing correlation and causation is one of the most common statistical errors people make.

Graphs, Charts, and Tables

Pie Charts

A pie chart states the proportion of each category within the whole. To construct a pie chart, the categories of a data set must be determined. The frequency of each category must be found and that frequency must be converted to a percent of the total. To draw the pie chart, determine the angle of each slice by multiplying the percentage by 360°.

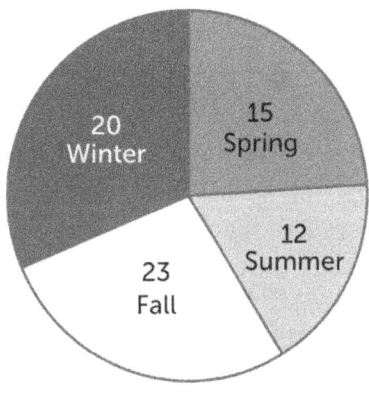

Figure 1.24. Pie Chart

Practice Question

73. A firm is screening applicants for a job by education-level attainment. According to the pie chart below, what percentage of applicants have earned a Master's degree?

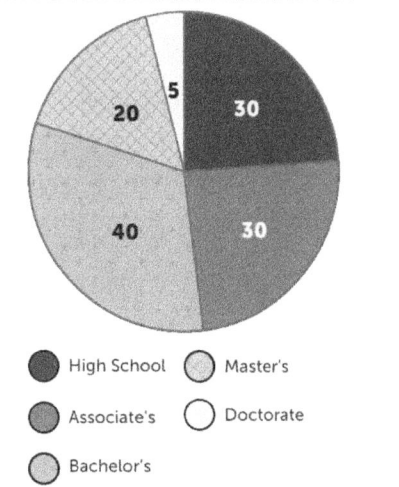

- A) 24%
- B) 4%
- C) 32%
- D) 16%
- E) There is not enough information to answer the question.

Measures of Variation

The values in a data set can be very close together (close to the mean), or very spread out. This is called the **spread** or **dispersion** of the data. There are a few measures of variation (or measures of dispersion) that quantify the spread within a data set.

Range is the difference between the largest and smallest data points in a set:

$$R = \text{largest data point} - \text{smallest data point}$$

Notice that range depends on only two data points (the two extremes). Sometimes these data points are outliers; regardless, for a large data set, relying on only two data points is not an exact tool.

The understanding of the data set can be improved by calculating **quartiles**. To calculate quartiles, first arrange the data in ascending order and find the set's median (also called **quartile 2** or **Q2**). Next, find the median of the lower half of the data, called **quartile 1 (Q1)**, and the median of the upper half of the data, called **quartile 3 (Q3)**. These three points divide the data into four equal groups of data (thus the word *quartile*). Each quartile contains 25% of the data.

Interquartile range (IQR) provides a more reliable range that is not as affected by extremes. IQR is the difference between the third quartile data point and the first quartile data point and gives the spread of the middle 50% of the data:

$$IQR = Q_3 - Q_1$$

The variance of a data set is simply the square of the standard variation. It measures how narrowly or widely the data points are distributed. A variance of zero means every data point is the same; a large variance means the data is widely spread out:

$$V = \sigma^2 = \frac{1}{N} \sum_{i=1}^{N} (x_i - \mu)^2$$

Practice Question

72. What are the range and interquartile range (IQR) of the following set?

    3, 9, 49, 64, 81, 100, 121, 144, 169

    A) 168 (range), 102 (IQR)
    B) 166 (range), 103.5 (IQR)
    C) 103.5 (range), 166 (IQR)
    D) 167.2 (range), 102 (IQR)
    E) 164 (range), 103.5 (IQR)

Other useful indicators include range and outliers. The **range** is the difference between the highest and the lowest values in a data set. The range of the set {16, 19, 19, 25, 27, 29, 75} is:

$$75 - 16 = 59$$

Outliers, or data points that are much different from other data points, should be noted since they can skew the central tendency. In the data set {16, 19, 19, 25, 27, 29, 75}, the value 75 is far outside the other values and raises the value of the mean. Without the outlier, the mean is much closer to the other data points.

$$\frac{16 + 19 + 19 + 25 + 27 + 29 + 75}{7} = \frac{210}{7} = 30$$

$$\frac{16 + 19 + 19 + 25 + 27 + 29}{6} = \frac{135}{6} = 22.5$$

Practice Questions

70. In 2016, LeBron James scored 1,954 points over 74 games. What was the mean number of points that he scored per game? Round to the nearest tenth.
    A) 74
    B) 26.4
    C) 3.8
    D) 25
    E) 27.1

71. In his class, Bart surveyed his classmates to determine their favorite pizza topping. The data he found was as follows:

Topping	Votes
Anchovy	1
Pineapple	2
Olives	4
Pepperoni	9
Bacon	2
Canadian Bacon	1

Which topping represents the mode?
   A) Anchovy
   B) Pineapple
   C) Olives
   D) Pepperoni
   E) Canadian bacon

Practice Questions

68. What is the slope of the line whose equation is $6x - 2y - 8 = 0$?
    A) -3
    B) $\frac{3}{4}$
    C) $-\frac{1}{3}$
    D) 3
    E) 2.25

69. In which quadrant is the point $(-5, 2)$ located?
    A) I
    B) II
    C) III
    D) IV
    E) None of the above

Data Analysis and Probability

Descriptive Statistics

Statistics is the study of data. Analyzing data requires using measures of central tendency (mean, median, and mode) to identify trends or patterns. The **mean** is the average; it is determined by adding all values and then dividing by the total number of values.

For example, the average of the data set {16, 19, 19, 25, 27, 29, 75} is found by adding the values and dividing by 7.

$$\frac{16 + 19 + 19 + 25 + 27 + 29 + 75}{7} = \frac{210}{7} = 30$$

The **median** is the number in the middle when the data set is arranged in order from least to greatest. For example, in the data set {16, 19, 19, 25, 27, 29, 75}, the median is 25. When a data set contains an even number of values, find the median by averaging the two middle values. In the data set {75, 80, 82, 100}, the two numbers in the middle are 80 and 82; the median will be the average of these two values:

$$\frac{80 + 82}{2} = 81$$

The **mode** is the most frequent outcome in a data set. In the set {16, 19, 19, 25, 27, 29, 75}, the mode is 19 because it occurs twice, which is more than any other number. If several values appear an equally frequent number of times, both values are considered the mode. If every value in a data set appears only once, the data set has no mode.

The most common way to write a linear equation is **slope-intercept form**:

$$y = mx + b$$

In this equation, m is the slope, and b is the y-intercept. The y-intercept is the point where the line crosses the y-axis, or where x equals zero.

Slope is often described as "rise over run" because it is calculated as the difference in y-values (rise) over the difference in x-values (run):

$$m = \frac{y_2 - y_1}{x_2 - x_1} = \frac{\text{rise}}{\text{run}}$$

To graph a linear equation, identify the y-intercept and place that point on the y-axis. Then, starting at the y-intercept, use the slope of "rise over run" to go "up and over" and place the next point. The numerator of the slope tells you how many units to go up—the "rise." The denominator of the slope tells you how many units to go to the right—the "run." If, however, the slope is negative, reverse the process and go down and over to the left before placing the next point. You can repeat the process to plot additional points. These points can then be connected to draw the line.

Helpful Hint:

Parallel lines have the same or equal slopes. The slopes of two perpendicular lines are negative reciprocals of each other.

To find the equation of a line, identify the y-intercept, if possible, on the graph and use two easily identifiable points to find the slope.

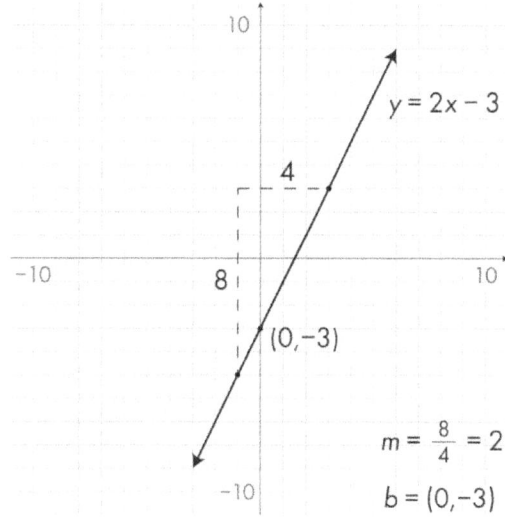

Figure 1.23. Linear Equation

to be similar, the ratio of their corresponding sides must be a constant (usually written as k). Similarity is described using the symbol $\sim$.

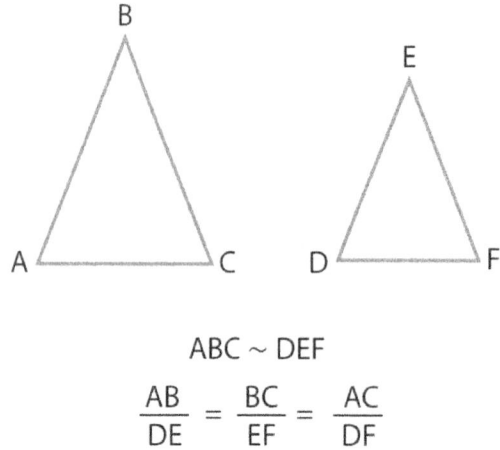

ABC $\sim$ DEF

$$\frac{AB}{DE} = \frac{BC}{EF} = \frac{AC}{DF}$$

Figure 1.21. Similar Triangles

Graphing Linear Equations on a Coordinate Plane

A **coordinate plane** is a plane containing the x- and y-axes. The x-axis is the horizontal line on a graph where $y = 0$. The y-axis is the vertical line on a graph where $x = 0$. The x-axis and y-axis intersect to create four **quadrants**. The first quadrant is in the upper right, and other quadrants are labeled counterclockwise using the Roman numerals I, II, III, and IV.

Points are locations on the graph are written as ordered pairs, (x, y), with the point $(0, 0)$ called the **origin**. Points are plotted by counting over x places from the origin horizontally and y places from the origin vertically.

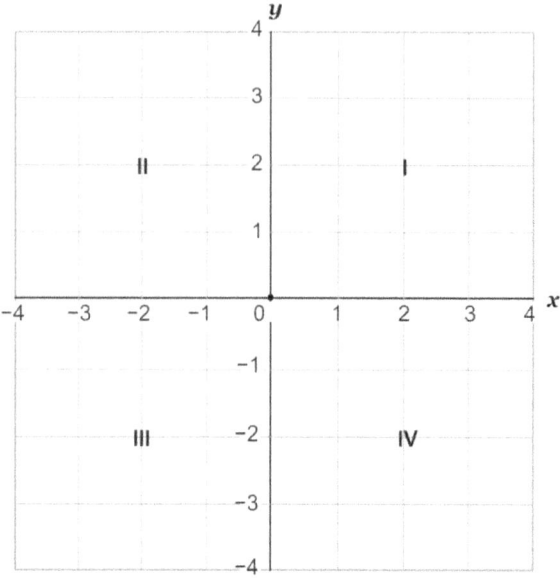

Figure 1.22. Four Quadrants

Chapter 1 - Quantitative (Math) Section

67. Given the diagram, if $XZ = 100$, $WZ = 80$, and $XU = 70$, then what is WY?

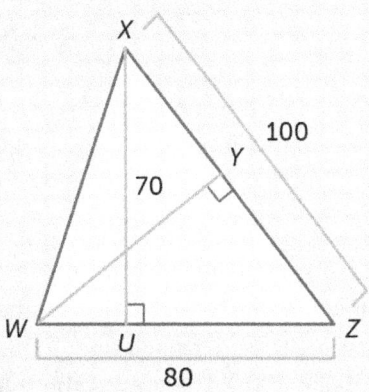

A) 54
B) 72
C) 61
D) 56
E) 48

Similarity and Congruence

In geometry, the term *congruent* means that two shapes have the same shape and size (but not necessarily the same orientation or location). For example, if the length of two lines is equal, the two lines themselves are described as being congruent. Congruence is written using the symbol ≅.

On figures, congruent parts are denoted with hash marks (#).

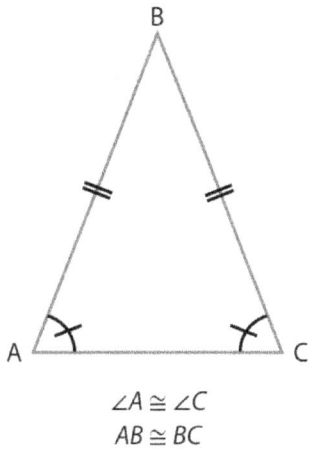

∠A ≅ ∠C
AB ≅ BC

Figure 1.20. Congruent Parts of a Triangle

Similarity means that although two figures share the same shape, they are not the same size. In other words, shapes that are similar have the same corresponding angles but different lengths. For two shapes

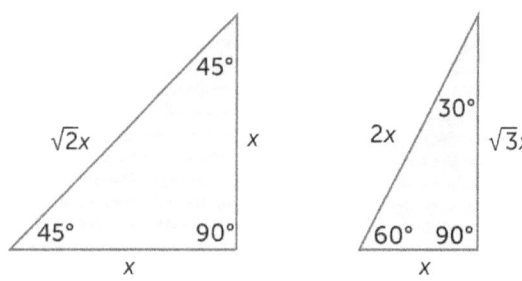

Figure 1.19. Special Right Triangles

For any triangle, the side opposite the largest angle will have the longest length, while the side opposite the smallest angle will have the shortest length. The **triangle inequality theorem** states that the sum of any two sides of a triangle must be greater than the third side; if this inequality does not hold, then a triangle cannot be formed. A consequence of this theorem is the **third-side rule**: if b and c are two sides of a triangle, then the measure of the third side a must be between the sum of the other two sides and the difference of the other two sides:

$$c - b < a < c + b$$

The relationship among a right triangle's sides is known as the **Pythagorean theorem:**

$$a^2 + b^2 = c^2$$

Here, c is the hypotenuse—the side across from the 90° angle. Right triangles with angle measurements of 90°–45°–45° and 90°–60°–30° are known as special right triangles and have specific relationships between their sides and angles.

Practice Questions

66. What are the minimum and maximum values of x to the nearest hundredth?

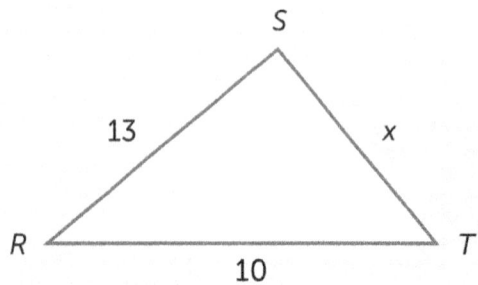

- A) 3.01 (min), 22.99 (max)
- B) 3.00 (min), 23.00 (max)
- C) 3.02 (min), 23.01 (max)
- D) 2.99 (min), 22.98 (max)
- E) 3.03 (min), 22.1 (max)

Triangles also have two "centers." The **orthocenter** is formed by the intersection of a triangle's three altitudes. The **centroid** is where a triangle's three medians meet.

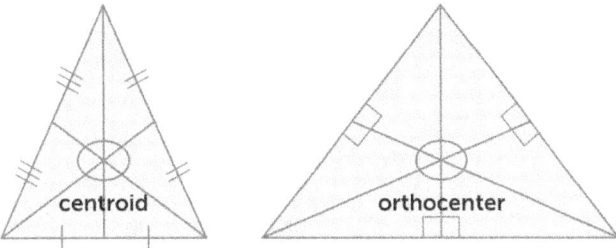

Figure 1.17. Centroid and Orthocenter of a Triangle

Triangles can be classified in two ways: by sides and by angles:

- A **scalene triangle** has no equal sides or angles.
- An **isosceles triangle** has two equal sides and two equal angles, often called **base angles**.
- In an **equilateral triangle**, all three sides are equal as are all three angles. Moreover, because the sum of the angles of a triangle is always 180°, each angle of an equilateral triangle must be 60°.
- A **right triangle** has one right angle (90°) and two acute angles.
- An **acute triangle** has three acute angles (all angles are less than 90°).
- An **obtuse triangle** has one obtuse angle (more than 90°) and two acute angles.

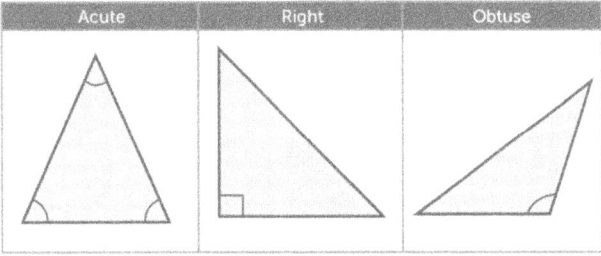

Figure 1.18. Types of Triangles

65. A chord is formed by line segment $\overline{QP}$. The radius of the circle is 5 cm and the chord length is 6 cm. Find the distance from center C to the chord.

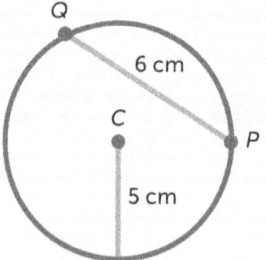

A) $d = 2\ cm$
B) $d = 5\ cm$
C) $d = 3\ cm$
D) $d = 4.25\ cm$
E) $d = 4\ cm$

Triangles

Triangles have three sides and three interior angles that always sum to 180°. The formula for the area of a triangle is one-half the product of the base and height (or altitude) of the triangle.

$$A = \frac{1}{2}(b \times h)$$

Some important segments in a triangle include the angle bisector, the altitude, and the median. The **angle bisector** extends from the side opposite an angle to bisect that angle. The **altitude** is the shortest distance from a vertex of the triangle to the line containing the base side opposite that vertex; it is perpendicular to that line and can occur on the outside of the triangle. The **median** extends from an angle to bisect the opposite side.

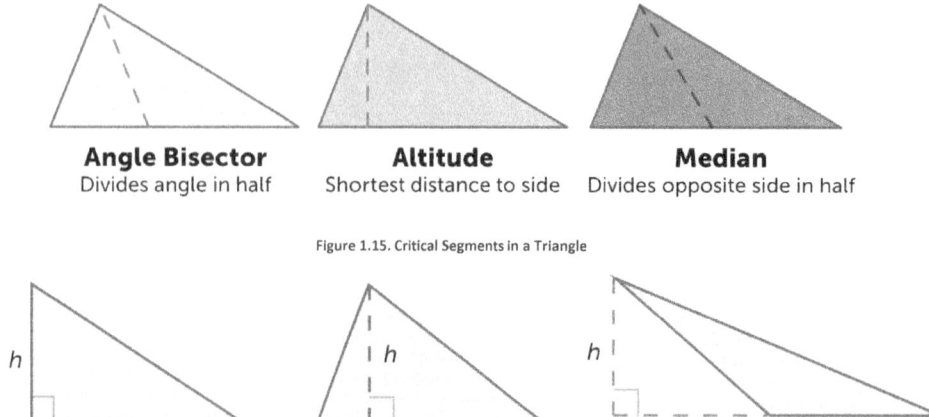

Figure 1.15. Critical Segments in a Triangle

Figure 1.16. Finding the Base and Height of Triangles

the radius of the circle r and the distance from the center of the circle to the chord d. (Note that d must be at a right angle to the chord):

- If you know the central angle, chord length $= 2r\sin\frac{\theta}{2}$.
- If you know the radius and distance, chord length $= 2\sqrt{r^2 - d^2}$.

A secant is similar to a chord in that it connects two points on a circle. The difference is that a **secant** is a line, not a line segment, so it extends outside of the circle on either side. A **tangent** is a straight line that touches a circle at only one point.

Did You Know?

The equation for a circle on the coordinate plane is $(x - h)^2 + (y - k)^2 = r^2$, where (h, k) is the center of the circle and r is the radius.

A **sector** is the area within a circle that is enclosed by a central angle. If a circle is a pie, a sector is the piece of pie cut by two radii. You can find the area of a sector if you know either the central angle θ or the arc length s:

- If you know the central angle, the area of the sector $= \pi r^2 \frac{\theta}{360°}$.
- If you know the arc length, the area of a sector $= \frac{1}{2}rl$.

There are two other types of angles you can create in or around a circle: inscribed angles and circumscribed angles.

Inscribed angles are inside the circle: the vertex is a point P on the circle and the rays extend to two other points on the circle (A and B). As long as A and B remain constant, you can move the vertex P anywhere along the circle and the inscribed angle will be the same. You can find the inscribed angle if you know the radius of the circle r and the arc length l between A and B:

$$\text{inscribed angle} = \frac{90°l}{\pi r}$$

Circumscribed angles are outside of the circle: the rays are formed by two tangent lines that touch the circle at points A and B. To find the circumscribed angle, find the central angle formed by the same points A and B and subtract that angle from 180°.

Practice Questions

64. A circle has a diameter of 10 centimeters. What is the intercepted arc length between points A and B if the central angle between those points measures 46°?
    A) 2.4 cm
    B) 4.0 cm
    C) 5.2 cm
    D) 4.3 cm
    E) 2.25 cm

Table 1.10. Three-Dimensional Shapes and Formulas			
Term	Shape	Formula	
Pyramid		$V = \frac{1}{3}Bh$ $SA = B + \frac{1}{2}(p)l$	B = area of base h = height p = perimeter l = slant height

Practice Questions

62. What is the surface area of a cube with a side length of 5 meters?
   A) 75 m²
   B) 125 m²
   C) 100 m²
   D) 150 m²
   E) 115 m²

63. A cylinder and cone both have the same radius and the same height. If the volume of the cylinder is 300 cubic meters, what is the volume of the cone?
   A) 100 m³
   B) 150 m³
   C) 300 m³
   D) 900 m³
   E) 225 m³

Circles

The definition of a **circle** is the set of points that are equal distance from a center point. The distance from the center to any given point on the circle is the **radius**. If you draw a line segment across the circle going through the center, the distance along the line segment is called the **diameter**. The radius is always equal to half the diameter:

$$d = 2r$$

A **central angle** is formed by drawing radii out from the center to two points A and B along the circle. The **intercepted arc** is the portion of the circle (the arc length) between points A and B. You can find the intercepted arc length l if you know the central angle θ and vice versa:

$$l = 2\pi r \frac{\theta}{360°}$$

A **chord** is a line segment that connects two points on a circle. Unlike the diameter, a chord does not have to go through the center. You can find the chord length if you know either the central angle θ or

Chapter 1 - Quantitative (Math) Section

Volume and Surface Area

Three-dimensional shapes have depth as well as width and length. The space that is occupied within the length, width, and depth of a shape is the **volume**, which is the number of cubic units any solid can hold; in other words, volume describes how much of something it takes to fill a three-dimensional shape.

Surface area is the sum of the areas of the two-dimensional figures that are found on its surface. Some three-dimensional shapes also have a unique property called a **slant height** (l), which is the distance from the base to the apex along a lateral face. The table below shows the formulas for three-dimensional shapes.

Table 1.10. Three-Dimensional Shapes and Formulas

Term	Shape	Formula	
Prism		$V = Bh$ $SA = 2lw + 2wh + 2lh$ $d^2 = a^2 + b^2 + c^2$	B = area of base h = height l = length w = width d = longest diagonal
Cube		$V = s^3$ $SA = 6s^2$	s = cube edge
Sphere		$V = \frac{4}{3}\pi r^3$ $SA = 4\pi r^2$	r = radius
Cylinder		$V = Bh = \pi r^2 h$ $SA = 2\pi r^2 + 2\pi rh$	B = area of base h = height r = radius
Cone		$V = \frac{1}{3}\pi r^2 h$ $SA = \pi r^2 + \pi rl$	r = radius h = height l = slant height

Practice Questions

58. A farmer has purchased 100 meters of fencing to enclose his rectangular garden. If one side of the garden is 20 meters long and the other is 28 meters long, how much fencing will the farmer have left over?
   - A) 4 meters
   - B) 2.5 meters
   - C) 1 meter
   - D) 5 meters
   - E) 4.5 meters

59. Taylor is going to paint a square wall that is 3.5 meters high. How much paint will he need?
   - A) 12.05 m^2
   - B) 11.15 m^2
   - C) 12.45 m^2
   - D) 12.25 m^2
   - E) 10.15 m^2

60. What is the perimeter of the regular polygon shown below?

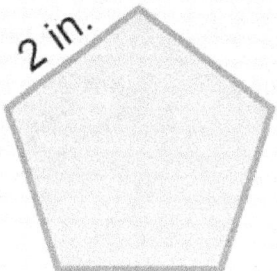

   - A) 6.88 inches
   - B) 8 inches
   - C) 10 inches
   - D) 12 inches
   - E) 9.5 inches

61. Examine (a), (b), and (c) to determine the best answer

(a) The perimeter of a square with side length of 6.

(b) The perimeter of a rectangle with a width of 4 and length of 8.

(c) The perimeter of an equilateral triangle of side length of 7.

   - A) (a) is greater than (c)
   - B) (a) is equal to (c)
   - C) (b) is equal to (c)
   - D) (a), (b), and (c) are equal
   - E) There is not enough information to determine the answer.

57. Which points and lines are contained in plane M in the following figure?

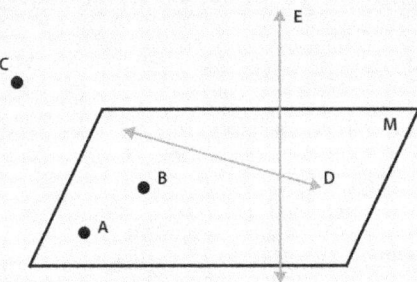

A) $\dot{A}, \dot{B}$
B) $\dot{B}, \overleftrightarrow{D}$
C) $\dot{A}, \dot{B}, \overleftrightarrow{D}$
D) $\dot{A}, \overleftrightarrow{D}$
E) $\overleftrightarrow{D}$

Properties Of Shapes: Area and Perimeter

Perimeter is the distance around a shape. It can be determined by adding the lengths of all sides of the shape. **Area** is the amount of space a shape occupies. The area of an object is its length times its width and is measured in square units. For example, if a wall is 3 feet long and 2 feet wide, its area is 6 square feet (ft²) because $3 \times 2 = 6$.

An **equilateral figure** has sides that are all the same length, and all of the angles have the same measurement:

- To find the length of a side in an equilateral figure, divide the perimeter by the number of sides.
- To find the measurement of each angle, divide the sum of all the interior angles by the number of angles.

Area and perimeter problems require you to use the equations shown in the table below to find either the area inside a shape or the distance around it (the perimeter). These equations will not be given on the test, so you will need to have them memorized.

Table 1.9. Area and Perimeter Equations		
Shape	**Area**	**Perimeter**
Circle	$A = \pi^2$	$C = 2\pi r = \pi d$
Triangle	$A = \dfrac{1}{2}(b \times h)$	$P = s_1 + s_2 + s_3$
Square	$A = s^2$	$P = 4s$
Rectangle	$A = l \times w$	$P = 2l + 2w$

Three-dimensional objects, such as cubes, can be measured in three dimensions: length, width, and height. Three-dimensional objects are also called **solids**, and the shape of a flattened solid is called a **net**.

Figure 1.13. Three-Dimensional Object

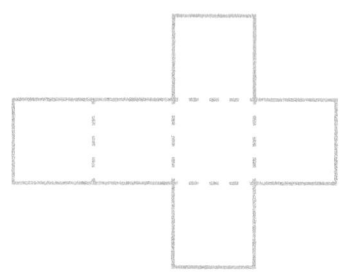

Figure 1.14. Net

Table 1.8. Basic Geometric Figures			
Term	**Dimensions**	**Graphic**	**Symbol**
Point	Zero	●	A
Line segment	One	A———B	$\overline{AB}$
Ray	One	A———B→	$\overrightarrow{AB}$
Line	One	←———→	$\overleftrightarrow{AB}$
Plane	Two	(parallelogram)	Plane M

Practice Questions

56. Angle M measures 36°. What is the measure of an angle supplementary to angle M?
    A) 180°
    B) 144°
    C) 36°
    D) 54°
    E) 138°

- Two lines that form right angles are **perpendicular**.
- Lines that do not intersect are **parallel**.
- Any two angles whose sum is 90° are called **complementary angles**.
- **Supplementary angles** have a sum of 180°.

Polygons are two-dimensional shapes that have three or more straight sides. Triangles and squares are examples of polygons. **Regular polygons** are polygons whose sides are all the same length. Angles inside a polygon are **interior angles**. Angles formed by one side of the polygon and a line extending outside the polygon are exterior angles.

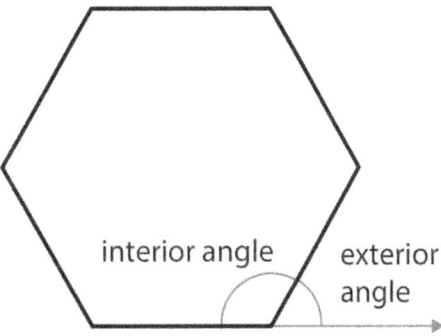

Figure 1.11. Interior and Exterior Angles

Two-dimensional objects can be measured in two dimensions: length and width. A plane is a two-dimensional object that extends infinitely in both dimensions.

Figure 1.12. Two-Dimensional Object

A collection of points that extends infinitely in only one direction is a **ray**. A ray is sometimes called a half line; it has one endpoint and extends indefinitely in one direction. A ray is defined by its endpoint, followed by any other point on the ray: $\overrightarrow{AB}$. The first letter represents the endpoint.

A section of a line that has two endpoints and a finite length is a **line segment**. The length of a segment, called the **measure of the segment**, is the distance from A to B. A line segment is a subset of a line and is also denoted with two points, but with a segment symbol: $\overline{AB}$.

The midpoint of a line segment is the point at which the segment is divided into two equal parts. A line, segment, or plane that passes through the midpoint of a segment is called a bisector of the segment, since it cuts the segment into two equal segments. Lines, rays, and line segments are examples of one-dimensional objects because they can only be measured in one dimension (length).

Figure 1.10. One-Dimensional Object

Angles are formed when two rays share a common endpoint. They are named using three letters, with the vertex point in the middle (for example $\angle ABC$, where B is the vertex). They can also be labeled with a number or named by their vertex alone (if it is clear to do so). Angles, which are measured in degrees or radians, are classified based on their measurements:

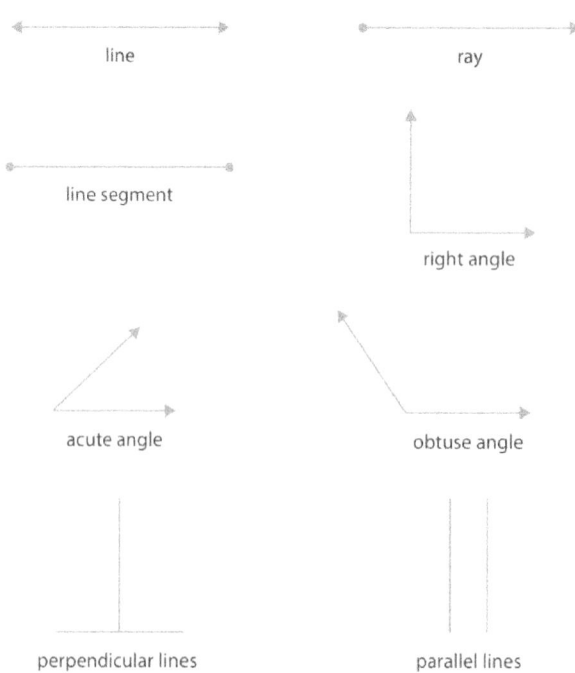

Figure 1.10. Lines and Angles

- Angles between 0° and 90° are **acute**.
- Angles between 90° and 180° are **obtuse**.
- An angle of exactly 90° is a **right angle**.

Practice Questions

53. Bridget can clean an entire house in 12 hours while her brother Tom takes 8 hours. How long would it take for Bridget and Tom to clean 2 houses together?
    A) $9\frac{3}{5}$ hr.
    B) $5\frac{1}{4}$ hr.
    C) 10 hr.
    D) $8\frac{2}{5}$ hr.
    E) 8 hours

54. Farmer Dan needs to water his cornfield. One hose can water a field 1.25 times faster than a second hose. When both hoses are running, they water the field together in 5 hours. How long would it take to water the field if only the slower hose is used?
    A) 12 hours
    B) 10.25 hours
    C) 11 hours
    D) 9.75 hours
    E) 11.25 hours

55. Ben takes 2 hours to pick 500 apples, and Frank takes 3 hours to pick 450 apples. How long will they take, working together, to pick 1000 apples?
    A) 1.5 hours
    B) 0.5 hours
    C) 45 minutes
    D) 2.5 hours
    E) 3 hours

Geometry

Properties of Shapes: Geometric Figures

Geometric figures are shapes made up of points, lines, or planes. A **point** is simply a location in space; it does not have any dimensional properties like length, area, or volume. A collection of points that extends infinitely in both directions is a **line**. At least two points are needed to define a line; any points that lie on the same line are **colinear**. Lines are represented by two points, such as A and B, and the line symbol $\overleftrightarrow{AB}$. Two lines on the same plane will intersect unless they are **parallel**; parallel lines have the same slope. Lines that intersect at a 90-degree angle are **perpendicular**.

A **plane** is a flat sheet that extends indefinitely in two directions (like an infinite sheet of paper). A plane is a two-dimensional (2D) figure and can always be defined through any three noncollinear points in three-dimensional (3D) space. A plane is named using any three points that are in the plane (for example, plane ABC). Any points lying in the same plane are said to be **coplanar**. When two planes intersect, the intersection is a line.

Distance Word Problems

Distance word problems involve something traveling at a constant or average speed. In a distance equation, d stands for *distance*, r stands for *rate* (i.e., *speed*), and t stands for *time*. Key words such as *how fast*, *how far*, and *for how long* indicate that you are dealing with a distance word problem:

These problems can be solved by setting up a grid with d, r, and t along the top and each moving object on the left. When setting up the grid, make sure the units are consistent. For example, if the distance is in meters and the time is in seconds, the rate should be "meters per second."

Practice Questions

51. Will drove from his home to the airport at an average speed of 30 mph. He then boarded a helicopter and flew to the hospital at an average speed of 60 mph. The entire distance was 150 miles, and the trip took 3 hours. Find the distance from the airport to the hospital.
    A) 74 miles
    B) 210 miles
    C) 83 miles
    D) 112 miles
    E) 120 miles

52. Two riders on horseback start at the same time from opposite ends of a field that is 45 miles long. One horse is moving at 14 mph, and the second horse is moving at 16 mph. How long after they begin will the two riders meet?
    A) 2 hours
    B) 1.5 hours
    C) 1 hour
    D) 2.5 hours
    E) 45 minutes

Work Problems

Work problems involve situations where several people or machines are doing work at different rates. Your task is usually to figure out how long it will take these people or machines to complete a task while working together. The trick to doing work problems is to figure out how much of the project each person or machine completes in the same unit of time. For instance, you might calculate how much of a wall a person can paint in 1 hour, or how many boxes an assembly line can pack in 1 minute. The next step is to set up an equation to solve for the total time. This equation is $work = rate \times time$.

Always read the entire problem before beginning to solve it. Remember that not all of the information provided in a problem is necessarily needed to solve it. When working multiple-choice word problems, it is important to check your work. Many of the incorrect answer options will be results from common mistakes; therefore, even if a solution you calculated is listed as an answer option, it does not necessarily mean that you have done the problem correctly—you must check your answer to be sure.

The following general steps can help you solve word problems:

- Read the entire problem and determine what the question is asking.
- List all of the given data and define the variables.
- Determine the formula(s) needed or set up equations from the information in the problem.
- Solve.
- Check your answer. (Is the amount too large or small? Is the answer in the correct unit of measure?)

Word problems generally contain key words that can help you determine which math processes may be required in order to solve them:

- **Addition:** *added, combined, increased by, in all, total, perimeter, sum,* and *more than*
- **Subtraction:** *how much more, less than, fewer than, exceeds, difference,* and *decreased*
- **Multiplication:** *of, times, area,* and *product*
- **Division:** *distribute, share, average, per, out of, percent,* and *quotient*
- **Equals:** *is, was, are, amounts to,* and *were*

Practice Questions

49. A store owner bought a case of 48 backpacks for $476. He sold 17 of the backpacks in his store for $18 each, and the rest were sold to a school for $15 each. What was the store owner's profit?
    A) $304
    B) $295
    C) $275
    D) $312
    E) $187

50. Thirty students in Mr. Joyce's room are working on projects over 2 days. The first day, Mr. Joyce gave them $\frac{3}{5}$ of an hour to work. On the second day, he gave the students $\frac{1}{2}$ as much time as the first day. How much time did each student have to work on the project?
    A) 45 minutes
    B) 52 minutes
    C) 1 hour and 4 minutes
    D) 54 minutes
    E) 42 minutes

46. The students on the track team are buying new uniforms. T-shirts (t) cost \$12, pants (p) cost \$15, and a pair of shoes (s) costs \$45. If the team has a budget of \$2,500, which of the following inequalities represents how many of each item the students can buy?
    A) $t + p + s < 2,500$
    B) $\frac{t}{12} + \frac{p}{15} + \frac{s}{45} > 2,500$
    C) $12t + 15p + 45s \leq 2,500$
    D) $12t + 15p + 45s \geq 2,500$
    E) $\frac{12t}{15p} + \frac{s}{45} > 2,500$

Absolute Value

The **absolute value** of a number (represented by the symbol | |) is its distance from zero, not its value. For example, |3| = 3 and |−3| = 3 because both 3 and −3 are three units from zero. The absolute value of a number is always positive. Equations with absolute values will have two answers, so you will need to set up two equations. The first is simply the equation with the absolute value symbol removed. For the second equation, isolate the absolute value on one side of the equation and multiply the other side of the equation by −1.

Practice Questions

47. Solve for x: $|2x - 3| = x + 1$
    A) 2
    B) 6
    C) $\frac{2}{3}$
    D) $\frac{3}{4}$
    E) 7

48. Solve for y: $2|y + 4| = 10$
    A) $y = 3$ or -9
    B) $y = 2$ or 4
    C) $y = 1$ or -9
    D) $y = 1$ or 7
    E) $y = -1$ or 9

Solving Word Problems

A **word problem** is an equation that is described using words. Your task when solving these problems is to turn the story of the problem into a mathematical equation. Converting units can often help you avoid operations with fractions when dealing with time.

Chapter 1 - Quantitative (Math) Section

Inequalities

Inequalities are similar to equations, except that both sides of the problem are not necessarily equal (≠). Inequalities may be represented as follows:

- greater than (>)
- greater than or equal to (≥)
- less than (<)
- less than or equal to (≤)

Inequalities may be represented on a number line. A circle is placed on the end point with a filled circle representing ≤ and ≥ and an empty circle representing < and >. An arrow is then drawn to show either all the values greater than or less than the value circled.

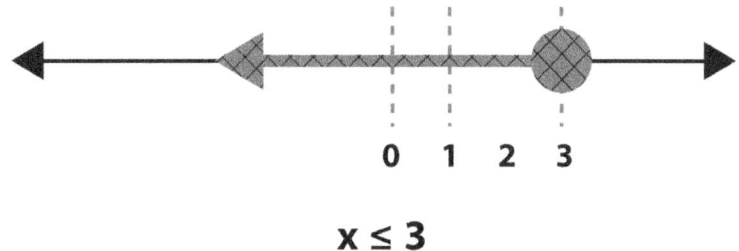

x ≤ 3

Figure 1.9. Inequality Line Graph

Inequalities can be solved like equations. The only difference is that the direction of the inequality sign must be reversed when the inequality is divided by a negative number.

Example:

$$10 - 2x > 14$$
$$-2x > 4$$
$$x < -2$$

The solution to an inequality is a set of numbers rather than a single value. In the example above, solving $10 - 2x > 14$ gives the solution $x < -2$. This means that every number less than -2 proves the inequality.

Practice Questions

45. Solve the inequality: $4x + 10 > 58$
    A) $x > 11$
    B) $x < 12$
    C) $x > 19.5$
    D) $x > 12$
    E) $x < 11$

Practice Questions

41. Solve for x: $5(x + 3) - 12 = 43$
    A) $x = 14$
    B) $x = 3$
    C) $x = 10.4$
    D) $x = 8$
    E) $x = 7.2$

42. Mandy babysits for families and charges $8 an hour for one child plus $3 an hour per additional child. The Buxton family has 4 children, and they ask Mandy to babysit for 5 hours. How much will Mandy make for babysitting the Buxton children?
    A) $163
    B) $104
    C) $220
    D) $85
    E) $75

Building Equations

Word problems require you to translate a scenario into a mathematical equation. To do this, first read the problem carefully and identify what value needs to be solved for. Identify the known and unknown quantities in the problem and assign the unknown quantities a variable. Once this is done, you can create equations that allow you to solve the problem.

Practice Questions

43. A school is holding a raffle to raise money. There is a $3 entry fee, and each ticket costs $5. If a student paid $28, how many tickets did he buy?
    A) 4
    B) 6
    C) 3
    D) 7
    E) 5

44. Kelly is selling shirts for her school swim team. There are two prices: a student price and a nonstudent price. During the first week of the sale, Kelly raised $84 by selling 10 shirts to students and 4 shirts to nonstudents. She earned $185 in the second week by selling 20 shirts to students and 10 shirts to nonstudents. What is the student price for a shirt?
    A) $7
    B) $5
    C) $6
    D) $5.50
    E) $6.75

Equations

An **equation** states that two expressions are equal to each other. Solving an equation means finding the value(s) of the variable that make the equation true. A **linear equation** has two variables with no exponents. To solve, isolate the variable for which you are solving on one side of the equal sign with all other terms on the other side. To do this, undo all of the operations that connect numbers to the variable of interest. To solve the following equation, isolate the variable. First, distribute the 2.

$$2(2x - 8) = x - 7$$
$$4x - 16 = x - 7$$

Subtract x to isolate the variable to one side.

$$3x - 16 = -7$$

Add 16 to both sides.

$$3x - 16 + 16 = -7 + 16$$
$$3x = 9$$

Divide both sides by 3.

$$\frac{3x}{3} = \frac{9}{3}$$
$$x = 3$$

Other ways to isolate the variable include:

- Eliminating fractions by multiplying each side by the least common multiple of any denominators.
- Combine like terms.
- Use addition or subtraction to collect all terms containing the variable of interest to one side and all terms not containing the variable to the other side.
- Use multiplication or division to remove coefficients from the variable for which you are solving.

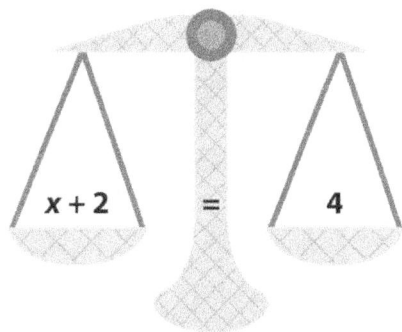

Figure 1.8. Equations

greatest common factor (GCF) among the terms. The remaining terms are placed in parentheses. Factoring can be checked by multiplying the GCF through the parentheses.

$$14a^2 + 7a = 7a(2a + 1)$$

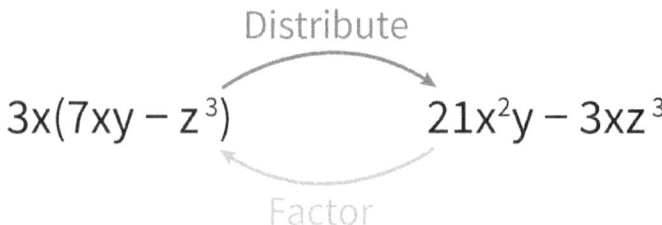

Figure 1.7. Distributing and Factoring

To multiply **binomials** (expressions with two terms), use the **FOIL** acronym:

- **F**irst: multiply the first term in each expression
- **O**uter: multiply the outer terms in each expression
- **I**nner: multiply the inner terms in each expression
- **L**ast: multiply the last term in each expression

The final step is to simplify the expression.

$$(2x + 3)(x - 4)$$
$$(2x)(x) + (2x)(-4) + (3)(x) + 3(-4)$$
$$2x^2 - 8x + 3x - 12$$
$$2x^2 - 5x - 12$$

Practice Questions

39. Simplify the following expression: $5x(x^2 - 2c + 10)$.
    A) $5x^3 + 10xc + 50x$
    B) $5x^3 - 10xc + 50x$
    C) $5x^2 - 10c + 50$
    D) $5x^3 - 2xc + 10x$
    E) $5x^2 - 2xc + 10x$

40. Evaluate $-3(b + 8c)$ if $b = -2$ and $c = -3$.
    A) -78
    B) -18
    C) 82
    D) 498
    E) 78

Adding and Subtracting Algebraic Expressions

Terms are any quantities that are added or subtracted in an expression. **Like terms** are terms with the same variable part. Expressions can be added or subtracted by simply adding and subtracting like terms. The other terms in the expression will not change. In the following expression, the like terms are $3xy$ and $2xy$:

$$2x + 3xy - 2z + 6y + 2xy$$
$$2x - 2z + 6y + (3xy + 2xy)$$
$$2x - 2z + 6y + 5xy$$

Practice Questions

37. Simplify the expression: $4x - 3y + 12z + 2x - 7y - 10z$
    A) $6x - 10y + 2z$
    B) $6x + 10y - 2z$
    C) $-2xyz$
    D) $-x + 14z - 17y$
    E) $-6xyz$

38. At the arcade, games give out green tickets or red tickets. The arcade also gives out small boxes to store tickets. Paul and Paula both play numerous games, and at the end of the day, Paul has 3 boxes of green tickets and 8 boxes of red tickets, while Paula has 6 boxes of green tickets and 2 boxes of red tickets. If the green box holds g tickets and the red box holds r tickets, write an expression that describes how many tickets they have together.
    A) $11g + 8r$
    B) $5g + 14r$
    C) $9g + 10r$
    D) $10g + 9r$

Distributing and Factoring

Simplifying expressions often requires distributing and factoring. To **distribute**, multiply the term outside the parentheses by each term inside the parentheses. For each term, coefficients are multiplied, and exponents are added (following the rules of exponents):

$$2x(3x^2 + 7) = 6x^3 + 14x$$

Factoring is the reverse process of distributing; it takes a polynomial and writes it as a product of two or more factors. The first step in factoring a polynomial is always to "undistribute," or factor out, the

Practice Question

34. Which equation demonstrates the associative property of addition?
    A) $2 + (1 + 5) = (2 + 1) + 5$
    B) $2(1 \times 5) = (2 \times 1)5$
    C) $1 \times 3 = 3 \times 1$
    D) $2(7 + 4) = 2 \times 7 + 2 \times 4$
    E) None of the above

Evaluating Expressions

A **variable** is an unknown number represented by a symbol (usually a letter such as x or a). Variables can be preceded by a **coefficient**, which is the number in front of the variable. A **constant** does not contain a variable and has a value that does not change.

- In $4x$, the variable is x, and the coefficient is 4.
- In $-2a$, the variable is a, and the coefficient is -2.
- In $4x + 7$, the constant is 7.

An **algebraic expression** is any sum, difference, product, or quotient of variables and numbers. The value of an expression is found by replacing the variable with a given value and simplifying the result.

For example, to solve the following expression given that $x = 4$ and $y = 9$, simply substitute and solve:

$$2x + 7y - 1$$
$$2(4) + 7(9) - 1 =$$
$$8 + 63 - 1 = 70$$

Practice Questions

35. Evaluate the following expression for $a = -10$:

$$\frac{a^2}{4} - 3a + 4$$

   A) 59
   B) -1
   C) -51
   D) 9
   E) 57

36. Evaluate the following expression for $a = xy$ and $b = x^2$:

$$2a + 3b$$

   A) $2xy + 3x^2$
   B) $3xy + 2x^2$
   C) $5xy + 5x^2$
   D) $6x^3y$
   E) $2xy + 9x^2$

The simplest forms of this rule are $x^{1/2} = \sqrt{x}$ and $x^{1/3} = \sqrt[3]{x}$. However, the rule can be applied to fractional exponents with denominators other than 1:

$$5^{2/3} = \sqrt[3]{5^2} = \sqrt[3]{25}$$

$$(6y)^{2/5} = \sqrt[5]{(6y)^2} = \sqrt[5]{36y^2}$$

Practice Questions

32. Simplify the following exponential expression: $\left(\frac{2^7 5^4}{2^{-1} 5^2}\right)^3$.
    A) $2^{18} 5^6$
    B) $2^{24} 5^6$
    C) $2^{24} 5^{24}$
    D) $2^{11} 5^5$
    E) $2^4 5^6$

33. Simplify the following: $(10^2 10^5)^{-2}$.
    A) 10^6
    B) 10^{14}
    C) 10^{-14}
    D) 10^3
    E) 10^{40}

Algebraic Properties

Algebraic properties describe basic rules related to addition, subtraction, multiplication, and division. It is important to understand what the properties are and how they are used.

Table 1.7. Algebraic Properties

Property	Explanation	Example
Commutative property of addition	Changing the order of the addends does not change the result.	$4 + 8 = 8 + 4$
Commutative property of multiplication	Changing the order of the factors does not change the result.	$5 \times 9 = 9 \times 5$
Associative property of addition	Changing the grouping of the addends does not change the result.	$(2 + 6) + 4 = 2 + (6 + 4)$
Associative property of multiplication	Changing the grouping of the factors does not change the result.	$(3 \times 5) \times 4 = 3 \times (5 \times 4)$
Distributive property of multiplication over addition	A factor outside parentheses enclosing a sum can be distributed to the terms inside the parentheses.	$7(10 + 3) = 7(10) + 7(3)$

Law of Power of a Power

The law of power of a power states that when you have an exponential expression raised to another exponent, to simplify this expression, just multiply the exponents together. The rule can be seen here:

$$(x^a)^b = x^{ab}$$

This rule can be applied to both positive and negative exponents:

$$(6^4)^5 = 6^{4\times 5} = 6^{20}$$

$$(7^{-2})^8 = 7^{-2\times 8} = 7^{-16}$$

$$\left(y^{\frac{1}{4}}\right)^5 = y^{\frac{1}{4}\times 5} = y^{\frac{5}{4}}$$

Law of Power of a Product

The law of power of a product states that if a product of two expressions is raised to the same power, each individual expression can be raised to that power. For instance, the rule is seen here:

$$(xy)^a = x^a y^b$$

This rule is helpful in clearing expressions of parentheses and simplifying algebraic expressions. Note that this rule applies to any number of individual expressions inside the parentheses:

$$(5x)^2 = 5^2 x^2 = 25x^2$$

$$(8xy)^4 = 8^4 x^4 y^4 = 4096 x^4 y^4$$

Law of Power of a Quotient

The law of power of a quotient is similar to the law of power of a product, although it deals with a quotient inside the parentheses instead of a product. If a fraction is raised to a power, both the numerator and denominator can be individually raised to that power.

$$\left(\frac{x}{y}\right)^a = \frac{x^a}{y^a}$$

$$\left(\frac{2}{y}\right)^3 = \frac{2^3}{y^3} = \frac{8}{y^3}$$

Fractional Exponent Rule

If an exponential expression has an exponent that is a fraction, it can be written as a rational expression (an expression with a root), where the denominator is equal to the radical:

$$x^{a/b} = \sqrt[b]{x^a}$$

Law of Quotient

When dividing two exponential expressions with the same base =, the law of quotient rule states that we subtract the exponents, finding the difference of the powers. This does not apply to expressions with different bases. The rule is shown here:

$$\frac{x^a}{x^b} = x^{a-b}$$

Examples:

$$\frac{3^9}{3} = 3^{9-1} = 3^8$$

$$\frac{6^{-2}}{6^3} = 6^{-2-3} = 6^{-5}$$

$$\left(\frac{1}{3}\right)^4 \div \left(\frac{1}{3}\right)^2 = \left(\frac{1}{3}\right)^{4-2} = \left(\frac{1}{3}\right)^2$$

Law of Zero Exponents

The law of zero exponents states that any base raised to a power of 0 is equal to 1. It doesn't matter what the base is; this rule always applies. The property can be seen here:

$$x^0 = 1$$

Law of Negative Exponents

The law of negative exponents states that we can rewrite the expression with positive exponents by placing the exponent in the denominator of the expression and then retaining the positive value of the exponent. The rule is shown here:

$$x^{-a} = \frac{1}{x^a}$$

Example:

$$4^{-2} = \frac{1}{4^2}$$

$$4y^{-2} = \frac{4}{y^2}$$

This property can also be applied to an expression in parentheses:

$$(6ab)^{-3} = \frac{1}{(6ab)^3}$$

Comparing Rational Numbers

Number comparison problems present numbers in different formats and ask which number is larger or smaller, or whether the numbers are equivalent. It's important to convert the numbers to the same format so that it is easier to compare them.

Practice Questions

30. Which of the following numbers has the greatest value?
    A) 104.56
    B) 104.5
    C) 104.6
    D) 104.47
    E) 104.04

31. Is 65% greater than, less than, or equal to $\frac{13}{20}$?
    A) Greater than
    B) Less than
    C) Equal to
    D) Greater than or equal to
    E) Less than or equal to

Algebra

Exponent Properties

Law of Product

When multiplying two exponential expressions with the same base, the law of product rule states that we add the exponents. This rule does not work if the bases are different. The rule is shown here:

$$x^a x^b = x^{a+b}$$

Examples:

$$3^5 3^9 = 3^{5+9} = 3^{14}$$

$$6^{-2} 6^5 = 6^{-2+5} = 6^3$$

$$\left(\frac{1}{4}\right)^4 \left(\frac{1}{4}\right)^2 = \left(\frac{1}{4}\right)^{4+2} = \left(\frac{1}{4}\right)^6$$

In the equations above, the percent should always be expressed as a decimal. In order to convert a decimal into a percentage value, simply multiply it by 100. For example, if you have read 5 pages of a 10-page article, you have read $\frac{5}{10} = .50$, or 50% of the article.

Note that when solving these problems, the units for the part and the whole should be the same. For example, if you are reading a book, it does not make sense to say that you have read 5 pages out of 15 chapters.

Helpful Hint:

The word *of* usually indicates what the whole is in a problem. For example, the problem might say, "Ella ate 2 slices of the pizza," which means that the pizza is the whole.

Percent change involves a change from an original amount. Percent change problems often appear as word problems that include discounts, growth, or markups. Certain words can indicate that you are dealing with a percent change problem, such as *discount*, *markup*, *sale*, *increase*, and *decrease*.

In these problems, it is necessary to identify and solve for the percent change (as a decimal), the amount of change, and the original amount. These values can then be substituted in the following equations:

- amount of change = original amount × percent change
- percent change = $\frac{\text{amount of change}}{\text{original amount}}$
- original amount = $\frac{\text{amount of change}}{\text{percent change}}$

Practice Questions

27. On Tuesday, a radiology clinic had 80% of patients come in for their scheduled appointments. If they saw 16 patients, how many scheduled appointments did the clinic have on Tuesday?
    A) 11
    B) 12
    C) 20
    D) 22
    E) 21

28. A TV that originally cost $1,500 is on sale for 45% off. What is the sale price of the TV?
    A) $675
    B) $825
    C) $1,455
    D) $2,727
    E) $850

29. Kevin is planning to host a party in a room that can hold 120 people. If he expects 30% of the people he invites not to attend, what is the maximum number of invitations he should send?
    A) 36
    B) 84
    C) 171
    D) 400
    E) 350

25. Twenty-four students recently took a math test and were given a grade of "pass" or "fail." If $\frac{1}{4}$ of the students failed the test, how many students passed the test?
   A) 6
   B) 96
   C) 18
   D) 16
   E) 12

Working with Ratios and Proportions

As discussed earlier, a **ratio** describes the quantity of one thing in relation to the quantity of something else, and a **proportion** is an equation that equates two ratios.

It is helpful to rewrite ratios as a fraction. For instance, say there are 7 total pieces of fruit: 3 apples and 4 oranges. The number of apples can be written as $\frac{3}{7}$, while oranges make up $\frac{4}{7}$ of the fruit collection. When working with ratios, always consider the units of the values being compared.

You may be given three of the values in a proportion and asked to find the fourth. In these types of problems, you can solve for the missing variable by cross-multiplying. **Cross-multiplying** involves multiplying the numerator of each fraction by the denominator of the other fraction to get an equation with no fractions, as shown below. You can then solve the equation using basic algebra.

$$\frac{a}{b} = \frac{c}{d} \rightarrow ad = bc$$

Practice Question

26. A train travels 120 miles in 3 hours. How long will it take for the train to travel 180 miles?
   A) 5 hours
   B) 4 hours
   C) 3.5 hours
   D) 4.5 hours
   E) 5.5 hours

Working with Percentages

A percent is the ratio of a part to a whole. Questions about percentages may ask you to find the percent, the part, or the whole. The equation for percentages can be rearranged to solve for any of these:

$$\text{percent} = \frac{\text{part}}{\text{whole}}$$

$$\text{part} = \text{whole} \times \text{percent}$$

$$\text{whole} = \frac{\text{part}}{\text{percent}}$$

There are several helpful techniques you can use to navigate between the two forms.

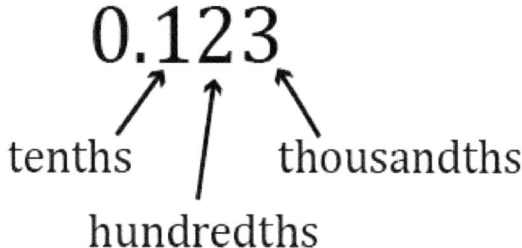

Figure 1.6. Decimal Places

The first thing to do is to simply memorize common decimals and their fractional equivalents. With these values, it is possible to convert more complicated fractions as well.

$$0.1 = \frac{1}{10} = \frac{10}{100}$$

$$.25 = \frac{1}{4}$$

Knowledge of common decimal equivalents to fractions can also help you estimate. This skill can be particularly helpful on multiple-choice tests like the SSAT, where excluding incorrect answers is just as helpful as knowing how to find the correct answer.

For example, to find $\frac{5}{8}$ in decimal form, you could eliminate any answers less than 0.5 because $\frac{4}{8} = 0.5$. You may also know that $\frac{6}{8}$ is the same as $\frac{3}{4}$ or 0.75, so anything above 0.75 could be eliminated as well.

Another helpful trick is to check if the denominator is easily divisible by 100. For example, in the fraction $\frac{9}{20}$, you know that 20 goes into 100 five times. You can therefore multiply the top and bottom by 5 to get $\frac{45}{100}$ or 0.45.

If none of these techniques work, you will need to find the decimal by dividing the denominator by the numerator using long division.

Practice Questions

24. Ari and Teagan each ordered a pizza. Ari has $\frac{1}{4}$ of his pizza left, and Teagan has $\frac{1}{3}$ of her pizza left. How much total pizza do they have left?

    A) $\frac{2}{7}$ pizza

    B) $\frac{1}{12}$ pizza

    C) $\frac{3}{4}$ pizza

    D) $\frac{7}{12}$ pizza

    E) $\frac{1}{5}$ pizza

23. Examine (a), (b), and (c) to determine the correct answer:
(a) 0.79

(b) 0.0122 + 0.7778

(c) 0.3 × 0.4

    A) (a) and (b) are equal
    B) (c) is greater than (a)
    C) (b) and (c) are equal
    D) (b) is greater than (a)
    E) (a) and (c) are equal

Working with Fractions

To **multiply fractions**, multiply numerators and multiply denominators. Reduce the product to lowest terms. To **divide fractions**, multiply the first fraction by the reciprocal of the second fraction. The **reciprocal** of a fraction is simply the same fraction with the top and bottom numbers switched. When **multiplying and dividing mixed numbers**, the mixed numbers must be converted to improper fractions.

> **Did You Know?**
>
> Inverting a fraction changes multiplication to division: $\frac{a}{b} \div \frac{c}{d} = \frac{a}{b} \times \frac{d}{c} = \frac{d}{bc}$.

$$\frac{a}{b} \times \frac{c}{d} = \frac{ac}{bd}$$

$$\frac{a}{b} \div \frac{c}{d} = \left(\frac{a}{b}\right)\left(\frac{d}{c}\right) = \frac{ad}{bc}$$

Adding or subtracting fractions requires a common denominator. To find a **common denominator** (a shared multiple of the bottom number of each fraction), multiply the denominators of the fractions. To add the fractions, add the numerators and keep the denominator the same.

$$\frac{a}{b} + \frac{c}{b} = \frac{a+c}{b}$$

$$\frac{a}{b} - \frac{c}{b} = \frac{a-c}{b}$$

To add mixed numbers, first add the whole numbers, and then the fractions. To subtract mixed numbers, convert each number to an improper fraction, and then subtract the numerators.

Converting between Decimals and Fractions

Since you may not use calculators on the Quantitative portion of the SSAT, it is important to understand how to convert fractions to decimals and vice versa. Understanding decimal placement is a key component in understanding how to convert between decimals and fractions.

21. Examine (a), (b), and (c) and find the best answer.

(a) $-5 + 25$

(b) $13 - (-10)$

(c) 2×14

    A) (a), (b), and (c) are equal
    B) (a) is greater than (b)
    C) (c) is greater than (a)
    D) (b) is less than (a)
    E) The answer cannot be determined.

Working with Decimals

Decimals can be added, subtracted, multiplied, and divided. To **add or subtract decimals**, align at the decimal point, and perform the operation. Keep the decimal point in the same place in the answer.

To multiply decimals, multiply the numbers without the decimal points. Add the number of decimal places to the right of the decimal point in the original numbers. Place the decimal point in the answer so that there are that many places to the right of the decimal.

Helpful Hint:

To determine which way to move the decimal after multiplying, remember that changing the decimal should always make the final answer *smaller*.

When **dividing decimals**, move the decimal point to the right in order to make the divisor a whole number. Move the decimal the same number of places in the dividend. Divide the numbers without regard to the decimal, and then place the decimal point of the quotient directly above the decimal point of the dividend.

Practice Questions

22. A customer at a restaurant ordered a drink that cost $2.20, a meal that cost $32.54, and a dessert that cost $4. How much was the total bill?

    A) $38.74
    B) $34.74
    C) $30.24
    D) $26.34
    E) $32.27

Working with Positive and Negative Numbers

Adding, multiplying, and dividing numbers can yield positive or negative values depending on the signs of the original numbers. Knowing the following rules can help you determine if your answer is correct:

- (+) + (−) = the sign of the larger number
- (−) + (−) = negative number
- (−) × (−) = positive number
- (−) × (+) = negative number
- (−) ÷ (−) = positive number
- (−) ÷ (+) = negative number

Helpful Hint:

Subtracting a negative number is the same as adding a positive number: $5 - (-10) = 5 + (+10) = 5 + 10 = 15$.

A **number line** shows numbers increasing from left to right (usually with zero in the middle). When adding positive and negative numbers, a number line can be used to find the sign of the answer:

- When adding a positive number, count to the right.
- When adding a negative number, count to the left.

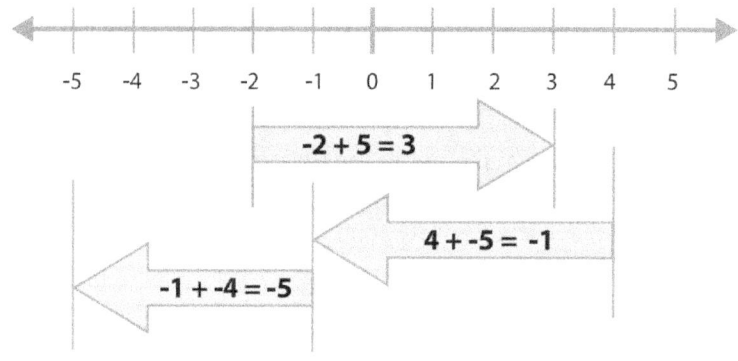

Figure 1.5. Using a Number Line to Add Positive and Negative Numbers

Practice Questions

20. The wind chill on a cold day in January was -3°F. When the sun went down, the temperature fell 5°F. What was the temperature after the sun went down?
    A) −2°F
    B) −8°F
    C) 2°F
    D) 8°F
    E) 0°F

Table 1.6. Operations Clue Words within Word Problems		
Addition	sum together (in) total all in addition	Leslie has 3 pencils. If her teacher **gives** her 2 pencils, how many pencils does she now have **in total**? $3 + 2 = 5$ pencils
Subtraction	minus less than take away decreased difference how many left? how many more/less?	Sean has 12 cookies. His sister **takes** 2 cookies. **How many** cookies does Sean have **left**? $12 - 2 = 10$ cookies
Multiplication	product times of each/every groups of twice	A hospital department has 10 patient rooms. If **each** room holds 2 patients, how many patients can stay in the department? $10 \times 2 = 20$ patients
Division	divided per each/every distributed average how many for each? how many groups?	A teacher has 150 stickers to **distribute** to her class of 25 students. If each student gets the same number of stickers, **how many** stickers will **each** student get? $150 \div 25 = 6$ stickers

Practice Questions

18. A case of pencils contains 10 boxes. Each box contains 150 pencils. How many pencils are in the case?
    A) 15
    B) 160
    C) 1,500
    D) 16,000
    E) 2,000

19. Solve $(12 - 8 \div 4)^2$
    A) 0.25
    B) 1
    C) 16
    D) 72
    E) 100

Practice Questions

16. Simplify: $-(3^2) + 4(5) + (5-6)^2 - 8$
    A) 2
    B) 22
    C) 4
    D) 29
    E) 12

17. Examine (a), (b), and (c) and find the best answer.

(a) $6 - (2 \times 3)$

(b) $(6 - 2) \times 3$

(c) $6 - 2 \times 3$

    A) (a), (b), and (c) are equal
    B) (a) is greater than (b)
    C) (b) is greater than (c)
    D) (b) and (c) are equal
    E) (c) is greater than (b)

Arithmetic Operations

There are four basic arithmetic operations: addition, subtraction, multiplication, and division:

- **Add** to combine two or more quantities ($6 + 5 = 11$).
- **Subtract** to find the difference between two or more quantities ($10 - 3 = 7$).
- **Multiply** to add a quantity multiple times ($4 \times 3 = 12 \Leftrightarrow 3 + 3 + 3 + 3 = 12$).
- **Divide** to determine how many times one quantity goes into another ($10 \div 2 = 5$).

Specific words are used to describe the answer to the four basic arithmetic operations:

- Adding creates a **sum**.
- Subtracting creates a result known as the **difference**.
- Multiplying creates a **product**.
- Dividing results in a **quotient**.

Word problems contain **clue words** that help you determine which operation to use; these words are described in Table 1.6.

Chapter 1 - Quantitative (Math) Section

Operations and Order of Operations

Order of Operations

Before understanding the order in which operations must be calculated, it is important to understand expressions. In terms of math, an **expression** is a statement that has at least two numbers and an operational sign (e.g., $+, -, \times, \div$) that connects all the numbers within the expression.

> **Helpful Hint:**
>
> The phrase "simplify the expression" just means that you need to perform all of the operations in the expression.

Expressions may also feature **variables**, which are letters that are used to represent unknown quantities.

Examples of basic expressions

$$1 + 2$$
$$(5 + 8) \times 7$$
$$397 \div 20$$

Examples of expressions with variables

$$x + 2$$
$$x(5 + 8) \times 7$$
$$397 \div 20x$$

Operations in mathematical expressions are always performed in a specific order, which is described by the acronym **PEMDAS:**

- **P**arentheses
- **E**xponents
- **M**ultiplication
- **D**ivision
- **A**ddition
- **S**ubtraction

> **Helpful Hint:**
>
> *Please Excuse My Dear Aunt Sally* is a helpful mnemonic you can use to remember the order of operations.

Operations within parentheses must be performed first, and then the exponents can be addressed. After those steps, all multiplication and division can be performed. The operations are carried out from left to right as they appear in the problem. Finally, do all required addition and subtraction—also from left to right—as each operation appears in the problem.

Most other countries use the **metric system**, which has its own set of units for variables like length, weight, and volume. These units are modified by prefixes that make large and small numbers easier to handle. These units and prefixes are shown in Table 1.5.

Table 1.5. Metric Units and Prefixes	
Variable Measured	**Base Unit**
length	meter
weight	gram
volume	liter
kilo	base unit × 1000
hecto	base unit × 100
deca (or *deka*)	base unit × 10
deci	base unit × 0.1
centi	base unit × 0.01
milli	base unit × 0.001

Conversion factors are used to convert one unit to another (either within the same system or between different systems). A **conversion factor** is simply a fraction built from two equivalent values. For example, there are 12 inches in 1 foot, so the conversion factor is $\frac{12 \text{ in}}{1 \text{ ft.}}$ or $\frac{1 \text{ ft.}}{12 \text{ in.}}$. To convert from one unit to another, multiply the original value by a conversion factor. Choose a conversion factor that will eliminate the unwanted unit with the desired unit.

For example, to find how many inches are in 6 feet, multiply the number of inches in 1 foot times 6.

$$\frac{6 \text{ ft.} \times 12 \text{ in.}}{1 \text{ ft.}} = \frac{6 \text{ ft.} \times 12 \text{ in.}}{1 \text{ ft.}} = 72 \text{ in.}$$

Practice Questions

14. How many centimeters are in 2.5 meters?
    A) 25
    B) 250
    C) 2500
    D) 25,000
    E) 0.25

15. Examine (a), (b), and (c) to determine the correct answer.
(a) 2 cups

(b) 0.5 quarts

(c) 16 fluid ounces

    A) (a), (b), and (c) are equal
    B) (b) and (c) are equal and less than (a)
    C) (c) is greater than (a) and (b)
    D) (b) is greater than (a)
    E) There is not enough information to answer the question.

12. Which number should come next in the series?

$$\frac{1}{5}, \frac{1}{25}, \frac{1}{125}, \frac{1}{625}, \ldots$$

A) $\frac{1}{15625}$

B) $\frac{1}{525}$

C) $\frac{1}{3125}$

D) $\frac{1}{625}$

E) $\frac{1}{15600}$

13. Which number should fill in the blank in the series?

$$74, 78, 82, \_\_, 90, 94$$

A) 98
B) 84
C) 88
D) 82
E) 86

Units of Measurement

The United States uses **customary units**, sometimes called **standard units**. In this system, several different units can be used to describe the same variable. These units and the relationships between them are listed in Table 1.4.

Table 1.4. US Customary Units		
Variable Measured	**Unit**	**Conversions**
Length	Inches, foot, yard, mile	12 inches = 1 foot 3 feet = 1 yard 5280 feet = 1 mile
Weight	Ounces, pound, ton	16 ounces = 1 pound 2000 pounds = 1 ton
Volume	Fluid ounces, cup, pint, quart, gallon	8 fluid ounces = 1 cup 2 cups = 1 pint 2 pints = 1 quart 4 quarts = 1 gallon
Time	Second, minute, hour, day	60 seconds = 1 minute 60 minutes = 1 hour 24 hours = 1 day
Area	Square inch, square foot, square yard	144 square inches = 1 square foot 9 square feet = 1 square yard

Arithmetic and Geometric Sequences

In an **arithmetic number series**, or **sequence**, the difference between each term is the same. This value is called the **common difference**.

For example, the following is a series:

$$15, 21, 27, 33, \ldots$$

To find the common difference, subtract each value by the one before it.

$$21 - 15 = 6$$
$$27 - 21 = 6$$
$$33 - 27 = 6$$

The series is arithmetic with a common difference of 6. Add 6 to find the next number that follows in the sequence.

$$33 + 6 = 39$$

In a geometric number series, the ratio between consecutive terms is **constant**. This value is called the **common ratio**. To find the common ratio, choose any term in the series and divide it by the previous term. To find the next term in the number series, multiply the previous term by the common ratio.

Example:

$$3, 9, 27, 81, \ldots$$

The number series is geometric with a common ratio of 3.

$$81 \times 3 = 243$$

The next term in the series is 243.

Practice Questions

11. Which number should come next in the series?

$$110, 99, 88, 77, \ldots$$

- A) 56
- B) 66
- C) 88
- D) 82
- E) 72

8. The populations of five local towns are given below.

Town	Population
A	12,341
B	8,975
C	9,431
D	10,521
E	11,427

Which of the following values is closest to the total population of the five towns?
- A) 50,000
- B) 53,000
- C) 55,000
- D) 58,000
- E) 52,000

Percentages

A **percent** (or **percentage**) means "per hundred" and is expressed with the percent symbol (%). For example, 54% means 54 out of 100. Percentages are converted to decimals by moving the decimal point two places to the left:

$$54\% = 0.54$$

Percentages can be solved by setting up a proportion:

$$\frac{\text{part}}{\text{whole}} = \frac{\%}{100}$$

Practice Questions

9. 45 is 15% of what number?
- A) 350
- B) 200
- C) 300
- D) 450
- E) 500

10. What percent of 65 is 39?
- A) 65%
- B) 60%
- C) 20%
- D) 45%
- E) 15%

6. Examine (a), (b), and (c) to determine the correct answer.

(a) 2^0

(b) 2^{-1}

(c) 2^1

   A) (a), (b), and (c) are equal
   B) (a) is greater than (b)
   C) (b) is greater than (c)
   D) (b) and (c) are equal
   E) There is not enough information to determine the answer.

Estimation and Rounding

Estimation is the process of rounding numbers to make it easier to perform operations. Estimation can be used when an exact answer is not necessary and to check work. To **round** a number, first identify the digit in the specified place value. Look at the digit one place to the right. If that digit is 4 or less, keep the digit in the specified place value the same. If that digit is 5 or more, add 1 to the digit in the specified place value; all the digits to the right of the specified place value become zeros.

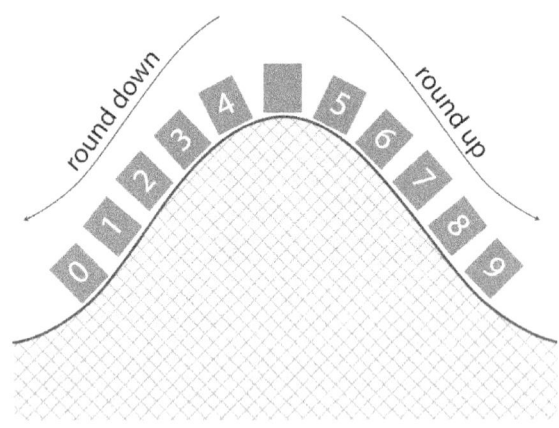

Figure 1.4. Rounding

Practice Questions

7. Voter turnout in a city election is estimated to be 80%. If Hank earns 4,000 votes (i.e., 40%) of the vote, how many registered voters live in the city? (Round to the nearest 100.)
   A) 5,000
   B) 8,000
   C) 10,000
   D) 12,500
   E) 7,000

Radicals are expressions (i.e., mathematical statements) that use roots. They are written in the form $\sqrt[a]{x}$, where a is the radical power and x is the radicand. Finding the **root** of a number is the inverse of raising a number to a power; in other words, the root is the number of times a value should be multiplied by itself to reach a given value. Roots are named for the power on the base:

- 5 is the square root of 25 because $5^2 = 25$
- 5 is the cube root of 125 because $5^3 = 125$
- 5 is the fourth root of 625, because $5^4 = 625$

The symbol for finding the root of a number is the radical: $\sqrt{\;}$. The number under the radical is called the **radicand**. By itself (when the radical power is not written) the radical indicates a square root.

$$\sqrt{36} = 6 \text{ because } 6^2 = 36$$

$$\sqrt{9} = 3 \text{ because } 3 \times 3 = 9$$

Other numbers can be included in front of the radical to indicate different roots:

$$\sqrt[4]{1{,}296} = 6 \text{ because } 6^4 = 1{,}296$$

The solution to the radical $\sqrt[3]{8}$ is the number that, when multiplied by itself 3 times, equals 8:

$$\sqrt[3]{8} = 2 \text{ because } 2 \times 2 \times 2 = 8$$

Radicals can also be written as exponents, where the power is a fraction:

$$x^{\frac{1}{3}} = \sqrt[3]{x}$$

Rules for working with radicals are provided in the table below.

Table 1.3. Operations with Radicals	
Rule	**Example**
$\sqrt[b]{ac} = \sqrt[b]{a}\sqrt[b]{c}$	$\sqrt[3]{81} = \sqrt[3]{27}\sqrt[3]{3} = 3\sqrt[3]{3}$
$\sqrt[b]{\dfrac{a}{c}} = \dfrac{\sqrt[b]{a}}{\sqrt[b]{c}}$	$\sqrt{\dfrac{4}{81}} = \dfrac{\sqrt{4}}{\sqrt{81}} = \dfrac{2}{9}$
$\sqrt[b]{a^c} = \left(\sqrt[b]{a}\right)^c = a^{\frac{c}{b}}$	$\sqrt[3]{6^2} = \left(\sqrt[3]{6}\right)^2 = 6^{\frac{2}{3}}$

Practice Questions

5. Which of the following values is equivalent to $\sqrt{48}$?
   A) $4\sqrt{3}$
   B) $24\sqrt{2}$
   C) $4\sqrt{12}$
   D) $3\sqrt{16}$
   E) $2\sqrt{4}$

Practice Questions

3. What is $\frac{7}{8}$ in decimal form?
   A) 7.8
   B) 0.78
   C) 8.75
   D) 7.085
   E) 0.875

4. What is the fraction $\frac{5}{11}$ as a decimal?
   A) 5.11
   B) $0.\overline{4545}$
   C) 2.2
   D) 0.45
   E) 1.15

Exponents and Radicals

Exponents, also known as **powers**, tell us how many times to multiply a base number by itself. The **exponent** indicates how many times to use the **base** as a factor. In the expression 5^3, 5 is the base and 3 is the exponent. The value of 5^3 is found by multiplying 5 by itself 3 times.

$$5^3 = 5 \times 5 \times 5 = 125$$

Some exponents have special names. For example, "x to the second power" is called "x squared"; it is displayed as x^2. Similarly, "x to the third power" (also called "x cubed") is displayed as x^3. Rules for working with exponents are provided in Table 1.2.

Table 1.2. Operations with Exponents

Rule	Example
$a^0 = 1$	$5^0 = 1$
$a^{-n} = \dfrac{1}{a^n}$	$5^{-3} = \dfrac{1}{5^3}$
$a^m a^n = a^{m+n}$	$5^3 5^4 = 5^{3+4} = 5^7$
$(a^m)^n = a^{m \times n}$	$(5^3)^4 = 5^{3(4)} = 5^{12}$
$\dfrac{a^m}{a^n} = a^{m-n}$	$\dfrac{5^4}{5^3} = 5^{4-3} = 5^1$
$(ab)^n = a^n b^n$	$(5 \times 6)^3 = 5^3 6^3$
$\left(\dfrac{a}{b}\right)^n = \dfrac{a^n}{b^n}$	$\left(\dfrac{5}{6}\right)^3 = \dfrac{5^3}{6^3}$
$\left(\dfrac{a}{b}\right)^{-n} = \left(\dfrac{b}{a}\right)^n$	$\left(\dfrac{5}{6}\right)^{-3} = \left(\dfrac{6}{5}\right)^3$
$\dfrac{a^{-m}}{b^{-n}} = \dfrac{b^n}{a^m}$	$\dfrac{5^{-3}}{4} = \dfrac{6^4}{5^3}$

A **ratio** describes the quantity of one thing in relation to the quantity of another. Unlike fractions, ratios do not give a part relative to a whole; instead, they compare two values. For example, if you have 3 apples and 4 oranges, the ratio of apples to oranges is 3 to 4. Ratios can be written using words (3 to 4), fractions $\left(\frac{3}{4}\right)$, or colons (3:4).

A **proportion** is an equation that equates two ratios. Proportions are usually written as two fractions joined by an equal sign $\left(\frac{a}{b} = \frac{c}{d}\right)$, but they can also be written using colons ($a:b::c:d$). Note that in a proportion, the units must be the same in both numerators and in both denominators.

Practice Question

2. What is 0.45 in fraction form?
   A) $\frac{45}{50}$
   B) $\frac{9}{20}$
   C) $\frac{5}{10}$
   D) $\frac{4}{5}$
   E) $\frac{1}{4}$

Decimals

In the base-10 system, each digit (the numeric symbols 0–9) in a number is worth ten times as much as the number to the right of it. For example, in the number 321, each digit has a different value based on its position:

$$321 = 300 + 20 + 1$$

The value of each place is called **place value**. It will be important to understand place value in order to estimate and round numbers up or down (discussed later in this chapter under "Estimation and Rounding").

Table 1.1. Place Value Chart

1,000,000	100,000	10,000	1,000	100	10	1	.	$\frac{1}{10}$	$\frac{1}{100}$
10^6	10^5	10^4	10^3	10^2	10^1	10^0		10^{-1}	10^{-2}
millions	hundred thousands	ten thousands	thousands	hundreds	tens	ones	decimal	tenths	hundredths

Practice Question

1. Which one of the following is an irrational number?
   A) $\sqrt{5}$
   B) $\sqrt{225}$
   C) $\sqrt{1}$
   D) $\sqrt{323}$
   E) $\sqrt{9}$

Fractions, Ratios, and Proportions

A **fraction** represents parts of a whole. The top number of a fraction, called the **numerator**, indicates how many equal-sized parts are present. The bottom number of a fraction, called the **denominator**, indicates how many equal-sized parts make a whole. Fractions have several forms. In a **proper fraction**, the numerator is less than the denominator. For an **improper fraction**, the numerator is greater than or equal to the denominator. A **mixed number** is the combination of a whole number and a fraction.

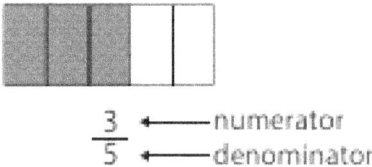

Figure 1.2. Parts of Fractions

Improper fractions can be converted to mixed numbers by dividing. In fact, the fraction bar also functions as a division symbol.

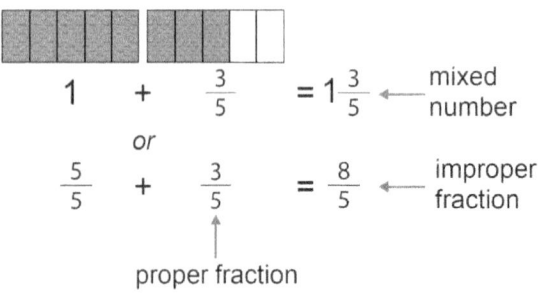

Figure 1.3. Types of Fractions

To convert a mixed number to a fraction, multiply the whole number by the denominator of the fraction, and add the numerator. The result becomes the numerator of the improper fraction; the denominator remains the same.

$$5\frac{2}{3} = \frac{(5 \times 3) + 2}{3} = \frac{17}{3}$$

Rational numbers are made by dividing one integer by another integer. They can be expressed as fractions or as decimals.

$$\frac{3}{4} \ (0.75)$$

Irrational numbers are numbers that cannot be written as fractions; they are decimals that go on forever without repeating.

$$\pi \ (3.14159\ldots)$$

Positive numbers are greater than zero. **Negative numbers** are less than zero. Using a number line (Figure 1.1.) can provide a helpful visualization of positive and negative numbers.

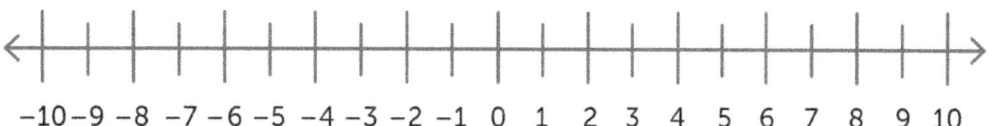

Figure 1.1. Number Line

To understand **prime** numbers, you must first understand factors. **Factors** are numbers that, when divided into other numbers, result in numbers that do not have fractions or decimals.

Factors of 6 include 1, 2, 3, and 6:

$$6 \div 1 = 6$$
$$6 \div 2 = 3$$
$$6 \div 3 = 2$$
$$6 \div 6 = 1$$

The following are NOT factors of 6:

$$6 \div 4 = 1.5$$
$$6 \div 5 = 1.2$$

A **prime number** is a number that has only two factors: 1 and the number itself.

$$5 \div 1 = 5$$
$$5 \div 5 = 1$$

If a number has two or more factors, it is called a **composite number**.

$$8 \div 1 = 8$$
$$8 \div 2 = 4$$
$$8 \div 4 = 2$$

All numbers can be even or odd. An **even number** is divisible by 2. An **odd number** is not divisible by 2.

Chapter 1 - Quantitative (Math) Section

There are numerous mistakes that can be avoided when taking the Quantitative portion of the exam. While many of these errors are considered simple mistakes, it is still important to avoid making them in the first place. These mistakes include answering with the wrong sign (positive/negative), mixing up the order of operations, misplacing a decimal, and not reading the question thoroughly (and therefore providing an answer that was not asked for).

Strategies for the Math Achievement and Quantitative Reasoning Sections

The following strategies can help you strengthen your performance on the SSAT Quantitative section:

Go Back to the Basics
First and foremost, practice your basic skills, including sign changes, the order of operations, how to simplify fractions, and equation manipulation. Remember that when it comes right down to it, all math problems rely on the four basic skills of addition, subtraction, multiplication, and division.

Do Not Rely on Mental Math
While mental math is great for eliminating answer options, always write the math down. Use the scratch paper or dry-erase board that is provided to draw out the problem. Students are more likely to catch mistakes when writing calculations down.

Use The Three-Times Rule
The three-times rule involves reading the question three times.

- **Step One—Read the question:** Write out the given information.
- **Step Two—Read the question:** Set up equation(s) and solve.
- **Step Three—Read the question:** Make sure the answer makes sense. For example, is the amount too large or small, is the answer in the correct unit of measurement?

Make an Educated Guess
Educated guesses can be helpful if a student is unsure how to solve a problem. Eliminate the answer options which you are relatively sure are incorrect, and then guess from the remaining options. In some instances (e.g., solving for an unknown variable), it may be helpful to plug in the answer options in place of the unknown variable to determine the correct answer.

Number Concepts and Operations

Types of Numbers

Integers are whole numbers, including the counting numbers, the negative counting numbers, and zero:

$$3, 2, 1, 0, -1, -2, -3$$

Scoring

Scores are calculated by giving one point per correct answer, while one-quarter of one point is taken away per wrong answer. No points are awarded or subtracted for unanswered questions. As stated above, the Experimental section is not scored.

For paper tests, scores are available within two weeks of the test date. For at-home tests, scores will be available on the Wednesday following the test date. For tests taken at Prometric sites, tests will be available on the Wednesday after the scoring period ends. In all cases, scores are available to families and schools on the same day.

Test Administration

The exam can be taken in three ways: on paper, at home, and at Prometric testing centers worldwide.

The paper SSAT is the traditional method of testing. The Standard SSAT is held on specific dates, while the Flex SSAT is given on a flexible schedule. The Standard and Flex tests are the same; the difference is the date and location of the test. Students can take up to six Standard tests and one Flex test per testing year.

The at-home test must be taken on designated testing dates. Students must have access to a computer or laptop with a webcam, speaker, microphone, and reliable internet to take the at-home exam. If needed, testers can request a free Equity Tech Kit, which include a laptop and mobile hotspot for internet access, that must be returned within two days of the exam. Students can take one at-home test per testing year.

Prometric tests are computer-based exams held at one of the many designated testing centers across the world. Test takers should arrive at least thirty minutes before the test's start time to allow time to check in and ensure they do not have any prohibited items, which includes cell phones, watches, calculators, and backpacks. Students will be given a dry-erase marker and board for note taking. Students can take two Prometric tests per testing year.

Test dates and locations for the SSAT Middle test in all forms can be found on the SSAT website: www.ssat.org.

Test takers will be given three hours and ten minutes to complete the exam. Students are allowed two ten-minute breaks: one after the Writing sample and one after the Reading Comprehension section. Please note that students may use the restroom or access snacks or drinks, but may not access prohibited items (such as cell phones) during this time. Students may take unscheduled breaks at any point; however, the timer will not stop.

Section	Subtests	Number of Questions	Time Allowed
Writing	Writing Sample	Two prompts to choose from	25 min
Quantitative (Math)	Quantitative #1 Quantitative #2	50 total: 25 in each subsection	60 minutes total, 30 for each subsection
Reading	Reading Comprehension	40 questions	40 minutes
Verbal	Synonyms Analogies	60 total: 30 synonyms and 30 analogies	30 minutes
Experimental		16 total: 6 Verbal, 5 Reading, 5 Quantitative	15 minutes

Keep in mind the Experimental section is unscored. This section tests new questions for acceptability for future SSAT Middle exams.

Introduction

The Secondary School Admission Test Middle Level exam is used to assess students in grades five through seven for admission to private middle schools across the world.

Test Format

The SSAT Middle exam consists of four main content areas: Quantitative (Math), Verbal, Reading, and Writing.

Writing
The SSAT Middle Level exam will provide two writing prompts: a creative story starter and a personal question prompt. The prompts will be displayed as sentences; test takers will choose one and have 25 minutes to write an essay. Schools use the writing sample to get to know the student better and to get an idea of their writing skills; it is therefore important to understand the basic mechanics of good writing and how to make sure ideas come across logically and clearly.

Math
There are two Math sections. The Quantitative portion of the Middle Level SSAT evaluates the student's ability to reason mathematically and solve problems without the use of a calculator. These problems will require the test taker to be comfortable using basic arithmetic, elementary algebra, and geometry. Additional math concepts, such as data and probability, will also be featured on the exam. Test takers are not allowed to use a calculator on this portion of the exam.

Verbal
The SSAT Middle Level Verbal Reasoning section includes two types of questions: synonyms and analogies. These questions test the candidate's vocabulary as well as their understanding of the logical relationships between words.

The SSAT synonym questions will provide a word and ask test takers to choose the word that has the most similar meaning. The analogies portion of the exam evaluates the taker's ability to understand the relationship between words. These questions will provide two words that have a relationship. The test taker will need to determine the relationship between those words and choose the answer that most closely recreates that relationship.

Reading
The SSAT Middle Level Reading Comprehension section of the exam evaluates the test taker's ability to understand the ideas and details of a text. There will be short passages and corresponding questions related to topics such as the main idea, supporting ideas and details, inferences, author's purpose, vocabulary, tone and style, opinions and arguments, and predictions. The passages will either be narrative or argumentative and may be taken from many genres or topics, including science, social studies, humanities, and literature.

Online Resources

Trivium includes online resources with the purchase of this study guide to help you fully prepare for the exam.

Review Questions

Need more practice? Our review questions use a variety of formats to help you memorize key terms and concepts.

Flash Cards

Trivium's flash cards allow you to review important terms easily on your computer or smartphone.

Cheat Sheets

Review the core skills you need to master the exam with easy-to-read Cheat Sheets.

From Stress to Success

Watch "From Stress to Success," a brief but insightful YouTube video that offers the tips, tricks, and secrets experts use to score higher on the exam.

Access these materials at: triviumtestprep.com/ssat-ml-online-resources

Practice Test #1 124
Quantitative Section #1 124
Quantitative Section #2 129
Reading 134
Verbal 143

Answer Explanations #1 149
Quantitative Section #1 149
Quantitative Section #2 154
Reading 158
Verbal 162

Practice Test #2 165
Quantitative Section #1 165
Quantitative Section #2 170
Reading 176
Verbal 186

Answer Explanations #2 196
Quantitative Section #1 196
Quantitative Section #2 200
Reading 204
Verbal 208

Practice Test #3 211
Quantitative Section #1 211
Quantitative Section #2 217
Reading 223
Verbal 233

Answer Explanation #3 243
Quantitative Section #1 243
Quantitative Section #2 248
Reading 253
Verbal 257

Appendix - Roots and Suffixes 260

TABLE OF CONTENTS

Introduction 1

Chapter 1 - Quantitative (Math) Section 5
Number Concepts and Operations 5
Operations and Order of Operations 16
Algebra 25
Solving Word Problems 35
Geometry 38
Data Analysis and Probability 53
Graphs, Charts, and Tables 56
Answer Key 67

Chapter 2 – Reading Comprehension 86
Ideas and Details 86
Literary Elements and Techniques 92
Using Context to Determine Word Definitions 94
Answer Key 96

Chapter 3 – Writing and the Writing Sample 97
Grammar 97
Constructing Sentences 100
Text Organization 109
Writing a Thesis Statement 110
Structuring the Writing Sample 110
Providing Supporting Evidence 111
Creative and Personal Knowledge Starter Examples 112
Creative Essay Example 112
Personal Essay Example 114
Answer Key 116

Chapter 4 – Verbal Reasoning 118
Word Structure 118
Synonyms 119
Analogies 120
Answer Key 123

Copyright ©2025 Trivium Test Prep

ISBN-13: 9781637989098

ALL RIGHTS RESERVED. By purchase of this book, you have been licensed on copy for personal use only. No part of this work may be reproduced, redistributed, or used in any form or by any means without prior written permission of the publisher and copyright owner. Trivium Test Prep; Accepted, Inc.; Cirrus Test Prep; and Ascencia Test Prep are all imprints of Trivium Test Prep, LLC.

SSAT® Middle Level Prep Book 2026-2027
3 Practice Tests and SSAT Study Guide

B. Hettinger